NARCISSISM, NIHILISM, SIMPLICITY AND SELF

NARCISSISM, NIHILISM, SIMPLICITY AND SELF

Karl M. Abenheimer

edited by

Robert R. Calder

ABERDEEN UNIVERSITY PRESS
Member of Maxwell Macmillan Publishing Corporation

First Published 1991
Aberdeen University Press
The Estate of Karl M. Abenheimer
Introduction © R. R. Calder

British Library Cataloguing in Publication Data

Abenheimer, Karl M., *1898-1973*
   Narcissism, nihilism: simplicity and self.
   I. Calder, Robert R.
   155.232

ISBN 0-08-041405-2

*Published with the assistance of a grant
from Leverndale Hospital Research Fund*

Keyed by Lothlorien, Edinburgh
Typeset by The Michael Press, Glasgow
Printed by Billing and Son Ltd., Worcester

There is no such one thing as 'Die Angst', there are only 'Ängste', anxieties of different origin and meaning. And there is no 'Die Angst als Krankheit' but anxiety as one aspect of diverse psychic illnesses. Nor is anxiety more predominant in Western man than, for example, in certain primitive civilisations.

[There is a danger of confusing] anxiety in general with the isolation of the narcissist, his inability to deal and communicate with the archetype of the terrifying mother and his flight from her into intellectualism. [However] intellectualism is only one form of narcissistic flight from the earth mother into spurious elevation. There are anti-intellectual positions which are no less narcissistic, such as aestheticism, lofty religion, dandyism, aristocratic snobbery, or the racial superiority of the Nazis. Narcissism is a specific danger of our civilisation. It is the inevitable shadow of our valuation of individual freedom of thinking and action and of the resulting secularisation and atomisation of social life. Within this civilisation one can overcome narcissism only by a deeper self-realisation and increased courage to lead an individual life.

Only very rarely in the history of western thought have the creative and original writers been the great examples for healthy and well balanced living. Those who impress us by their exemplary 'existence' have usually been no writers of books, and those who have written books (philosophical, scientific or poetic) usually have done so under the pressure of an inner disharmony which forced them to face what others bypassed.

This usual neurosis of the writer is no reason to neglect his insights and teachings. He who wants to eliminate the creative intellectual because he usually is a Luciferic character, a narcissistic neurotic, will end by rejecting the whole western and Christian tradition and embracing one of the totalitarian creeds. If one believes in our tradition then one has to know with Thomas Mann that the Christian and Luciferic figures are inseparable and supplement one another.

(from review of Die Angst als Abendländische Krankheit, *by Arnold Künzli. Zürich; Rascher Verlag, 1948)*

Contents

Introduction 9

On Narcissism, with Reference to Shakespeare's *King Lear* 29

Shakespeare's *Tempest*: A Psychological Analysis 39

On Narcissism *(1968)* 53

The Heart of Man (Erich Fromm) 59

Shakespeare's Sonnets 120 and 121 61

The Problem of Individuation in the Writings
of Friedrich Nietzsche 70

Rilke and Nietzsche 87

Some Answers to Nihilism 100

The Individualistic Ego 113

Reflections on Gunter Grass's Novel, *The Tin Drum* 129

Patrick White's *Voss* 140

On Simplicity
  with reference to Patrick White's novels *The Solid Mandala*
  and *Riders in the Chariot* 152

APPENDICES:
  1. From 'Jung in His Letters' 164
  2. On 'The Group' 166

BIBLIOGRAPHY 170

INDEX 174

Editorial Introduction

The major part of the present book began as an exile's meditation in time of war. Over the following thirty years Karl Abenheimer wrote a great deal more, for various reasons never publishing a book, but amid a considerable range of work continuing the developed series now put together as this book. It reveals a very considerable thinker, and not only in the field which was his as an extremely gifted psychotherapist. He began these writings at a time when the humane civilisation of Europe was under threat from a monstrous and murderous regime. By reference to some of that civilisation's crucial literary elements he says a great deal on its behalf, addressing the widest range of human issues from a psychologically informed viewpoint.

Exile is perhaps Abenheimer's central theme, not least the self-exile which all too unconsciously lets things happen. His own physical exile he saw as a product of such psychological self-exile, and of various consequences of the latter which many witnessed in his day, and which better than most he understood.

The Man

Karl Markus Abenheimer was born in Mannheim on November 2nd 1898. His father, Heinrich Ferdinand Abenheimer (1860-1938), was descended from Jewish families which had been settled since the middle ages in South West Germany around Speyer and Mainz and the Rhine. The surname derives from the village of Abenheim near Worms, where one forebear was a notable Rabbi. The paternal family moved in the early 19th century to Feudenheim, on the Neckar, a village subsequently incorporated in the growing city of Mannheim. In 1895 Heinrich married Wilhelmina Weill (1863-1915), born in Kaiserslautern in the Palatinate near the border with France, a region in which the Weill family had lived since at least the 14th century. The composer Kurt Weill was a none too distant cousin.

The Abenheimer family was a prosperous bourgeois one, H. F. Abenheimer having taken over his father's business as a grain importer in the busy river port of Mannheim. Earlier he had travelled widely on the firm's behalf, widely in America and North Africa. He had not attended university but was a gifted man, had some command of Latin, and was fluent in German and Arabic. Highly musical, like many a German he took a leading part in a local choral society. His son had music lessons, and became an accomplished pianist and cellist. The only other child of the family was a daughter, Lilly, born in 1897. The family enjoyed walking tours in the nearby Odenwald and the Black Forest, and spent summer holidays in Switzerland. Wilhelmina, unfortunately, was a victim of diabetes, considerably debilitating in the days before insulin, and a causative factor in her death from tuberculosis in 1915.

By that time war had begun, and while his final school examination should have been in mid-1917, Karl Abenheimer was one of eight pupils at the Realgymnasium (*anglice* High School) in Mannheim who took the exam early, in November. He joined the army in December 1916, (horse) Field Artillery, training not far from home at Rastatt, then transferring to the Eastern Front. He served in Poland, where as well as the extreme squalor of living conditions he recalled lice which no amount of washing could get rid of, apparently frost-resistant even as uniforms froze stiff on the line.

Conditions improved very considerably with the peace of Brest Litovsk, ending formal hostilities between Germany and the former Tsarist Russian territories. Abenheimer's unit was transferred into the Ukraine, to Kiev. Rule from Moscow having been in effect suspended, there were hopes of an independent Ukrainian state and the German force was accepted not as an occupying army but as a garrison. The situation became progressively more complex, with the end of the war. There were even hopes that the German force might be detained to forestall Bolshevik incursions. Abenheimer left, it would seem, with some slight regret. He had made friends, and following promotion had been duty officer in attendance at the Kiev Opera during performances. The return journey was to be a sore trawl, lack of rations demanding the slaughter of horses. Army service however also found Abenheimer sharing an experience with other German Jewish soldiers, of encounter with the eastern Jewry in the pale of settlement, both witnessing appalling living conditions and general deprivation, and experiencing a certain uplift in contact with a far from attenuated Jewish cultural life, participating in communal celebration.

Back home, he resumed the expected formal education, able to accelerate his studies, graduating in law at Heidelberg in record time, prior to the extensive practical training of the German lawyer. Two other factors have to be noted in his student years, his encounter with Ernst Simon and membership of one of the Zionist groups which were then forming in German universities, and attendance at the psychology lectures of the young Karl Jaspers. Students were obliged to attend classes outwith their principal course, and while no great involvement was necessary it is plain that Jaspers' teaching had some impact on Abenheimer. Quite possibly he was attracted by what he had heard of the young philosopher, initially a medical psychologist but teaching within the philosophy department, and with considerable freedom as to what he taught. Jaspers was 'a teacher of clear thinking to many,' including himself, Abenheimer wrote much later. He heard lectures which were the basis of Jaspers' *Psychologie der Weltanschauungen*.

Abenheimer was already working as a prosecuting counsel by 1921, and his other legal experience included a spell as regional magistrate, not to mention fulfilling the obligation to be present when a sentence of death was carried out. He joined and became partner in a legal firm in Karlsruhe, Fürst and Abenheimer, in 1924 marrying the senior partner's daughter, Friederike (Fritzi) Fürst. There were three children, but the marriage was not a success. It was finally dissolved in the 1940s in Glasgow.

With the advent of Hitler in 1933 came the laws which denied Abenheimer as a Jew any career in law. On the basis of growing interests he entered his second career, as psychotherapist. Living not far away in Karlsruhe, he had from 1931 attended the South West German Training Institute in Heidelberg, working with Frieda Fromm-Reichmann, herself Jewish and later to have an exceptionally brilliant career in American exile. Abenheimer, who had in 1932 begun publishing small papers on legal-psychoanalytic topics, went from that more Freud-irientated centre to Gustav Richard Heyer's circle in Munich, travelling to Munich on the night of long knives when Roehm and his associates were slaughtered. Heyer was a friend of and influential on the novelist Hermann Broch, as well as of C. G. Jung, and it was undoubtedly through Heyer that Abenheimer met Jung, whom he heard in person at the Berlin seminar of 1933 deliver an all too notorious speech on the German spirit.

Abenheimer retained one broad lesson taught by Fromm-Reichmann and by Heyer, as indeed Jung in his approving reviews of Heyer's books in the early 1930s. This is, simply, that there is such a thing as psychological understanding; while the work of any "school" ought definitely to aim to serve that understanding, there is a consideration distinct from fidelity to any one school approach. The lesson was also taught by Jaspers, who made his name with the *Allgemeine Psychopathologie* (1916), which is a critical account of the effectiveness of various distinct and different methods of treatment. Not least is it the case that no terminology is final. The value of any approach is in its doing justice to fact, and accomplishing certain objectives. It may well be that two writers are saying almost the same things, but in different words. Freud had remarked that the knowledge which had been his concern had long been a possession of poets. Heyer insists that the poets rather than the psychologists have the language which alone does justice to the case. If the essays in this book very much follow that up, the importance of a convergent understanding was a major concern with Abenheimer throughout.

Abenheimer had it seems been free with legal advice during a period when Jews still had recourse in law, and this did not endear him to the Nazi authorities. Quite how urgent was his exit from Germany is uncertain, but he seems to have considered emigration at least as early as his exclusion from the practice of law, or even earlier, reading the signs. He had a meeting with Martin Buber (they did not get on) in the autumn of 1935, arranged from his Karlsruhe address, though he was by this time working in Munich. By the end of that year he was writing from there to Jung, and he was in Zurich by March 1936. October of that year found him in the Beaumont Hotel in Glasgow, investigating prospects of settling in the city.

Much later he was amused to recall one Glasgow Jewish 'entrepreneur' who had assured him that the need and prospects of a psychotherapist in

Glasgow were great. Abenheimer settled in Glasgow in the spring of 1937, and it was obvious that the 'entrepreneur' had been referring to his own 'need.' Other patients followed him, and over the next few years Abenheimer consolidated a substantial practice.

He was soon recruited to a post as visiting psychotherapist at Gartnavel Hospital in the west of Glasgow, where Dr. Angus MacNiven was assiduous in efforts both to help refugees and to apply their gifts and learning to better mental health provision in the west of Scotland.

Only by the end of 1938 did Abenheimer finally have all his family together in Glasgow. His two sons had been some time at a prep school in Surrey, and his daughter with a group of German Jewish girls at a home maintained by Sir Albert Kahn in Nottingham, until he was able to make a home for them and leave their places for others in urgent need in that year of pogroms. Through the local Glasgow refugee committee he found a foster-home for his sister's son, who travelled from Germany to Glasgow with Abenheimer's wife in December. Abenheimer's sister had taken charge of their father's household on her mother's death in 1915. After her marriage the old man was part of her household, until his death in June 1938. Abenheimer had also been able to exert some influence with German contacts, under the counter, to help her husband get out of an internment camp. After a few months the man had been so starved and ill-treated that his wife scarcely recognised him. They reached Glasgow in July 1939 only weeks before war was declared.

Amid ordeals Abenheimer had begun a considerable contribution in his new field, delivering lectures, circulating an occasional paper and being available for discussion with other professionals. Having made a particularly full study in relation to different inter-school movements in southern Germany, not merely by any restricted standard was he remarkably learned in the literature; as the texts of his earliest lectures reveal. The perspective is wide and there is no parroting of others. There is a point of view, clearly informed by important predecessors but critically very much worked out in Abenheimer's own mind, in relation to his own experience. He at one point corresponded with a publisher on the question of writing a short primer, from a point of view more or less Jungian. While his command of English was very considerable, it bears very much the marks of not having been acquired in an environment of native speakers. This may have been an important factor in the book's regrettable non-appearance. By the middle 1940s Abenheimer had established himself in practice in Glasgow, published or circulated several papers, and earned some reputation as a lecturer.

Subsequently he suffered one considerable blow, when in 1948 the National Health Service was instituted in Britain. He welcomed the institution, but its regulations abruptly declared him unwelcome as a staff member at a psychiatric hospital. He lost his post of some 12 years at Gartnavel, because he was not a qualified doctor of medicine. More than 40 years after, it was still possible to feel a certain outrage on the part of surviving colleagues at the unceremonious dismissal. He was, it is plain from report, wounded by the impersonal decision; and while there are mss. for a book on ego psychology dated 1947-48 it seems around then to have been abandoned as an immediate project. Yet this is a complex period of Abenheimer's career, with a difficult paper offered to the *British Journal of Medical Psychology*, for which he had been writing since 1942, on the basis of a review of Jaspers' *Allgemeine Psychopathologie* in its 1946 fourth edition. Extensively updated by Jaspers during years during years of suspension from his post at Heidelberg, during wartime years under constant threat of transportation with his Jewish wife, this was a book of the first importance to Abenheimer, which he believed could transform British therapeutic practice.

The pitch at which his mind was working is well indicated notably by the unpublished paper 'The Concept of Spirit in Analytic Psychology' of 1947 (a cut-back, rather schematic version in a kind of Jungian style appeared later, 'Notes on the Spirit as Conceived by Dynamic Psychology,' *Journal of Analytic Psychology*, Vol. 1 No. 2, 1956). The 15,000 word original goes well beyond current British thinking, working out a convergence between lessons of Freud and Jung, and Existential Psychology and Philosophy. Into the 1950s he felt a continuing exasperation at a growing trend toward ever more orthodox Freudianism in the *British Journal of Medical Psychology*, if anything exacerbated by a tendency toward polarisation between 'Jungian' and 'Freudian.' In sending in the cut-down review of the Jaspers book which did appear, he expressed concern that the journal might cease to be a 'neutral forum' for discussion of all 'scientific' views, and become 'more popish than the Pope' in its discouragement of papers critical of Freud. With the rejection of his 1957 paper 'Existentialism and Psychotherapy' by the journal he considered his worst fears justified.

He was also not encouraged by the occasional dismissal of a paper by a psychoanalytic journal as 'too philosophical,' so that while it is plain that he continued to write, his publications very much tail off after the middle 1950s. His good humour and serenity are on record from friends and associates, and reported by his widow on the subject of non-publication, which he came to learn to live with.

His domestic life had changed for the good at the end of the 1940s, when he remarried. His wife, Irene Thorburn, was a Glasgow woman and a niece of the poet Edwin Muir, and they had two sons, born 1949 and 1951.

And he was by no means isolated in Glasgow, a city with a large university and a varied population including a considerable complement of immigrants, not least a community of Jews from the Eastern *shtetl*, arrived at the beginning of the 20th century. In the late 1940s there came to Glasgow, too, the astonishing Joseph Schorstein (1910-76), son of a Rabbi from Brno, and Abenheimer's close friend for the rest of his life. Together they somehow contrived a constellation of gifted individuals around them, theologians especially of Existentialist orientation (Ian Henderson, Ronald

Gregor Smith, John Macquarrie);churchmen of pastoral concern (A. C. Craig, Murdo Ewen MacDonald), the philosopher J.J. Russell, of wide European interest, plus as "devil's advocate" the Bertrand Russell follower D. R. Bell; Classics scholars, specialists on (mainly Soviet) totalitarianism, psychotherapists and others in that field. These included the young R. D. Laing, whose mentors Abenheimer and Schorstein were (*see* Appendix). Abenheimer also founded a group for co-operative discussion between practitioners of psychoanalytic therapies of different sorts. He had a context, within and for which the previously unpublished papers in this volume were written.

From the 1950s until his death Abenheimer continued in private practice, working too at different clinics in the Glasgow area, the Lansdowne and the Davidson. Qualified doctors of medicine continued to refer patients to him, or came to him to train. One reported having come with an initial dream of being a prisoner in the dock. "Did you know I used to be a judge?" Abenheimer asked him wth much amusement.

He lived and worked in Belmont Street, in the West End of Glasgow, with a weekend cottage at Garelochhead, to which he would retire for a weekend with family and friends, or for instance his sometime protege R. D. Laing, working over the text of *The Divided Self*. With his sister and her family living on the other side of the street there was something between an extended family and a miniature German community. (Liszt's pupil the pianist Frederick Lamond, a sometime neighbour in Mannheim, lived around the corner in Lacrosse Terrace).

Maintaining continuity too, the catering explosion of the German Christmas occurred each year. He did not retire, and perhaps with some international recognition had by the early 1970s resumed the project of a book, of which some earlier chapters are in typescript. He is reported as having seemed in fine health, but in late summer 1973 his wife was concerned by expressions of tiredness, and there was talk of slackening off soon, to concentrate on the book. He suffered a heart attack at his cottage at Garelochhead on a weekend when the *Glasgow Herald* published a particularly full and vigorously critical review by him of books by and about Jung. A final and fatal heart attack followed in Vale of Leven Hospital some eight days later, on August 26th 1973.

THE WRITINGS

Karl Abenheimer left a considerable volume of papers. While happily a general catalogue was made of them shortly after his death, other commitments denied any possible editor time and opportunity to make the necessarily full survey of the whole *Nachlass*. The present editor was invited to make a survey of the papers in the late 1980s, and thus this book came about, following the appearance of some previously unpublished papers in the *Edinburgh Review*.

While the select listing of Abenheimer's papers suggests what might yet be done, the present book stands out as one which pretty nearly edited itself. With three additions, two preliminaries published with this appendix, and the *summa* on 'The Individualistic Ego' the work is rooted in Abenheimer's confrontation with questions as expressed in different literary texts. Here the empirical or observational character of his approach can be seen demonstrated most clearly. Unlike in the work of a number of supposed literary specialists, he does not pick up a theory and impose it. He is in fact an excellent literary critic in classical terms, though of course dealing mainly with the import of certain texts as psychology, or in relation to the questions of the *Verstehende Psychologie* which is the business both of the therapist and the man in the street. How is one to understand oneself and others, to live with oneself and others? The work of psychoanalysis has not always been appropriated to any such end.

Abenheimer's Psychology

Abenheimer differed from the immediately preceding, pioneering generations of psychoanalysts in having no background in medical study and practice. Any deficiency there was more than offset by the special factors in his case, not the least of which was an early extensive experience of persons from other European cultural backgrounds, in those backgrounds. As schoolboy-turned-soldier he moreover approached this range of empirical encounters without the specific interest, or unconscious pretence, of the professional psychologist.

He also differs from such predecessors as Freud and Jung, not to mention others such as Jaspers, in having had a range of predecessors. When he began to train as analyst/therapist sometime around 1930 there was a new challenge in the field. It was to appropriate the "findings" (Abenheimer's preferred word) of an already considerable number of differently orientated approaches, each with a sizeable literature.

He had begun the study of psychology under Karl Jaspers in 1919-20, and had plainly to some extent appropriated the more commonsensical view expressed by Jaspers and his friend Max Weber. Investigations are not to be judged in relation to their fidelity to a prescribed method, but rather in their production of sound results. Disciplined method is not unimportant, but method is justifiable only insofar as it results in new understanding of reality. It must do more than merely work out implications internal to its own assumptions. To say nothing of the other and still contentious philosophical issues raised by Weber and Jaspers (on which Abenheimer elsewhere sheds light) a receptiveness toward the possibility of different approaches was valuable to him in relation to his three teachers in the psychoanalytic therapies—Fromm-Reichmann, Heyer and Jung. All of them made notable attempts in the 1930s, and to differing extents later, to appropriate the various findings of different schools and approaches. The Jung Abenheimer

met in 1933, and worked with during the next three years, was different
from the later figure more concerned with religion and often thought of in
terms refracted through the writings of later 'Jungians.' When Abenheimer
in 1940 circulated a critique of the leading English Jungian H. G. Baynes'
Mythology of the Soul, its preference of the Freudian reading of one case was
by no means alien to Jung himself.

A further difference between Abenheimer and for instance the young
Freud is also worth note. While the precise extent of his knowledge of
neurochemistry remains obscure, he was by no means conditioned to seek an
oversimple psychoanalytic picture by acceptance of an overly crude view of
brain functions (and Fromm-Reichmann had worked on cerebral lesions
among brain-injured 1914-18 soldiers). The difficulty of Abenheimer for
'strict Freudians' may be in his manifesting a modernity too easily thought of
as confined to a purely biochemical approach. The need and validity of more
than one school's approach may best be understood in relation to the
physical complexity of man.

He had arrived at his final views on the development of mind quite
clearly by the time of a 1938 lecture in Glasgow, where they are sketched.
What is properly to be thought of as an *id* is not a separately developed dark
wild and repressed part of the psyche. *Id,* rather, is the pretty well undifferentiated or unorganised in mind, and the beginning of mind (not a 'ghost in
the machine' but the human being as apperceived in certain terms) is an
undifferentiated 'unorganised mass of tendencies.' There may well be doubt
as to whether it makes sense to talk of 'tendencies,' implying as that does a
degree of differentiation above what is the case with the newborn.

There is really no primary unity, for while the newborn as an entity may
be unitary there is no co-ordination. Not only does the right hand not know
what the left is doing, there is no consciousness of hands, and indeed no
consciousness of a tie to the mother. That comes only later, as the child's
awareness forms and he/she/mind becomes sufficiently differentiated to
differentiate his/her separate existence and the existence of others. There
may even be doubts about deeming so dependent a helpless creature a
separate organism. Man's separate existence always remains a question.

There remains the problem of differentiating the origins of particular
feelings, whether they come from within or outside or some combination of
the two. There is also the problem of differentiating between different
entities, things or persons. To conceive of things which are not persons is by
no means straightforwardly the case for the infant, so dominant are parental
presences in the early period of entire dependency. Much of this may be seen
in accounts of primitive tribes, and in the psychoanalyst's experience of
neurotics.

The differentiation which begins to occur within, or of, the infant's
psyche, Abenheimer (who studied Piaget) treats of as the formation of
complexes. He does not use Jung's special term 'complex' for the precise
reason that Jung has no special term 'complex' and uses the word 'complex'

as in ordinary language. It applies as a description in this case as elsewhere, and in psychology avoids problems of defined terms which imply characters these complexes have not been experienced as having. Because of this differentiation into complexes identifiable feelings, desires and imperatives become possible. In these terms the ego, what I think of as 'I,' forms as one complex no different in kind from others. To regard psychoanalysis as a science proceeding toward a specific result which can be prescribed without making value-judgements, is for Abenheimer wrong. Why prefer one complex rather than others? Why be concerned about a seedy child rather than glad on account of the success of the internal parasites which cause the seediness?

Freud, to use the Scots philosopher A. D. Ritchie's amusing phrase, was an apostle of the hard-boiled in contrast with the half-baked. Among those who claimed to dislike Freud Abenheimer regarded quite a number as apostles of the half-baked. Freud propagandised for a recognition of science which seemed to him to have exposed superstition and also to have enabled understanding and some means of managing a dangerous animality. The latter point did not impress Abenheimer, who apart from knowledge of the work of Bowlby was able to describe the animal in man as consisting in his descent from 'harmless vegetarians.' Not an antecedent animality but processes of human development are what underlie the violent darkness of the repressed content.

Human drives and differentiations are various. In tribal settings and custom-bound societies, as in the infant's relation to the mother, the basis of unity and control is the social setting. This is to say the recognition of an external authority, in its quiet effect reinforced by familarity, and in cases of conflict uncomforting sanctions. Abenheimer clearly did not believe that human life in any setting was necessarily always free of conflicts and anxieties—one need only read the reports of anthropologists. His concern was with the specific conflicts and anxieties of modern man, flung out of or compelled to be in a situation where no authority is sure. And where the seeking of such a security as was perhaps once possessed, more certainly dreamed of, has been disastrous.

He says much in a few words about the obvious group psychology problems involved in totalitarianism. His insight into the inner anxieties of the psychological exile it allayed had no shortage of experience on which to feed, whether as schoolboy-turned-soldier in 1916, or as a German Jew in the 1920s and 1930s. He also draws attention to othere factors relevant in Weimar Germany, the apparently self-sufficient independence and real isolation of the academic. To understand his relentless analysis of Prospero it is useful to relate it to the non-political man of the Weimar republic. The 'controlled' Ulrich, Musil's *The Man Without Qualities,* is also apostrophised as 'sick.' What are the objectives of psychoanalysis?

It is no wonder that the 'therapeutic' seen in isolation has no appeal for Abenheimer. It is an ethically ignorant, rather than indifferent, mode of control. Freud too essayed a mode of control, polemicising on behalf of a view which pretended not merely to be scientific in psychology but in meeting dangers for society. Abenheimer also shows signs of believing his psychology capable of beneficial effect on society's self-understanding and self-management. He did not scorn Freud's hope, but disagreed with certain crucial contentions of Freud.

Freudian theory resembles a scientific presentation in its degree of abstract generality, order and clarity. Yet these characteristics do not themselves amount to science. Generality is not by itself comprehensiveness, mankind across the world have a lot in common as regards native endowment and in the circumstances and experiences which meet them. This broad view is not the whole. We can know that human beings are human beings quite without having to say why, and without needing to articulate or own to any very involved precise theories about them. Meeting some theories about them, it is possible that we may have no experience which goes against such theories. They seem fair enough, but it is careless to go that much further.

Other theories strike us differently, especially when stated in either half-baked or hard-boiled terms. Hard-boiled Freud offended the half-baked, as he intended. Abenheimer certainly disagreed with Jaspers where in the *Allgemeine Psychopathologie* the latter is entirely dismissive of psychoanalytic theories of the unconscious. He however defends those passages of Jaspers, for while they misunderstood Freud and Jung they attacked quite well various ideas which appeal to those who, with no profound understanding of psychology, accept and parrot Freudian formulae from a mere hard-boiled point of view.

If therapists they are liable to impose a model on people come to them for treatment. If writers they will perpetuate errors with unduly reinforced false confidence. In either regard they will not understand, and will be unable to see what is before them. They will regard sundry generalities referring fairly enough to innumerable people as the whole truth about all. That this has been the case with Freudians is perfectly clear, so that the critique of the paper on *Snow White* is a valuable introduction, especially with its continuation by way of a different, properly philologically reading, and the early statement of that need for an ego-psychology so much of Abenheimer's work sought subsequently to answer.

His different papers are not purely a linear series but worth taking together. Thus for instance one might re-read him on *Snow White* beside 'Rilke and Nietzsche.' The ostensive theme is hard-boiled misreading, relevant both as literary criticism and as something of an example for therapists and psychological understanding in general. The earliest form of the 'Rilke and Nietzsche' paper was merely on Rilke, from 1941, and demonstrates the importance to Abenheimer of an intensive reading of Rilke—the paradigmatic figure who attempted to explore his humanity by sheltering his life from historical-political accident. It was reworked in relation to Kaufmann's book, which Abenheimer attacked in a *Glasgow Herald* review with specific reference to Kaufmann's claim to be expressing a modern 'Nietzschean' point of view. There was something other than hard-boiledness to Nietzsche, as Abenheimer indicates elsewhere. He emphasises the changeableness of Nietzsche, but between one fixed form and another. Without necessarily saying that much specifically about everyone he ostensibly discussed, Nietzsche generated a remarkable mass of psychological descriptions, and lived a succession of psychologies.

It is important that Abenheimer represents each of these psychologies as it was. It is no less important that he brings out Kaufmann's error so clearly. There is a general point throughout these papers of misunderstanding others by an illicit too close relating to oneself.

This recurs to the problems of development, that 'man does not know how anthropomorphic he is.' The child, for whom the world is dominated by the defending parent, finds difficulty in distinguishing things and indeed persons from the parent. Toy horses and alas for instance living cats are often subjected to the kind of cajolery and so forth as the parent. One begins by expecting things to be and be moveable in a certain way. Seeing them as they are is difficult, and the corollary of finding appeal in the works of a poet, or the supposed person of someone else, is to mistake the other for an image of oneself, something or someone else congenial. Thus they cannot be recognised, and thus cannot be loved. The at first apprently uncongenial may continue to be the object of marks of misunderstanding, if there is persistence in mis-apperceiving them as another kind, thing or person. If I can like or know only what I have hitherto liked and known, and can see nothing else, I will never learn and likely never love.

The respective character of each person is bound up very much with factors special to him or her, and factors by no means special. In a many transactions between people this does not to a great extent matter. People do not need to worry about understanding each other beyond a certain point *and* should be wary of misunderstanding. A fair degree of acceptance is necessary, while at the same time rejections are not entirely out of the question. For the therapist another consideration arises, where nothing has prepared him or her to understand some very different person who appears as a patient. Abenheimer urges, against the view that different schools cannot reach truth, the fact of a therapist imposing the model of his own developed psyche beyond where it can cognise the other. The difficult case is impossible for that therapist and must be referred to another practitioner, or less should be hoped for or claimed.

For Abenheimer mind is in a very real sense a community. It becomes a community, rather than a chaotic dependency ruled from outside, by dint of the differentiations which occur. Complexes form, autonomous, refracting and shaping lessons and (true or false) convictions which have formed. In the journalistic Freudian model one such complex is called super-ego, and as such it operates as a spectre of most obviously parents, teachers, urging various priorities, feelings, wishes, from within. It is apprehended only in relation to another complex, ego, with its own autonomy and priorities, its own standards and desires. On kindred lines there may be a 'dark' complex of repressed, violent or otherwise disturbing elements, and on this fairly standard model these non-ego elements are hostile and conflict with ego. They have to be modified and incorporated within it. All must be comprehended and controlled by a central progressive scientific understanding.

Abenheimer demurs. The trinity of 'dark' with ego and superego represents three in mutual opposition. While there are plainly intrapsychic oppositions and conflicts manageable only by hard work at understanding, tracing histories and questioning beliefs, the community character of all mind is not comprised entirely by either mutual conflicting parts or a dominance of one over others. There are quite beneficial conflicts, marginal or unhappily absent from various pathological cases he describes in novels and the drama. Co-operation between complexes is perfectly well the case in many people. It is possible only by dint of an appropriate attitude to life, beyond narcissism and nihilism and facing conflicts whose origin is in dealing with external situations.

The ego is central inasmuch as it is the complex identified with 'I' in willing, in setting up oppositions within and with the external, in relating other than submissively toward othere persons. It is central and a focus of ethical thinking and of power. Problems arise when it seeks to be all, fixed and tyrannical, coveting monopoly of control. Where that happens. the condition can be recognised by extension of tyranny beyond the person's own being, seeking to subdue and being unable to recognise othereness or to love. It is wrong to prescribe that always 'where id is should ego be.'

'Id' is for Abenheimer the not-organised-together, and such a loose community within mind is crucial to various performances demanding rather responsiveness than deliberation. Spontaneity can be possible, only through ego maintaining an untyrannical attitude. Ego must however have some power and stability as against the mere play of impulse. It must seek to be governed by wisdom. Highly structured, it must not be immutable. The trauma of overcoming the worst narcissism is that whiles a bad ego must necessarily break: where he that would find himself must lose himself.

The achievement of what might be called selfhood or integration in the world, is acceptance of community, of the whole of a psychic totality which has attained to a certain condition, of course somewhat short of perfection. Anothere concept to which Abenheimer refers in relation to the psychic totality of the person is Existence, a term he takes not uncritically from Jaspers. He speaks of Existential Decision, which is not ego's decision about anything but a decision of the whole being to which ego is subject, compelled. In a field in which Abenheimer was properly attentive toward appropriate description—a field which demands literary awareness—it might be said that an Existential Decision is decided. One's existence is committed, to a profound relationship in marriage, devotion to a moral or religious cause, to the process of deeper discovery when the result is a revelation of oneself.

A NOTE ON THE TEXT

Abenheimer's command of English was in general admirable, and the reader may gather that he could put of putting difficult matters extraordinarily well. He continued however to write as one who had learned his English in Germany, and characteristically strays now and again from common English idiom. This is notable in the tenses of verbs and also in the presence of the definite article where none would normally appear. In editing, verbs have been silently corrected, to avoid awkwardness, as have various obvious intrusions of 'the'. Sometimes, however, to have altered Abenheimer's German-English idiom seemed by no means to leave his meaning unaffected. Where there was any doubt on that point, no change was made.

Other slight intrusions were made in consultation with associates of Abenheimer, where plainly an emphasis had been insufficiently pointed, and the proper force of a conclusion had not emerged without re-readings. Nothing at all extensive was involved, but the modification should be noted.

The sole intrusion of any extent was made in consultation with Abenheimer's friends Christopher Small, and J. A. M. Rillie of Glasgow University, in the paper on Shakespeare's Sonnets. Some passages from Shakespeare's text have been incorporated in a paper initially delivered to an audience with the Sonnets before them.

It also seemed necessary to emend an opening passage in which Abenheimer gave the unintended impression of rejecting various scholarly views as to the order in which the sonnets had been composed. Quite plainly Abenheimer wished to essay no such rejection, his concern being simply with the validity of the standard published sequence as in effect a dramatic text of psychological moment and validity. As such it stands.

Robert R. Calder

ACKNOWLEDGEMENTS

The editor must thank Irene Abenheimer for her considerable hospitality, and clerical assistance, in the process of sorting through the papers. For biographical material, as well as to Mrs. Abenheimer considerable thanks must go to Abenheimer's nephew, Dr. Hans Wagner, as to family and friends including Matthew Abenheimer, Dr. Jacob Miller, Aileen Campbell Nye, Susan Golombok, Jack Rillie, Dr. Cameron MacDonald and others. Particular thanks in that and other regards go to Christopher Small for proofreading, and for initiation of the project and financial support Dr. David Forrester, through whose good offices the Royal Philosophical Society of Glasgow awarded a bursary to facilitate research into the Abenheimer/Schorstein Group.

ON A FREUDIAN INTERPRETATION OF THE STORY OF SNOW WHITE (1942)

This is one of those papers which try to find a connection with Freud's sex theory in every incident of the story. It is much more a collection of associations from Freudian readings which come to the author's mind *a propos* of the story, than an interpretation of the story itself; all sound rules which safeguard the accuracy of the interpretation are neglected. The snow in the first scene brings 'frigidity' to the mind of the authors, and the good loving mother queen has to be frigid in spite of this being just meaningless. That the snow falls outside her room and her window and not in her or in her house does not bother these interpreters. Another 'principle' of this type of interpretation is *once a sex symbol, always a sex symbol*: for example, mountains sometimes symbolise breasts, and therefore any mountain must mean breast; and Snow White being exposed in her glass coffin on the mountain 'suggests continued contact with the poisoned breast though the mountain might also be the loving mother.' I wonder who beside a Melanie Klein adept would think of this on listening to the story. Other people probably see the summit of the mountain as a place of isolation and aloofness from the world.

Nobody, of couse, can go mining in the mountains without intercourse coming to the authors' mind, and it does not matter to them that the dwarfs are, if anything, representative of desexualised (harmless, undangerous) forces. When Snow White is lying dead in her glass coffin, then this 'represents an extraversion of libido by Snow White herself', which is just the opposite of what the story says. Parallels of other fairy tales or mediaeval legends which could have elucidated unclear incidents are never consulted. For instance, the long period which Snow White spent in the glass coffin has a parallel in the hundred years sleep of the Sleeping Beauty, or in Brunnhilde's sleep on the mountain surrounded by fire; or, more important still, the enclosure of the white (Snow White) and the red (apple) elements in the hermetically sealed glass vessel for putrefaction (death) and transformation in mediaeval alchemy.

According to the authors, everything in the story has to do with death and the sexual love, hatred and jealousy between parents and child. We never get away from this, with the result that nothing happens in the whole story. No sooner does Snow White leave her parents, being driven into the woods, than she is back with them; for the little house of the dwarfs and the dwarfs themselves are the parents again. When she dies she cannot escape the parents, for the authors decide that the birds who watch at her coffin are again the mother; and when she finally marries, the prince then is the father, for he has slept in the house of the dwarfs, with whom he gets identified in his feelings for Snow White.

This type of interpretation is a frequent one in Freudian papers, and has frequently also been criticised on the lines I have pointed out. What makes people go on with the same faulty interpretations year in year out? We get some insight into this if we ask ourselves what is wrong with the general trend of this interpretation. The authors say that the story is chiefly concerned with the relationship between a mother and a daughter from the child's birth till her development to womanhood, and that the chief villain of the piece is mutual sexual jealousy. This is however only half of the truth. The story deals not only with the mother-daughter relationship, but also with the development of a human individual from birth to marriage, when the circle of birth and maturation starts again.

The difficulties between mother and daughter are only incidents in this development of Snow White. Already the first scene, when the three drops of blood fall out of the mother's room into the cold snow outside, anticipates the theme of the child being born out of the mother and pushed into the cold world. This theme is then more explicitly pursued in the incident of the mother's death and Snow White's actual expulsion from the parental house by the stepmother. Now a complete change of scene takes place, Snow White is no longer with her parents in the flesh but in the wood with the trees and the wild animals, and behind the seven hills with the dwarfs.

It may be that these are symbols akin to those forces which originally were included in the parental *imagines*, but this only obliges us all the more to emphasise the features which differentiate the new symbols from the original ones. For example, the diffusion of the mother *imago* into the larger image of mother nature can be a step forward in the solution of the mother fixation and the transformation of the original childish parental *imagines*. Here original mother qualities are distributed not only over the trees, the kind and helpful animals, the house in the wood, but the dwarfs also participate in these qualities. These helpful earth spirits who appear only at night, and who work during the day inside the mountains, are symbols of helpful subconscious forces (and the subconscious is, of course, connected with the original mother *imago*). Snow White, last but not least, also acts as the caring mother to the dwarfs. The whole scene in the wood behind the seven hills symbolises introversion and the introjection of the qualities of the good mother. Now Snow White finds helpful forces in herself which carry the development further.

These forces are akin to the former *imagines* of the good parents, but belong no longer to the outside world, but to a mystical place behind the seven hills; that is, Snow White's inner world. The one helpful mother *imago* has become split up into many forces, thus enabling the development of the child's ego: for as long as the original parental *imagines* remain compact and undissolved, the ego has no chance to grow. How should it be able to compete with those outsized *imagines*? Yet the *imago* of the cruel mother has not yet undergone this transformation and remains still an overpowering, paralysing force. Twice does Snow White, turning away from the inner helpers, become paralysed (especially sexually paralysed) by the encounter with the cruel mother *imago*. Only at the third encounter does she really get to grips with this evil force. She now incorporates some of its poison, and what looks like a victory of the stepmother is the beginning of a new transformation of Snow White herself. This happens in the familiar form of death, incubation period when the destructive poison is inside Snow White and contaminating her, and resurrection.

The result is an assimilation into Snow White's ego, of some of the aggressive forces which before were all dissociated and projected on to the evil stepmother. Now Snow White is able to assert herself enough to live her sex life, and in the heat of the slippers (her awakened sex) which she and the prince have brought for the stepmother, the *imago* of the restricting superego perishes. This is a rough outline of what one could call the ego psychology in the story of Snow White, or the anagogic meaning (Silberer) or the process of individuation (Jung) in the story.

MacQuisten and Pickford's paper interprets the story on the basis of Freud's pre-ego psychology theory. This older theory has a special appeal to natural

scientists because it is of the type of a generalising natural science interested in one
or two general forces (instincts) which are supposed to work behind the individual
variety of psychological happenings. To discover these, is the aim of the
'interpretation'.

Ego psychology, though empirical and scientific too, is not a natural science but
is interested in the development of the individual personal unity which is spoken of
using the first person, 'ego', personal pronoun. In spite of many articles on the
subject in recent years (1942), ego psychology is still a neglected step-child of
Freudian theory. Only rarely is it realised that it is the psychology of personal unity
and its development. Among the roughly twenty different ego concepts and definitions which (have been) used in the Freudian literature, scarcely one (has emphasised) this personal moment which so obviously is the distinguishing feature
between *Ego* (personal pronoun) and *Id* (impersonal pronoun).

The two different 'interpretations' of a fairy-tale, the 'analytical' and what
Silberer calls the 'anagogic', the search for vestiges of general instinctual forces and
the individualising search, are not two interpretations on the same level. The one
deals with the origin of certain symbols, with the raw material which is used in the
story, while only the second type of interpretation aims at finding the meaning
which the story wants to convey. To call the first an 'interpretation of the story' is
like calling a discourse on mahogany wood or on organic chemistry an 'interpretation of the Chippendale style of my furniture.'

EXISTENTIALISM *(1951)*

(1) Existentialism may be described as a philosophical anthropology, i.e. a body of
philosophical ideas about man and the human situation. As such it can form part of
various general philosophies, and there are existentialists who adhere to a religious
Weltanschauung and others who profess atheistic views.

(2) The existentialist speaks of how man experiences himself subjectively, particularly how he experiences his total being, his existence. He holds that this cannot be
the subject-matter of any objective science because every science approaches man
from one particular point of view only, and even the sum-total of all the sciences
concerned with man does not give us a concept of man's wholeness. Man is always
more than his actuality. He always turns against his finite stability and when he gets
stuck in fixed forms or is levelled down to something merely average he becomes
sub-human. Man is incomplete and not to be completed. His entirety cannot be
made the subject-matter of theoretical knowledge but can be experienced only in
those existential decisions, actions and situations in which the individual entirety
shapes and expresses itself.

(3) Further characteristics of existentialism demand consideration of what we
mean by the 'subject' and 'subjective'. The subject is first and foremost the doer of
actions, or more accurately he wills the action ('will' is here used in the widest sense
of the word, so that it comprises desiring, aiming at, having purpose, preferring,
intending, experiencing urges and drives, and so forth). When we think of subjects
we deal with the motives of subjects, with the subjective experiences of what ought
to be or to happen, with their will, and, in this sense, with the normative acts of
subjects. This is different from causal or scientific thinking. The progress of science
could be described as a progressive elimination of the subject and its purposive will,

and as the replacement of subjective will by endless causal connections which have no starting point and are not wilfully directed and goal-seeking, but are purely objective and independent of subjective interpretations. Psychology too had the ambition to become an objective natural science which eliminates the subject and replaces its normative acts by causal connections. Yet man in his pre-scientific thinking still experiences himself and his fellow-men as subjects. Therefore a need for another, not natural-scientific psychology arose, which would aim at describing and understanding the pre-scientific comprehension of self, which would continue to reckon with subjects and their motives and wills and which would approach man in the same subjective way as the existentialist does. The psychology of the various analytical schools is of this nature.

Another branch of psychology which tries to describe and investigate our pre-scientific ways of experiencing ourselves and the world is the phenomenological psychology which Edmund Husserl, Heidegger's predecessor in the Chair of Moral Philosophy at Freiburg, started.

(4) The following conclusions can be drawn from the previous reflections:

(a) The subject is the starting point of will and normative acts and exists concretely only in its concrete decisions. Irrespective of its strivings, will, decisions, norms, the subject is a mere abstraction. Existentialism is interested in the concrete individual as he appears in his existential decisions.

(b) The statement that a subject willed an event is identical with the statement that the subject is responsible for it, and *vice versa* the rejection of responsibility is identical with the imputation of the event to the will of another subject. The concept of subject and of responsibility are inseparable. That is the reason why formerly psychology and moral philosophy were regarded as one subject-matter. Yet even nowadays, when subjective psychology deals with a far more comprehensive body of empirical observations than the psychology of old, subjective psychology cannot wholly be separated from moral philosophy.

(c) Subjective thinking inevitably reckons with freedom. A subject acts either by complying with another subject's will, dependent, heteronymous, subjected; or is a law unto himself, independent, autonomous, free. Subjective thinking must by definition arrive somewhere at free subjects. The opposite of freedom is heteronymy, not determinism. Determinism and indeterminism are concepts belonging to objective causal thinking, not to subjective thinking. These are two different methods of viewing man. Both are true statements of the case within the system of thought to which they belong. Neither can be used to refute the correctness of a statement belonging to another system of reference. All that can be said is that there is more than one way of experiencing man, and that the various methods of thinking which we employ in these experiences are mutually incompatible.

(5) The various philosophical anthropologies and subjective psychologies are characterised by the choice and description of the subjects which they regard as autonomous. For instance among psychologists C.G. Carus regarded the 'Unconscious' as the autonomous subject, McDougall 'the sentiment of self-esteem'. Freud 'the instincts', Jung 'the Self', and so forth. Examples of autonomous subjects from the realm of philosophy are 'God', 'the Spirit', Reason', 'the Soul', 'the Will to Power', 'the State' ... All existentialists have in common that they regard 'exis-

tence', as it is experienced in decisions which concern our whole being, as free and autonomous. Existential freedom is neither a 'freedom *from*' nor 'freedom *for*', but the freedom *of* being at one with oneself and *of* honouring the necessities of one's whole being in a concrete situation irrespective of the approval or disapproval of others. The concept 'existence' therefore implies a number of challenges:

    (a) An appeal to accept responsibility for one's own life and not to surrender it to heteronymous forces; for this would be the end of 'being'.

    (b) An appeal to be honest and sincere with regard to oneself. Everything insincere is make-believe and not 'existence'. Therefore what counts is the life one actually lives, not intellectual or symbolic imaginings of oneself, which are usually tinged with wishfulfilling illusions. It is in the existential decision that one discovers oneself, for one cannot know oneself in advance.

    (c) An appeal to express the wholeness of one's being in the concrete situation. The existentialist does not speak of the freedom of the personality because by 'personality' we usually mean the individual outside the concrete life-situation as an isolated abstraction. The existentialist also rejects the idea of the freedom of isolated mental functions such as the reason, the spirit, the instincts, or of isolated structures like the ego, or certain sentiments or the unconscious. Through emphasis on the interweaving of one's individual being with the concrete life-situation existentialism tries to prevent the misinterpretation of freedom as libertinism or paranoid solipsism.

Within these limitations every possible choice is regarded as existentially valuable. This wide tolerance together with the high valuation of honesty and the fearless acceptance of the total reality of our whole being, is akin to the professional attitude which the psychotherapist adopts towards his patients.

Moral tolerance of every decision which is the sincere expression of one's whole existence leaves man in a state of uncertainty and anguish when decisions have to be made which affect his whole being. He has nothing on which to rely except faith in his whole being and in the freedom of his existence, a faith which is itself an existential decision and which can neither be proved nor logically deduced (as for instance Sartre erroneously tries to do from Descartes' *Cogito ergo sum*).

(6) 'Existence' cannot be defined. It 'is not a concept but an index which points to what is beyond all objectivity', says Jaspers. 'Existence' is paradoxical in many ways. One paradox is that 'existence' means being, and yet it is something which is constantly created in the course of the existential decisions throughout life. It means 'being' yet as an autonomous subject it is a supreme value, and it is something that does not 'exist' in the sense that natural science uses the word 'being', but exists only because it is believed in. The same paradox can be found in other subjective systems of thought. The supreme value, the free subject, is of a different nature from the derivations from it, from the consequences it entails, from its passing individual utilisations and expressions. These are valuable because the supreme value is believed in, the supreme value is because it is. Therefore the supreme value is often defined in ontological terms. The best-known example of this is Rousseau's 'Nature'.

'Existence' like 'Nature' or Freud's 'Life and Death instincts' is not a natural object which natural science can investigate, but only an idea of moral philosophy. The ambiguity of the term 'existence' affects the whole of existentialist teaching, which at times reads like a theoretical exposition of what man is when it is really a valuating belief in the supreme value of individual existence and the assertion of profound respect for man whatever he decides to do as the sincere expression of his whole being in a concrete situation.

(7) Existentialist anthropology does not claim to be new. Existentialists all maintain that it is a restatement of philosophical beliefs already contained either in the religious beliefs of Western man or in the philosophical humanism of our tradition (e.g. Goethe's). The need for a new formulation of these beliefs arose out of various circumstances of which I want to mention three:

(a) Moral and political turmoil particularly in Germany and France faced many individuals with moral decisions which in stable societies will only rarely confront man.

(b) Existentialism takes into account the criticism of conventional moral teaching which not only Kierkegaard and Nietzsche have voiced but which follows also from the findings of modern subjective psychology. In many ways existentialism can be regarded as a formulation of the supreme ideals of health toward which psychotherapy aims. It formulates in a positive way the aim which we are accustomed to formulate negatively as the overcoming of compulsive submission to heteronymous authorities, or to fixed defence mechanisms. It values action on one's own responsibility in accordance with the necessities of one's whole being, and the progressive discovery and clarification of self and of the situation of the self in the world in the course of these existential decisions. On the other hand the actions which existentialist plays and novels describe as the opposite of existentially free decisions, those actions which are based on blind submission to conventions, on moral delf-deception, perfectionism, despair, laziness of heart, and so forth, could in most cases equally well be described in terms of psychopathology.

(c) Finally the new formulation of old beliefs is intended as a criticism of current divergent beliefs in the supremacy of non-individual and (in this sense) heteronymous authorities and forces. Existentialism criticises all forms of political authoritarianism which regard any deviation of personal decision as treason and morally despicable. It also rejects all forms of so-called scientific *Weltanschauung*. These represent the isolated natural laws (or historical laws in dialectical materialism) which natural science discovers as supreme values having precedence over individual existence. Every finding of objective science may influence our subjective will in many ways, but is never by itself an existential value of compelling validity. Its meaning and value derive from the existential interpretation it receives from the valuating agent, the individual existence. Existentialism therefore disagrees with Freud's philosophical belief that his subjective psychology is objective natural science and as such the necessary basis for a scientific *Weltanschauung*. Psychoanalysis cannot replace moral philosophy.

On Narcissism, with Reference to Shakespeare's *King Lear*

The word 'ego' is the personal pronoun of the first person singular. As such it relates to those concepts, models and schemata which we ourselves have. Each person uses a number of such models of himself. The particular interest of the psychotherapist is in the models and schemata which refer to organisation of the desires, impulses and emotions. In this sense the ego is experienced as the subject and the origin of the desires, impulses and emotions. We know that not all desires and so forth are included in ego organisation, and as far back as 1906 Jung referred to the ego as an emotional complex which stands beside other emotional complexes. Freud and the Gestalt psychologists followed later with similar descriptions.

The ego, as the subject of desires, meets with difficulties which cause anxiety, and Freud has shown how this leads to repressions, dissociations and displacement of impulses. Yet often the ego fights anxiety in different ways. If an individual has sexual urges which tend to cause conflict, he may, instead of giving them up or repressing them, try to change his way of expressing them and pursuing them, so that the conflicts may be avoided, i.e. he will modify the ego and ego-expression. To avoid opposition, the individual may remain passive and wait until others fulfil his wishes voluntarily; or he may aim at full domination over his environment and in this way exclude conflicts; or he may try to avoid contact with others, and exclude the possibility of friction by means of solipsism. To be at peace with the world may in the course of this development become an aim in itself. Yet his efforts to avoid conflict do not extinguish his demands to have his sexual and other urges satisfied.

Insatiable demands of the ego are one of the main characteristics of narcissism. Freud and his school have shown that reactions to early childish aggression and destructive tendencies play a paramount role in these modifications of the ego. Aggressive and destructive impulses various in origin, purpose and fate (not, therefore, to be classified as one instinct), probably the first to bring the child face to face with strong opposition to his desires. They create a more or less comprehensive fear of being the subject of desires, impulses and emotions.

Yet this alone is not narcissism, for the avoidance of conflicts cannot produce that emphasis on the ego which gives that impression of self-love which led to this ego attitude being named after Narcissus. Again, Freudian research into the development and fate of the early aggressive and destructive urges has shown that attempts to master these urges always leads to aggressions against oneself, and to self-destructive tendencies. These self-destructive tendencies have to be answered by increased ego-defences and ego emphasis and there is no narcissism (I use this term only for what Freud called secondary narcissism) without this defence purpose.

Thus narcissism could be defined as a definite ego attitude by which a person attempts simultaneously to gratify ego urges without conflict, and to defend himself against self-destructive tendencies. Narcissism is a response to two contradictory fears: the fear of being an ego, (i.e. an independent subject of desires and so forth), and the simultaneous fear of not being an ego. The narcissist wants to have the advantage of being an ego without the commitments of having to rely upon himself and to face conflicts; and he wants the advantages of not being an ego without the limitations of liberty and independence which it entails. (I prefer this, based on formulations of the Danish philosopher and psychologist Kierkegaard, to the possible Freudian formulation that narcissism is a response to sado-masochistic tendencies. The latter formulation leaves connexion with the ego unmentioned. It uses terms originally coined to describe specific sexual perversions, and cannot be sufficiently neutralised to describe also non-sexual, aggressive and destructive tendencies adequately.)

That narcissism tries to serve two masters, and to pacify simultaneously two contradictory fears, accounts for its inner paradoxes. The attempt to have desires satisfied without conflict is most often made by regression to the longing to be cared for and looked after like a baby. If one were contained in the love-object as in the mother's womb, or at the breast of an all-loving mother, one could get satisfaction without conflict. Yet the narcissist is not able to accept care and attention naively as the baby does, for he has experienced the disappointment of frustration by the mother, and the restriction of his liberty. These experiences have aroused fears of being left helpless, and the babyish submission has therefore to be coupled with attempts to dominate. He can feel safe only on the proviso that the person who is supposed to play the role of the good mother can be forced to serve him perpetually and exclusively. The narcissist submits in order to induce the object of his love to be more assertive and indulgent to his wishes. By his submission, he wants to enslave the love-object. Symbolically speaking, the wish to be contained in the love-object is coupled with the wish to contain it and thus have full control over it. Hidden or open, narcissism must always aim at domination, for only in this way can gratification without conflict be safeguarded.

The aloofness which some narcissists display is not genuine detachment, and it is true to say that a narcissist never withdraws his object libido. He is always more dependent on others than anybody else; for he is unable to satisfy his desires against opposition and needs reassurance from others.

When he cannot find anybody sufficiently dependable in the outside world, he may be forced to turn to introjected objects. Or he may stop looking altogether for the service of one individual, and transfer his need for reassurance to anonymous masses whose approval and admiration he may court by being perfectionistic and outstanding. If both these methods fail, he will become helpless and develop a paralysing sense of futility which Fairbairn rightly found characteristic of schizoid and schizophrenic personalities. All this can be clearly observed in the life stories of dandies.

The dandy is a prototype of narcissism. One of his characteristics is his snobbish aloofness and feeling of superiority toward the masses. He constantly claims to be an independent individual who does not care what other people think of him, he indulges in all kinds of extravagances. yet is at the same time extremely conventional. To be perfectly dressed, shine as a wit, and be admired, is more important to him than to anyone else. Oscar Wilde never ceased to claim his independence from moral and social conventions, at the same time courting public attention and admiration with showman-like propaganda worthy of any modern dictator. In every party he had to be the central figure. After his trial and imprisonment, when he lost public attention he also lost all direction, leading the life of a desperado, drinking and depending on the charity of friends for his existence. Everything had become futile. The paradoxes of narcissistic love are well illustrated in the film *Citizen Kane*. It contains an excellent portrait of a paranoid narcissist.

Kane's first marriage fails because he cannot love and respect a self-reliant personality beside him, and he attaches himself to a girl whom he has picked up in the street — a complete nonentity. Her emptiness and lack of character lead him to expect her complete submission and the possibility of moulding her according to his wishes and needs. He believes that he really loves her and that he is proving this by overwhelming her with presents, valuable beyond measure, and by fulfilling all her wishes. Yet even this silly and empty-headed woman comes to realise that he never can express his real feelings towards her, but is using her only for the purpose of his own reassurance. He needs to feel that he is loved, that he can give love, and that he is not alone; apart from this the girl means nothing to him. This is the essence of all narcissistic love: to be reassured that conflictless unity exists, that self-destructive attacks are unjust, and that one is lovable after all. To obtain this reassurance narcissists go to every possible extreme; they are prepared to sacrifice all money, reason, and dignity. They may falsify every genuine feeling and suppress all justified criticism. They constantly try to be kind and good in order to show others the loving way in which they want to be treated themselves. They may speak incessantly of love (narcissism is a real hotbed of sentimentality: spurious and exaggerated expressions of sentiment which are required to hide the lack or suppression of true and genuine feelings). Yet a loved one never means anything in his or her own right, apart from a value as reassurance against the two fears of being an ego and of not being an ego. The narcissist remains in his or her bastion of self-defence, even in love. No matter how kind and considerate he may be towards the love-object, all his love is basically nothing but dependence for the purpose of reassurance.

Narcissists treat themselves in the same way as they treat the love-object. They are often morbidly introspective and self-centred, but this does not prevent them from being quite blind about themselves. Vast parts of the personality always have to remain unnoticed in order to pacify their fears. Therefore the narcissist may be said to love himself as little as he loves others. He rejects the greater part of himself and is interested only in those qualities which help to reassure him. Thus whilst he considers himself to be good and kind to everybody, he is simply choked with hatred and resentment.

Another may display extreme humility and self-abasement, thinking that he is being perfectly honest with himself in seeing nothing but faults in himself. He fails to realize the conceit and perfectionism on which his criticism is based. There is no acceptance of the irrational totality of his being, no naivety towards himself. Every self-expression is controlled so that it may fit into a picture acceptable to his self-esteem. (McDougall's description of the integrated personality as a pyramid of purposes, with the sentiment of self-esteem at the top, is in reality the description of the narcissist. Freud's concept of the super-ego even belongs to the sphere of narcissism).

Even the autoerotic narcissist, who is supposed to be in love with his own body, aims only at reassurance. Freudian authors maintain that all exhibitionism is a compensation for a strong castration complex, and I have found this confirmed by my own experience. The woman who narcissistically displays her body has rejected herself as a woman and is trying to reassure herself about not being male; and the male who displays his body has rejected his manly urges towards the other sex and mentally castrated himself.

In so far as a person rejects himself he is by necessity unindividual. Wherever he does not allow himself genuine self-expression, he is either conventional and suggestible, or else is rebelling against conventions and suggestions: in which case his reactions also remain ruled by those outside forces, although in the negative way. One can study this well in schizoid personalities whose attempts to be egos are reduced to negativism. All parties and movements which are 'in opposition' have a large following of narcissists, who join such bodies for no positive reason but only for opposition's sake.

Another way open to the narcissist to express individuality, is to attempt to become outstanding in a certain direction and thus to escape the conflict of competition as well as the sufferings of self-criticism. The narcissist may be outstanding by real achievements, as is the case with so many artists and scientists, or he may at least fancy himself to be outstanding, as for example Oscar Wilde did when he wrote his first plays. These were complete failures but nevertheless convinced him that he was greater than Shakespeare. Every form of snobbishness and eccentricity serves the purpose of appearing outstanding. To be an individual on the common human plane is impossible for the narcissist, He needs a big distance between himself and the masses, in consequence of fear of losing his ego.

Narcissism is ambiguous and lacks genuineness and sincerity. It is the main source of what Pfaender called *Unechtheit*, which is to say spuriousness of personality.

If we co-ordinate and contrast this description of narcissism with other psychological concepts, we may be able to elucidate it further and to find and describe the healthier opposite towards which psychotherapeutic efforts are directed.

The narcissistic ego attitude may be present in any psychotic or neurotic illness and is actually to be found in most cases. Longing for reassurance and for gratification without conflict finds most often a perfect expression in longing for the perfect mother, and regressions to oral urges are prominent. On the other hand, anal tendencies, in so far as they symbolise independent ego assertion and aggression, are usually repressed. Yet one will find not seldom narcissistic fantasies of union with the love-object *per anum*. Nor does emphasis on oral urges exclude desires for conflictless gratification of genital urges. It is well known how obsessed many schizoid personalities are with cravings for sexual intercourse, mainly because it serves them as a reassurance against the fear of being powerless and not likeable. That other perversions, especially homosexuality, masochism and exhibitionism, go well together with narcissism, has been frequently described. Also most sadists can indulge in their perversions only when conflicts are excluded, that is, with willing or powerless victims.

The relationship between narcissism and aggressions is rather complex. We saw that narcissism develops as a response to fears of conflicts and aggressions. Perhaps it was for this reason that Freud regarded narcissism as a libidinal force, turned towards the ego. Narcissism and aggression are not, however, opposites. Many narcissists can use aggression freely for self-defensive purposes, or can react with thoroughly destructive aggressiveness when their demands for gratification of desires and reassurance are frustrated. This aggression is just as narcissistic as the original demands for love were. Apparently the narcissist changes from an outwardly submissive or aloof, to an openly domineering or possessive attitude; but we have seen that attempts at domination have always been present behind the submissive role. Cyclic changes from submission and aloofness to destructive and domineering attitudes, and back, are characteristic of most forms of narcissism. Therapeutically, nothing is gained by liberating narcissistic destruction. Fear of aggression certainly has to be decreased if narcissism is to be overcome, not for the purpose of becoming domineering, but in order to enable the person to express and pursue desires and feelings spontaneously. I call this freedom of positive self-expression *self-assertion*.

Because the earliest forms of self-assertion are coupled with aggressions against the parents the neurotic regards all the various forms of self-assertion as aggressive. In hysteria, sex is regarded as aggressive, in schizophrenia every form of ego abstraction, even every form of thinking, may be feared as something aggressive. This does not however justify the conclusion that there is really an element of aggression contained in these activities, any more than it is justified to assume that all drugs contain excreta because a neurotic who is afraid of incorporating excreta also fears drugs. Self-assertion, not aggression, is the opposite of narcissism; and self-assertion, not giving, is the opposite of narcissistic demands. The therapist helps the patient to follow his own heart where it is necessary, instead of being hindered by self-protection, or that pseudo-kindness which makes him afraid to hurt because of the fear of being hurt himself.

Linked to the therapeutic aim of liberating self-assertion is the other aim of helping the narcissist to overcome his self-rejection. He has to learn to accept himself as he is, and not as he for safety's sake pretends to be. Therapy has to bring about active introversion if it wants to overcome narcissistic ego emphasis. (Jung discriminates between active and passive introversion, the first meaning that detachment from objects and self-introversion from the ego which is unknown to the narcissist; the second coincides largely with the narcissistic introjection of love-objects and dissociation of vast parts of his personality.) Not all turning to oneself is narcissism, but it is narcissistic to turn inward with the unconscious aim of escaping into an imaginary paradise or to the introjected good mother. It is not narcissistic to turn inward for the sake of self-realisation.

Neither is narcissism identical with regression, and many forms of healthy regression exist. For instance, we regress temporarily in sleep, love and all forms of productivity, and this regression is of a more genuine type than the narcissistic one. Certainly the narcissist longs for complete union with the good mother, but he cannot really regress to the original unity of child and mother, because he cannot give up his ego. All his ego-negation and ego-dissolution serves paradoxically only the purpose of safeguarding and reassuring his ego. The young child has not yet developed an ego in our sense. He is part of the total situation, to which he reacts like an animal. Only later and slowly does the child realise himself to be the subject of desires, impulses and emotions. This happens first only at moments, and throughout our lives a great part of our behaviour is conducted without clear ego segregation. What Levy-Bruhl describes as participation mystique rules not only the activities of primitives but to a large extent also the activity of modern man. The narcissist, with his fear of losing himself, constantly meddles and interferes with this participation and tries to be an ego where he should react spontaneously and naively.

In the earliest experiences of ego segregation power, mastery and will play a great role, and so do aggression and opposition to people on whom one depends. The narcissist tries to be an ego by the application of one or several of these concomitant characteristics of early ego assertion. Therapy has therefore to aim at relaxing this defective ego emphasis and ego control, to help the patient to 'let himself go' and *be*, to let things happen without interfering, to trust himself and others, to be like others, and to assimilate the common man in himself. The maxim 'where *ego* was should *id* be' is as important in the therapy of narcissism as the rule 'where *id* was should *ego* be'. No one-way path of strengthening or development leads from the narcissistic to the healthy ego, but the narcissistic attitude has to collapse and a new one to be discovered. It is for this reason that I think it right to distinguish more clearly than does Freud between narcissism and the primal identity of the child with the surrounding world, which he called primary narcissism. He describes it as a state where all libido is stored up in the ego. This description is obviously based on secondary narcissistic fantasies, for the baby has no ego, nor is he or she, as Freud implies, passive; the baby turns actively to the breast, or expresses discomfort. Freud's ideal of health is equally hostile to narcissism and to primal participation mystique, and this accounts for the aloofness, rationalism, and solipsism of this ideal.

The choice of the name narcissism is not so arbitrary as might be assumed by those who see in the myth of Narcissus a description merely of love of one's own body. Many features of narcissism described above can be found in the different interpretations of the myth since ancient times.

The oldest form of the myth is regarded by Frazer as a mythical description of the widespread primitive fear that the soul of a man whose shadow falls upon the water may be dragged down into the depths by water spirits. The myth might thus be seen as having originated in the fear of losing one's soul or ego through the fascination of the inner world; and this has little reference to the love of one's own body.

In the Alexandrian period of Greek literature the myth was elaborated in the form which many will know from Ovid's *Metamorphoses*. Narcissus was so beautiful that he attracted everybody's love. Yet he did not respond, and proved to be a despiser of Eros. The nymph Echo died from unanswered love for Narcissus, and another lover, a male called Ameinitis, killed himself (according to Konon). This roused the wrath of the gods, who took vengeance by making Narcissus fall in love with his own image. It was clearly realized that Narcissus was unable to love others. It may be that Narcissus's surname 'The Taciturn', which Strabo mentions, also relates to the shut-in character of the narcissist.

In a version of the myth provided by Pausanias, Narcissus does not fall in love with himself but takes his reflection for his twin sister, his exact counterpart, who had died. Similarly, in a French poem of the twelfth century it is said that Narcissus believed his reflection to be the apparition of a '*fee de mer que la fontaine ait a garder*': that is, for a mother image, for his mother was a nymph. In these two versions it is realised that the narcissist loves not himself but introjected objects. The version of Peutadius says that Narcissus committed suicide by throwing himself into the water, because he

wanted to unite with his father, the river-god, Cephissus. Here you have the
attempt at complete union with the love-object by disappearing in it. That it
is the father, not the mother, into whom Narcissus retires, is a homosexual
displacement frequently found in male narcissists. Let me quote two more
modern interpretations of the myth.

R.M. Rilke's poem *'Narziss'* describes how Narcissus, on seeing his
reflection in the water, experiences what women felt when they fell in love
with him. Again Narcissus does not love but feels only the love for which he
longs. This identification with feelings of the love-object is a specifically
hysterical form of narcissism.

Finally,in 1891 Andre Gide wrote a *Traite du Narcisse* in which Narcissus's love for himself is a symbol of longing to escape from the world and
conflict and change, and to return into a timeless and perfect paradise. In the
paradise, tensions do not exist. Adam is described as *Androgyne* and not yet
separated from the things around him, he is not yet an ego. The myth
symbolises the attempt to undo ego-segregation.

I want to finish with some remarks on the greatest description of
Narcissism in literature, Shakespeare's *King Lear*. This play shows the
vehemence with which people cling to their narcissistic attitudes, the tragic
implications to which this leads, and the crushing experiences which are
needed before a person is prepared to give up his narcissism. The deep
impression which the play makes on spectators proves the ubiquity of the
narcissistic longing to discard the burden of being a self-reliant ego without
losing the sovereign independence of the ego.

At first glance the fable of the play appears artificial and one wonders
why it is so deeply moving; Goethe even called it absurd. That an old man
should make himself dependent on his children, that he can take seriously
the flattery of his two eldest daughters, that he cannot understand Cordelia's
deep sincerity, and that he then reaps what he has sown: all this seems
nothing but the story of personal foolishness and its consequences.

Lear, however, is not simply an old man who wants to retire, and who
does so somewhat inefficiently. He is a king of limitless power and wealth,
he wants to strip himself of all his power, but only to obtain something still
more valuable in its place, namely unrestricted love. He cannot tolerate the
slightest limitation of this love, no matter how sensible that might be, and
he meets Cordelia's qualification with an extreme and exaggerated reaction:
any qualification whatever makes the love which is offered valueless, he
desires a perfect and absolute love which he does not have to share with
anybody. Such is the love which the narcissist expects from the perfect
mother.

The king's fool clearly sees, and says, what Lear is after. He wants to
make his daughters his mother. Thus he in old age and at the end of his life
makes a last desperate effort to have his deepest and most regressive
longing fulfilled, the longing for the perfect mother. Lear's whole behaviour, which seems so strange and unreasonable, now becomes understan-

dable. His exaggerated sovereignty, his attempt to be even above common reason, parental love and obligations, or loyalty towards devoted friends, all express the narcissistic intolerance of any limitation of the ego. He at the same time craves liberation from the burden of being an ego, and therefore throws away all his power and makes himself weak like a little child who has to be cared for and looked after. His daughters' boundless love is expected to safeguard his sovereign freedom, he believes the lies and flatteries of Goneril and Regan because he prefers, to sight of reality, the promises which gratify his longing. Blindly he chases after the impossible aim of sheltering in the love of the perfect mother.

Lear himself, like every narcissist, is unaware of his true motives. He believes that by transferring his power to his children he is exercising the wisdom of old age, but really he is seeking the fulfilment of narcissistic regressive desires. He thinks he is abdicating and renouncing all his powers, whereas really he wants to gain even greater power, perfect devotion, from mother substitutes. He imagines that he is extremely generous, and that the gratitude which he expects is normal, but really he is demanding something quite impossible, unlimited boundless love. It is misleading to think that he is going mad under the weight of the disappointments which he has to experience. From the very beginning of the play he has been insane, and he has lost all sense of reality. The disappointments shatter his personality, but they at the same time free him from the captivity of his overwhelming longing for mother love. They open the door leading back to reality and to human relationship.

The process of cure reaches its climax in the highly symbolic scene on the heath. Lear is locked out of his daughter's castle and exposed defenceless to the storms of the elements. This symbolises perfectly all the narcissistic fears and what he would have to face if he were to overcome his narcissism. Here on the heath Lear meets the naked madman, Tom. His nakedness signifies that he is without any of those defences behind which Lear has always sheltered, power and prestige, wealth and loving support from others. Lear understands the message of this encounter; he sees in Tom the symbol of the 'unaccommodated man' who is no more than such a poor forked animal, and Lear knows that he has to become like that.

Goneril and Regan are narcissistic figures no less than Lear himself. Without love for anybody, they hate and distrust as a possible danger every person who possesses independent power, and their obsessive need for self-defence through selfish power is no less urgent than Lear's craving for mother love. Their destructive hatred of power other than their own, finds probably its most concentrated expression in Regan's active participation in the blinding of Gloucester. Blinding is symbolical of castration, the destruction of man's physical power. Women who narcissistically crave omnipotence always include this destruction among their fantastic destructive aims. Every psychotherapist will have much experience of such dream fantasies of women.

Shakespeare couples the Lear tragedy with that of Gloucester, in so many ways similar to Lear's. Yet Gloucester's misfortune is not as tragic in the Greek meaning of the word as the fate of Lear, who destroys himself by his own *hybris*. He aims at the impossible and cannot other than fail. In an analogous way Edmund differs from Goneril and Regan. Lear's daughters are possessed by their power-craving, and blindly storm along their destructive path, without any choice. Edmund knows every moment what he is doing. His lies are well-calculated intrigues, whereas Goneril's and Regan's flatteries in the first scene come to them without thinking. It never occurs to them that they could say something other than what would please Lear, as long as he is in power and they themselves powerless. To express feelings, as Cordelia does, for the sole reason that self-respect demands such, and to value this self-respect higher than material advantage, is beyond their imagining.

Cordelia does not submit to Lear's madness. She remains true to herself. Neither consideration of material advantage nor false kindness for Lear nor the fear of hurting him could tempt her to adulterate and falsify her feelings. There could be no finer example of sanity and mental and moral health in the distorted world of narcissism than is provided by Cordelia in the short first scene of the play.

SUMMARY

This paper describes ideo-typically an ego attitude which develops when self-assertion is excluded by fear and when, at the same time, the ego has to be defended against self-destructive tendencies. The description serves also to define the ideal of health which has to be approached in overcoming the narcissistic ego attitude.

To view psychopathological material from the standpoint of this paper is only one of many different approaches necessary to comprehend the totality of a psychically ill subject. The examples quoted serve however to show that this point of view is useful and important.

References

Freud's paper '*Zur Einführung des Narzissismus*' (1914) is for the most part out of date even from Freud's own later standpoint. Amongst papers which have criticised and developed his views I am indebted mainly to:

J.G. Frazer (1911), *Perils of the Soul*, p.49.

André Gide, 'Le Traite du Narcisse', in *Le retour de l'enfant prodigue précédé de cinq autres Traites*. Edition de la N.F.R.

Karen Horney (1939), *New Ways in Psychoanalysis*.

R. M. Rilke, '*Narziss*', Gesammelte Werke (1930) 3: 415.

Roscher, *Lexicon der Mythologie*, '*Narkissos*'.

Lou Andreas-Salome (1931), *Mein Dank an Freud*.

Shakespeare's *Tempest*
A Psychological Analysis

To Professor C.G.Jung on his Seventieth Birthday

Shakespeare's writing, particularly in the period after the sonnets, shows a constant preoccupation with the problems of individuation. The problem of how man may be able to renounce the child's longing for parental love and shelter, and live a life of his own without such demands, is the constantly recurring theme. *The Tempest* too deals with this question, and represents the final answer which Shakespeare arrived at.

To submit *The Tempest* to a psychological interpretation and analysis is tempting for the reason that it is in all essential parts the product of Shakespeare's own imagination: no 'sources' of any importance are known. It thus promises a direct insight into Shakespeare's creative imagination and the underlying motives and problems. In addition it is a play which challenges our wits with many obscure and irrational passages. We sense meaning in them without being able to grasp it easily. It may be as well to start our analysis with the most glaring of these puzzles.

What strikes one as most puzzling on reading *The Tempest* is that Shakespeare, at the height of his mastery as a playwright, suddenly seems to have violated all the most basic rules of dramatic art. In a play one ought to see what happens as action on the stage, and the unfolding of the action ought to awaken the spectator's sympathetic interest. He should be able to fear and rejoice with the persons on stage, and share their emotions. n *The Tempest* an unusually large part of the story is only recounted, not acted out on stage. The whole story of how Prospero was deprived of his dukedom by his treacherous brother; how he and his daughter came to the island on which the play is set; and how he has managed to live there during the last twelve years, we only hear narrated. And the same is true of the story of Ariel's enslavement by the witch Sycorax, and his liberation through Prospero; or the history of Sycorax' son Caliban and his meeting with Prospero.

When Shakespeare proceeds to show us some happenings on the stage, such as the shipwreck and the fate and reactions of the ship's company after the shipwreck, our sympathetic participation in their feelings is hindered by our knowledge that they are victims of magic deception. No sooner has our pity and anxiety for the ship on the storm-beaten sea been awakened, than we meet Prospero telling his daughter that the tempest was caused by him and that he has made sure that nobody came to harm in it. From then onward we constantly know that the mourning of the king for his son, or the son for his father, are unnecessary; and that all the plotting of the courtiers against the king, or of Caliban and the drunkards against Prospero, will come to nothing: the omniscience and omnipotence of Prospero and Ariel will interfere in time.

What is the dramatic meaning of this play, in which the dramatic sympathy of the spectator is nipped in the bud by his partaking in the action on a double level: that of the people who are the object of Prospero's magic, and that of Prospero, who controls all external events? Yet do we really take part in all that happens in this double role? There is certainly one person in the play whose weight and importance overshadows every other figure, and we can participate sympathetically in his fate without without being disturbed by this knowledge at another level. This one person is Prospero himself. He is certainly not the God of Destiny where his own fate is concerned, and he is as much exposed to the transforming influence of the tempest as any other mortal person. Prospero's transformation may well be the dramatic core of *The Tempest*.

Prospero, when he was Duke of Milan, lived the life of a recluse and indulged in his predilection for mystical studies. He turned away from the outside world to a world of invisible powers and magic. He therefore is not an introvert who has turned to himself and accepted himself. Extroversion and introversion are a pair of opposites not of the same logical character as *a* and not-*a*, where everything which is not *a* must of necessity be not-*a*, and all not not-*a* must be *a*. If one is not extrovert one need not necessarily be introvert. A man may be turned away from the outside world and from himself as well, and his whole interest may be taken up by an imaginary world and by introjected objects, but not by his own self, which may remain rejected and unknown to him. Such a man is neither extrovert not introvert.

The affairs of the world and the actual rule of his dukedom he has left to his brother, trusting completely in his loyalty. This childlike trust was disappointed when his brother, together with the King of Naples, betrayed him. Deprived of all power and help, he was exiled and exposed to the play of the elements on the stormy sea in a small boat. Lear, in a similar situation, perished. Prospero however managed to survive this first tempest. Nevertheless, the manner in which he succeeded in withstanding catastrophe was not altogether satisfactory. He certainly saved his own and his daughter's life, he acquired full mastery over the outer circumstances of life and gained magical powers far beyond the mere necessities of life. Yet, at the same time, he became completely isolated, living on a small island (*isola*) away from all human contact (save that of his child-daughter).

The psychological cause of this isolation is clearly visible. Prospero, who as duke expected to live in the parentlike care and shelter of his brother, did not succeed in giving up completely his longing for such care when he was betrayed. He introjected the images of the caring and protecting parents and played their role himself. Instead of being mothered he now mothers Miranda, and he also identifies himself with the image of the omnipotent and omniscient father. Such identification with archetypal images leads inevitably to isolation, for no longer can such a person react to events as his own heart and feelings would demand: he has to hide his own personality and play the part of being nothing but a good and protective parent. There is a striking example of this in the second scene of the first act. Prospero has raised the tempest because he wanted to revenge himself on his enemies and because the stars told him that his own fortunes would decline unless he seized the chance offered to him. Yet when Miranda is upset by the sight of the ship struggling with the storm, Prospero does not tell her these true motives for causing the tempest — he tries to quieten her with the remark:

> I have done nothing but in care of thee,
> O thee my dear one; thee my daughter.

This is sentimental pretence of having no interests of his own and acting only out of care of others in conformity with the wishful fantasy of the loving parent. Prospero, the magician, patronises others or rules over them and orders them about, but does not expose his own personality to relations and the influence of others. He thus is isolated. The breaking down of this isolation is the central dramatic theme of *The Tempest* The same dominating and patronising relationship as with Miranda exists between Prospero and Ariel. Ariel is a figure not easily understood. Superficially he seems to be a nature spirit like Puck in *A Midsummer Night's Dream*, but this similarity is deceptive. *The Tempest* has far less connection with *A Midsummer Night's Dream* than is often assumed. *A Midsummer Night's Dream* is the vision of a state outside time (Midsummer Night) and outside social and moral bounds. It is the vision of an ecstatic state of liberty in a world where action has no irreversible consequences and where everything is mere play; the world of nature spirits as opposed to the world of tragic consequences and moral demands. *The Tempest* is on the other hand the symbol of the fateful storms which cause the deepest moral crises, such as being driven out of the shelter of the family and social tradition, or the crisis which brings Prospero back into social contact. *The Tempest* is therefore more the the epilogue to the great tragedies than a play on the free level outside human tragical entanglements.

Ariel's rather human feelings, his longing for freedom, his compassion with Gonzalo's suffering, and his often expressed wish to please his master, contradict any suggestion that he is of a kind with Puck. When Prospero asks him about the sea storm,

> My brave spirit,
> Who was so firm, so constant that this coil
> Would not affect his reason?

He too presupposes human feelings and a human psychology in Ariel.

We come nearer to understanding this figure if we remember that this male spirit has to appear in a female disguise (as a nymph, or as Ceres) several times. Thus he is reminiscent of many ambisexual girls and sweet-hearts in Shakespeare's other plays: it is not by chance that Ariel is often played by actresses on the modern stage. He is most akin to the male beloved in the sonnets, like whom Ariel has 'a woman's face, a woman's gentle heart' (*Sonnet* 20), and Prospero constantly addresses him in various terms of endearment like a sweetheart. When Ariel asks 'Do you love me, master?' Prospero answers 'Dearly, my delicate Ariel,' and later he confesses that he will miss his 'dainty Ariel' when he is set free. Of Ariel, as of the male addressee in the Sonnets, can be said:

The other two "elements", slight air and purging fire,

Are both with thee wherever I abide.

He represents Prospero's spiritual love, cleansed and divorced from material and physical aspects. He is childlike and impish as befits the *anima* of so inflated and pompous a man as Prospero.

Like all *anima* figures Ariel was originally connected with the mother image. He was Sycorax the witch-mother's servant. She imprisoned him in a cloven pine but Prospero broke this material entanglement and freed him as Eros freed Psyche. Yet Prospero's relation to this *anima* figure has become ambiguous. In the Sonnets the young nobleman is the idol to whom Shakespeare looks up, and whom he admires most self-effacingly and submissively. Prospero's attitude to Ariel is quite different. He keeps him as his slave and is his absolute master. He masks this possessiveness, however, with sentimental justifications. When Ariel impatiently asks for release from his slavery, Prospero maintains that he has a rightful claim to it because Ariel owes him gratitude for his liberation from Sycorax' tortures.

How spurious this claim is becomes apparent when Prospero adds the menace that he will torture Ariel as Sycorax did if he refuses to obey. He will force him back into the material prison of a cloven tree, where he would share in the contempt with which Prospero treats everything material. In subjects whose love still follows the pattern of child-parent relationship, we can often observe how submissive dependence on a greatly overvalued love object changes into open possessiveness as soon as the lover passes from a self-effacing phase into an inflated megalomaniac phase. Then the formerly dependent one tries to force the beloved one into submission by open threats, or by the expression of utter contempt, self-deceptively justifying his or her claims by citing the debts of gratitude which the beloved owes them. Such is the nature of Prospero's debt to Ariel. His love of Ariel is insincere and only a thin veil over frank possessiveness. This also explains why Prospero continually has to repeat his promise to set Ariel free after two days. It sounds as if neither Ariel nor Prospero himself had much faith in Prospero's given word.

The paradox of this situation in which Prospero wants to master the *anima* is that he himself becomes possessed by the *anima*. The *anima* who is always supposed to be obedient and is never allowed a will of her own, is identical with the ego ideal. She is not an independent being outside Prospero's ego but the image of the immaterial spirituality, justness and goodness to which he himself aspires. Prospero is so lonely and isolated because he tries to force the ego as well as every beloved figure to comply with the same ideal of the kind and asexual parent. *Anima* and ego are enslaved by the same emotional anima image of perfection. Any deviation from it arouses Prospero's contempt and utter rejection.

Ariel and Miranda are very much akin, particularly in the time before Miranda meets Ferdinand. She is an image of *woman* as Prospero desires woman to be, all pleasing, all obedient, all submissive. In consequence she is as unsubstantial and impersonal as Ariel himself. Prospero's relationship to her is also cleansed of physical aspects through the incest taboo. Thus she is as childlike, pure and immaterial an *anima* as Ariel. Yet she, as a human being, has the potentiality of transformation into something completely human which is lacking in Ariel. This is probably the deeper reason for the duplication of the *anima* in the play

Caliban's name is a near-anagram of the word 'cannibal', but his character has very little to do with that of aborigines. He is Prospero's shadow, the personification of all those qualities which Prospero, in his identification with the kind and omnipotent parental images, and with the spiritual *anima*, excludes from his ego. This is why Prospero despises him so utterly. He is only half-human, like all the personifications of dissociated complexes. He is lecherous and his sexual desires are turned toward Miranda (who, as the only woman on the island, cannot have escaped some subconscious incestuous interest on Prospero's part). Caliban is earthy and dirty and stinking (anal), animalic and selfish, all qualities which are opposed to the good, loving parent with whom Prospero is identified.

His arch-crime, however, is that he does not repay kindness with kindness and unfaltering goodness. This seems to Prospero to justify every form of abuse and utter contempt. People who are, like Prospero, isolated and unable to make contact, often try to establish a semblance of relationship by an exchange of kindness according to the principle of *do ut des*. They try to bribe others into conforming to their ideal of spirituality and kindness, and thus, of course, achieve the very opposite of their intention. Instead of creating relationship with independent beings they try to submit them to the same super-ego figures by which they themselves are enslaved. Every kindness on their part justifies in their eyes a claim not only for equal kindness in return, but for absolute perfection on the part of the other. Any imperfection in the other is a sign of ingratitude and a justification for unqualified rejection. There is no personal relationship in which one person as a whole reacts with differentiated feelings to another person as a whole, and experiences his defections in the setting of the total personality.

As a result, kindness seems to produce impersonal claims for gratitude, claims as abstract as legal claims are. If they remain dissatisfied, every form of punishment seems permissible. Thus the overdone longing for kindness

leads to a world where only cold and impersonal obligations exist, sanctio-
ned by the threat of disproportionate punishment. Shakespeare's writing is
full of such demands for gratitude and of disproportionate threats or
reactions in the case of frustration. Examples are to be found not only in
Prospero's behaviour toward Ariel and Caliban, but also in Lear's behaviour
towa d Cordelia, or in Timon or in Coriolanus.

No useful quality of Caliban which Prospero exploits can diminish
Prospero's contempt. Caliban, like a true god of the material, chthonic
world, has both physical strength and a deep knowledge of the earth and its
helpful forces, fresh springs, brine pits, fertile places and all the qualities of
the island. Prospero contemptuously rejects everything material. He wants
the Madonna-like kind of mother, or the pure immaterial spirit, but fears
and hates the earth mother, who appears to him as an evil witch. Caliban,
son of the evil witch Sycorax, is her heir and representative in the play.

Here, however, we come again across a curious paradox in Prospero's
character, a paradox quite co.   .on in men like Prospero. In spite of their
attempt to identify themselves with the good parent(s), they begin in their
inflated state to display some qualities of the very opposite, which is to say
the witch. Prospero rules over his two slaves by menacing them with exactly
the same type of cruel punishment which Sycorax used to employ. This
cruelty clashes curiously with Prospero's role as the all-providing benevo-
lent wizard. Yet if one tries to protect oneself against disappointments by
absolute superiority and control of everything, one simply cannot help
assimilating and using some of those hated, aggressive qualities which one
wanted to ward off. If one starts to play the role of God one cannot avoid
playing the role of the Devil too. When Prospero became the magician by
identifying himself with the omnipotent and omniscient father, he simultaneously took possession of the witch's island and made his home there. As
little as Apuleius could Prospero remain unaffected by such an excursion
into the country of the witch.

The wreck of Naples' ship exposes the ship's company to a plight similar
to that which Prospero had to master twelve years before. We take part in
their anxiety and grief but share at the same time Prospero's knowledge that
the catastrophe may turn out to be the beginning of psychic progress and
moral development. Now we can understand this double knowledge, not as a
violation of the rules of dramatic art, but as a very daring attempt at the
dramatic representation of the truth that the tempests which separate us
from the shelter of social and family security have a double aspect: a
horrifying one, and a beneficial one. They may lead into emotional crisis, but
can result in progress and conversion.

The different reactions of the various members of the ship's company
provide Shakespeare with an opportunity also to show some other aspects of
the problem of separation from the sheltering parental world which the
main hero, Prospero, has by-passed and avoided. Thus Shakespeare accom-
panies the main theme with a counterpoint of variations on the same theme.

As a linking together of various solutions to the same problem is often found in dreams, it is probable that the accompaniment by these themes to the main theme in *The Tempest* is the result of Shakespeare's autonomous creative fantasy and not of his conscious deliberations as author.

The King is another representative of the all-powerful father image. He, in his aloof superiority, had never appreciated what injustice and injury had been done to Prospero. Now, under the influence of grief over the loss of his son, he opens his mind to the sufferings of others and repents his treachery toward Prospero.

Gonzalo, too, is a believer in the ideal of a world in which everybody behaves like a good parent or a good child. He gives this vivid description of how, according to his ideal, the world should be:

> *I' the commonwealth I would by contraries*
> *Execute all things; for no kind of traffic*
> *Would I admit; no name of magistrate;*
> *Letters would not be known; riches, poverty*
> *and use of service, none; contract, succession*
> *Bourn, bound of land, tilth, vineyard, none;*
> *No use of metal, corn, wine or oil;*
> *No occupation; all men idle, all;*
> *And women too, but innocent and pure ...·*
> *All things in common nature should provide*
> *Without sweat and endeavour: treason, felony,*
> *Sword, pike, knife, gun, or need of any engine*
> *Would I not have; but nature should bring forth,*
> *Of its own kind, all foison, all abundance,*
> *To feed my innocent people.*   (Act II, Scene i, 152-171)

No experience can shake Gonzalo's wishful optimism that there will always be good fathers whom one can serve; nor can anything shake his own kindness and helpfulness. He does not react to disappointment with self-isolation and the attempt to force the world into his ideal pattern by master-like superiority, as does Prospero. Shakespeare knows that unfailing loyalty toward parental figures can be achieved only at the expense of the loyalty which one owes to oneself and to other values; and which is thus found together with a shallowness of personality, and a certain cynicism as regards all values other than of parental and of filial loyalty. Gonzalo does not show these traits so sharply as Polonius, and is not so free of them as Kent and Bellarius, but all these figures are creations arising from the same emotional source.

Ferdinand too gets over the presumed death of his father without Prospero's self-isolation. On the contrary, he is now able to turn his love to the other sex and finds a new love in Miranda. This can be the beginning of a healthier development than that of Prospero if Ferdinand is able to concede some independence to Miranda, and to maintain some measure of independence for himself as well. Certainly Ferdinand's sudden infatuation is based on a projection of the *anima* image on to Miranda, but all youthful love begins like that. Whether it will be the first step of a healthy development or of a development in the direction of Prospero's difficulties, depends on Ferdinand's reactions to the realisation that the real Miranda does not coincide with his image of the longed-for woman, a realisation which has inevitably one day to come. If he then can stand the tension between her and himself without retreating into himself, and without trying to crush Miranda's independence, or forcing her to conform with his fantasies, or without self-effacement, he will have succeeded in avoiding Prospero's isolation. It is for this reason that Prospero's problems are predominantly those of middle age (after the age of 35); at Ferdinand's age they usually have not crystallised.

Antonio and Sebastian rebel against paternal authority. When they are freed from the restrictions which the stable social world imposes on them, they plan regicide. Shakespeare abhors such a treacherous attack upon authority. Prospero circumvented it in his own case by identifying himself with the omnipotent father image, after the world had refused to shelter him like a child. He jumped the gap between the small child and the outsized father, whereas in a healthy development the gap would disappear through the growing up of the child and the transformation and deflation of the father image. The first step in a transformation of this kind is the imaginary attack on the father, and patricide, for symbolically death does not annihilate but transform the father image. Maybe the very lenient treatment meted out by Prospero to Sebastian and Antonio is to be explained by Prospero's dim awareness that their crime has not been so alien to his own subconscious tendencies, and that he would have dealt better with these tendencies in a less repressive way.

Trinculo and Stefano also enter into a homicidal conspiracy, but on a different level from the two noblemen. Simple men who do not live in a hierarchical world, they are blind to the different dignities of people and are interested only in animalic pleasures which are common to all human kind. Because of this common animalic nature they are identified with Caliban, the personification of Prospero's *shadow*, and are despised like him. Their conspiracy is the rebellion of the suppressed shadow, the attempt of the evil forces to seize power and to overwhelm and destroy those who want to do only good.

The believer in the hierarchy of absolutely good parental figures, obedient servants or children, stands in constant fear of rebellion and has every reason so to do. This is not because the power of evil is so much greater than the power of goodness, but because he is hostile to not only the purely evil but also to the mature man who has made peace with the animal in himself, who has gained confidence by the assimilation of his shadow. There is at least one figure among the ship's crew who seems to be definitely more mature than the noblemen, and who nevertheless is treated by the noblemen without the respect which is his due. This is the boatswain, and he has weathered so many storms that the present tempest and his landing on an apparently deserted island in no way unbalance him. He goes to sleep as soon as the ship is safe in harbour.

Yet Prospero too is affected by the tempest. His transformation begins when he realises that he has been presented with a chance which will not return, and that his fortunes would forever after droop were he to miss it. There, for the first time since his isolation, he recognises the existence of forces outside his ego and ego domination. He causes the storm and he revenges himself on his enemies, giving vent for the first time to self-assertive feelings other than those needed to ensure his domination and aloof superiority.

This is immediately followed up by his first friendly contact with a human being, when he lays aside his magic isolating mantle and tells his daughter the story of his life. He conceals no longer the fact that he too is a suffering human being, who has made grave mistakes and, without Gonzalo's help, would have lost everything through the neglect and carelessness with which he treated the affairs of the world. The depth of his loneliness, how unaccustomed he is to opening out and conversing with others on the same level, is shown by the three questions with which he interrupts his narrative. Again and again he has to make sure that Miranda is listening. It is more than twelve years since he has asked anybody to be a sympathetic listener, and he can scarcely believe that such personal contact is still possible.

Next, he loses Miranda to Ferdinand, losing his parental domination over her ends. The awakening of Ferdinand's and Miranda's love is only indirectly Prospero's doing. While he gave Miranda an opportunity to meet Ferdinand, the love between them sprang up as a free reaction in them. Miranda, the *anima*, got the freedom to act on her own.

Then Prospero's two slaves get somewhat out of hand. Caliban sees a chance to rebel when he meets Trinculo and Stefano. This rebellion, unfortunately, ends in nothing and leads to no revision of Prospero's attitude toward his shadow. Ariel, however, does get his freedom. As long as Prospero kept his *anima* in slavery, deluding himself that he was treating her lovingly, demanding nothing but what Ariel owed him in gratitude, he had no chance of establishing healthier and free-er relations with other people. Not only is love impossible as long as the *anima* is enslaved, it is self-deception to imagine that the domination over the *anima* is something in the nature of a relationship: the fact of isolation is concealed. People often believe that they are loving most passionately when they are only in a half demanding half domineering dependence on another person. They cannot begin real relationship until they break this dependence and give back to the objects of their love their proper freedom.

At the same time as he frees Ariel, Prospero promises that he will renounce his magics, break his magic staff and drown his book, thus ending

the inflation caused by the identification with the image of the omnipotent
and omniscient father. He does not carry the revenge against his enemies to
its ultimate possibility by annihilating them. That would have left him once
again isolated. He forgives them and returns into contact with others. The
result of Prospero's transformation is described in the Epilogue in these
words:

> Now my charms are all o'erthrown,
> And what strength I have's mine own,
> Which is most faint.

Too little attention has been paid to these verses, with the result that the
most unsound theories have been propounded about the meaning of Ariel's
emancipation and Prospero's drowning of his magic book. Prospero here is
really describing Shakespeare's last ideal and aim of personal development,
an aim which has found similar expression again and again in the history of
the human mind. Goethe, at the end of the second part of *Faust* lets him
burst out into expressing nearly identically the same longing and desire:

> Noch hab ich mich ins Freie nicht gekämpft.
> Könnt ich Magie von meinem Pfad entfernen,
> Die Zaubersprüche ganz und gar verlernen,
> Stünd ich, Natur! vor dir ein Mann allein,   .
> Da wäre's der Mühe wert, ein Mensch zu sein.

(Faust Part II, Act v scene 6)

> I am not wrestled into freedom yet.
> If I could magic from my path dispel,
> wholly unlearn the words of sorcery,
> and stood, Nature, before you, as but a man,
> that would be worth the toil of being human.

Modern psychotherapy has repeatedly defined its aim in similar terms.
Freud and his followers have wanted to help the patient to overcome
archaic, magical forms of thinking, to lead him into a realistic outlook as
regards himself. Jung's essay 'The Relations between the Ego and the
Unconscious' (*Two Essays in Analytical Psychology*, London 1928) describes developments very similar to Prospero: how the archetype of the
magician takes possession of the ego because of the ego's dream of a victory
over and enslavement of the *anima*. His therapeutic aim, too, coincides
largely with Prospero's verse above quoted, but it is not merely in modern
descriptions of the goal of personal development that one finds agreement
with Shakespeare's: the Christian virtue of humility too seems to me aptly
described in these verses.

Jung however points out that a formulation of the aim of development is
not quite satisfactory which contains no mention of something in us which
transcends the ego. Goethe mentions this 'something' by contrasting the ego
with the transcendent '*Natur*'. Shakespeare does not recognise anything

transcendent and remains a-religious to the end, and that is the point where doubt begins whether Prospero actually managed to overcome his isolation and to return to society as a free-er and more mature man than he had been twelve years before.

Has the development which *The Tempest* describes only the character of a dreamlike vision which anticipates something that was not yet accessible for active use in Prospero's life (something which has not yet been 'worked through') or does it indicate that Prospero can now live humbly, using nothing but his own strength, no longer relying on charms and magics?

I am inclined to answer this question according to the first alternative. When Prospero joins the ship's company at the end of the play, he meets them in an entirely conventional manner, and not as a man who has found a relationship to human beings on a more personal level than the merely conventional. He is immediately identified with the noblemen, no matter how unworthy they are, and he finds no kind words for those who are socially inferior. His approach to Gonzalo seems to me particularly stilted and out of focus. He calls him 'holy', says 'Let me embrace thine age whose honour cannot be measured or confined', and he promises ' I will pay thy graces home, both in word and deed'. All this is both too much and too little.

It is too little because it is aloof, and we expect some warmth of friendship and love, not only 'paying home' and reverence for honourable old age. It is too much because Gonzalo, the kind but shallow old man, is not holy. Prospero meets Gonzalo not as a man who has matured and been made wise through his own sufferings, but as a young man who looks up to the old man because he represents the unfailing loyalty and helplessness of the good father.

What Prospero's future relationship to Caliban will be remains unclear in the play, but certainly there are signs that his contempt has slackened, and that he is about to realise that Caliban is a part of himself, and a necessary one.

He goes on with his witchcraft to the very end of the play, arranging calm seas and auspicious gales for the King's journey home. (Contrary to his previous promise to abjure this rough magic as soon as he had lifted the spell from the senses of the King and his company.) On the other hand he envisages his own future as a retirement where every third thought shall be his grave. This sounds far too similar to his state of mind before his expulsion from Milan, the only difference being that in his retreat he will indulge in depressed rather than magical fantasies.

Here Jung's criticism comes in. If one tries only to eliminate the magician (and the *anima*) and not to put something in their place, one will remain suspended between three dangers: *first*, of beginning to do magic again, *second*, of overvaluing other people and expecting them to have magical powers and to play the parents' role, or *third*, of falling into an abyss of depression. All these dangers are visible in the third act of the play.

Last but not least, Prospero's attitude to women shows no change. The only woman who appears in the play (apart from the Masque) is Miranda. She is the image of the all-pleasing child as Prospero might wish her to be. As such, the aspects of the earthy mother which Prospero abhors are also absent in her. She is, like Athene, the product of her father's wishful thought. She has grown up without the influence of a mother and does not remember her mother at all (whereas she remembers other servant women in Milan).

The mother aspect of woman is under a peculiar taboo in *The Tempest*, the only mother of whom we hear being Sycorax, the evil witch mother of Caliban. Ferdinand never mentions his mother, nor does any of the men of the King's ship's company mention his wife or his mother. It is from men, Prospero, his brother the Duke, Gonzalo, that kindness is given or expected. A mental outlook which is quite intolerant to the realistic woman, which fears and avoids women as horrible witches unless they are Mirandas, is, of course, still archaic and magical. As long as Prospero keeps to it his statement that he has overthrown his charms remains incorrect and an anticipation of an aim which he actually has not yet reached.

We read *The Tempest* as a dramatic representation of the inflated loneliness and paranoid isolation into which Prospero had retired after his expulsion from Milan; and of his attempt to overcome it and to return to the social world. It remains to be discovered whether the other plays of the same period, *Cymbeline* and *The Winter's Tale* tally with this interpretation. It seems to me that the motive behind the writing of these two plays was already the same as that for *The Tempest*, but that it was not yet clear enough to find more than a dim expression.

The Winter's Tale shows how the King of Sicily through a sudden fit of jealousy isolates himself from wife, children and friends, and how after sixteen years this isolation is miraculously undone. This action takes up four-fifths of the play, but the love intermezzo between Perdita and Florizel surpasses the rest of the play so much in charm and liveliness that the first three acts read like a mere exposition of the idyll in Bohemia. The King's jealousy remains psychologically incomprehensible, his liberation from his isolation is the result of mere outer circumstances and miraculous events, so that it becomes nearly impossible to take a sympathetic interest in him and his fate. Nevertheless he is intended to be the hero of the play, as is confirmed by comparison of the play with its source. The play is a dramatisation of Robert Greene's novel *Pandosto, or the Triumph of Time*. Pandosto, the jealous king of the novel, is the King of Bohemia. His friend whom he suspects unjustly is the King of Sicily.

Shakespeare reverses their parts and lets the jealous King reign and reside in Sicily. It is easier for an English audience to identify with the king of an island, and to take sympathetic interest in his fate, than to look upon the king of a remote continental country as the hero of a play.

Pandosto commits suicide after the return of his daughter, in desperation over his previous mistakes, which caused so much harm. Shakespeare changes this because he is concerned with the problem of salvation from paranoid self-isolation, with no wish to write another *Othello* or *Lear*, in which jealousy or paranoid self-estrangement leads to the death of the hero. He therefore also removes one of the motives of Pandosto's death. Where in the novel Pandosto's wife dies in grief over her husband's unjust jealousy, in the play Hermione remains alive and joins her husband after Perdita's return. The only permanent victim of the King, Leontes' jealousy in *The Winter's Tale*, is his young son, unable to survive the separation from his mother. It seems rather symbolic that the mother-fixated youth has to disappear for good, as this is the problem in all the three late comedies: how mother-fixation can effectively be conquered without paranoid sham solutions.

Perdita, like Miranda, grows up without a mother. She has not even a foster-mother, and the shepherd who brings her up is a widower. In Greene's novel the equivalent figure was married to Mopsa, who took the mother's place in Perdita's life. Shakespeare transforms Mopsa into a mere playmate of Perdita's.

In *Cymbeline*, interest in the hero of the play is completely swamped by the side action: Posthumus' test of Imogen's fidelity, the life of Belisarius and his foster-sons in the wild woods. Nobody who reads the play without knowing its title would regard Cymbeline as the title hero: he appears only five times on the stage, in a completely passive role. Only because his fate mirrors the problem with which Shakespeare was occupied at that time, does he have this position. Cymbeline, by his unjustified banishment of Belisarius, and his undue trust in his second wife, lost his children and his true friends. The play ends in the miraculous reunion.

The same basic motif of isolation through paranoid folly, and reunion, is repeated in Posthumus' loss of his wife through the foolish test of her fidelity, and in Belisarius' retreat into the woods. There Belisarius plays the part of the faithful father to the King's son, after the King's betrayal of his father obligations toward him; thus Belisarius introjects the father image which he could not find outside. He anticipates Prospero more than does either Cymbeline, or Leontes in *The Winter's Tale*. The Queen and her son Cloten are the forerunners of Sycorax and Caliban. Imogen is related to both Ariel and Miranda: significant is her description in the 'Sooth' as 'tender air' or 'mollis aer-mulier'. This, in addition to her ambisexual part, connects her with Ariel, whose name was chosen for its aural connection with 'air' and not in its Hebrew meaning of 'Lion of God'. Hatred of woman is rampant in *Cymbeline*. noone of the four youthful heroes or heroines having been brought up by his or her mother. The fantastic paragon of goodness, Imogen, contradicts as little as Miranda a rejection of woman: the presence of this character confirms that other than those born out of the thoughts and wishes of a man, women were at that time unbearable to Shakespeare.

Comparison of these three plays gives us an opportunity to observe the unfolding and clarification of a set of ideas in Shakespeare's mind. In the two plays which precede *The Tempest* the return from isolation is only the conclusion of a play in which circumstances which cause the isolation, or events which have no direct connection with the hero, take up most of the action. Only in *The Tempest* does Shakespeare find a highly artful way of making the play centre on the hero's transformation from isolated magician to humble human being within the social world. Only in *The Tempest* does he gain considerable insight into the psychological causes both of the hero's isolation and of his liberation. In the previous plays he only states the problem, and does not see through it with psychological understanding. For in spite of the superficial impression that *The Tempest* is fuller of magic, spirits and fairy-tale motifs than the other plays, it surpasses them incomparably in psychological realism and insight.

This insight was, of course, not of the kind which modern psychology has: it resulted not from scientific reflection but from Shakespeare's inner necessity of struggle with these problems. The depth of his insight is unique and *commands* admiration in spite of any criticism that Prospero only saw but did not reach the final aim of self-realisation.It is equally unique how this insight finds immediate expression in the dramatic events of a play which does not strike us either as strange or mystical, or as a mere allegory of ideas which could be equally well expressed in an abstract rational form. Shakesspeare's best plays are truly symbolic in Jung's sense, which is to say that they are the best possible expression of some insight for which no more rational formulation had yet been found. Shakespeare was the creator of a mythology of modern man.

I characterised Prospero's struggle as a struggle with paranoid difficulties. Thus I hinted at the similarity of his problems to those with which other people too have to deal. I refuted the romantic prejudice that a genius is different from all other human beings in the respect of not being troubled with the common human difficulties and problems. *Paranoid* expresses a negative valuation with regard to the value *mental health*. Naturally, it intends no valuation whatsoever with regard to other values, moral, artistic, intellectual; nor does it imply that a person troubled with these difficulties is 'generally inferior'. Mentally healthy people may be absolute dullards, whereas a paranoid person may have great moral strength, an outstandingly rich imagination, powers to express this, intellect, and whatever makes a 'generally superior' man.

What we may learn from the fact that a man like Shakespeare had these difficulties, and that the plays in which he tried to solve them appeal to so many people as they have over centuries, is that paranoid problems are extremely common in our culture. In particular a person who is forced to aim at individuation will know from his inner experience the deceptive victories and perils of the paranoid attitude.

On Narcissism *(1968)*

Narcissism is a term which describes a set of purposes which motivates behaviour and explains its variety in a unified way. We can of course describe these purposes only in a typical way. We construct an ideotype to which the individual case corresponds only more or less. It is no argument against such a description that other descriptive concepts can also justifiably be applied to the same behaviour. What may be called narcissism may also be described as separation anxiety, or oral fixation, or reaction-formation to destructive urges, and so on. Narcissism describes a rich complexity of motivation, it makes contradictory and paradoxical behaviour understandable as resulting from the same motives and clarifies the changes necessary if therapy is to be successful.

Narcissism has been defined in various ways. A common but superficial description is self-love or infatuation with one's physical appearance. This is superficial because more important than self-love is rejection of all aspects of self which contradict a fixed and very narrow concept of self which the narcissist alone accepts and displays.

Freud has described narcissism with the help of the libido theory. In the 'primary narcissism' of the infant all the libido is contained in the ego. In secondary narcissism the ego becomes the object of the libido, often via incorporation of or identification with a previous outer love object.

This description of of primary narcissism presupposes that one can speak of an 'ego' of the very young infant, and that the libido is a quantity of energy which if not turned on to outer objects must be stored and invested somewhere else. Both these assumptions I regard as erroneous. This description of secondary narcissism also omits to mention that the narcissist typically hates many aspects of himself. In addition, the description of the ego as love object suffers from failure to differentiate between wanting to be loved, and active outward-going loving: this lack of clarification makes all Freudian teaching on 'love objects' unsatisfactory. The narcissist cannot love (this the Greek myth of Narcissus already emphasises) but he wants intensely to be loved. He does not love even himself, his 'self-love' only emphasises those features of himself which he believes make him lovable to others.

It is on this account that Lou Andreas-Salomé calls narcissistic man's striving for unity with others and the world: for that unity which exists at birth between mother and child, and which there is a later striving to re-establish or to perpetuate. Opposite to this longing for total integration in a comprehensive whole are the ego tendencies which aim at selfhood, and at being able to express and pursue aims of one's own irrespective of the approval of others. These tendencies, though opposing one another, also further one another dialectically. Every advance in the particularisation of the ego stimulates strivings for unification on a higher level, and *vice versa* all unification creates the need for re-definition and assertion of the place of the individual self within this unity. Andreas-Salomé's description of narcissism and ego tendencies as the two healthy human motive forces elaborates Freud's early theory of the libido and ego instincts as the basic conflicting drives.

Freud later modified this theory considerably, yet his final definition of the libido corresponds closely to what Andreas-Salomé calls narcissism. According to this definition the aim of Eros is 'to establish ever greater unities and to preserve them—in short to bind together'. Jung occasionally remarked that his description of the *anima* corresponded to what in Freudian terms is called narcissism. He too must have had in mind Andreas-Salomé's definition of narcissism as the healthy opposite and dialectical complement of the ego tendencies.

Andreas-Salomé's identification of narcissism and libido ignores the fact that we usually mean by narcissism not a healthy striving for unity but a disturbance of the emotional balance, and often a disturbance of a most serious nature. This has clearly to be brought out in the definition of narcissism. I agree that a striving for unity is characteristic of narcissism, but would use this term only if two other conditions prevailed, namely, (a) that unity is aimed at by way of the repression, dissociation, ignoring or any other suppression of all ego tendencies experienced as jeopardising the longed for union, and (b), that the ego aims at being acceptable either by being lovable or by being able to enforce acceptance by others. These functions of the ego, and other functions regarded as innocuous with regard to unity, are overemphasised to compensate for the ego weakness which results from suppression of ego tendencies which seem to jeopardise unity.

Occasionally everybody puts his or her most likeable aspects on show, and hides hostile or critical ego tendencies in social intercourse; but I shall speak of narcissism only when such behaviour becomes compulsive and forms a style of life. In my paper published twenty-five years ago (see above) I therefore described narcissism in Kierkegaard's terms—a desperate attempt not to be a self and concurrently a desperate attempt at being a self.

The aspects of selfhood experienced as incompatible with union will differ from case to case, just as do also the aspects of selfhood which are overemphasised. Narcissistic motivation can start at or regress to any developmental state.

Some schizophrenics experience as detrimental to unity every form of being an active subject, and of actively expressing or gratifying needs of their own. Even the privacy of thinking may be denied, and all thoughts be imagined as known to others while simultaneously all direct communication of them appears unnecessary. One assumes one is fully understood without explicit communication, yet the unity which originally existed between mother and infant cannot be perpetuated indefinitely, and some selfhood is socially demanded of everybody. The schizophrenic may therefore act like a most conventional ego, yet emphasise concurrently by subtle exaggerations that he regards this as a phoney display in which he does not himself believe. The schizophrenic really wants to be no ego at all, and his debunking of the conventional ego-pose does not (as R. D. Laing has mistakenly believed) hint at awareness of a true self-assertive ego which is repressed.

The depressive regards destructive urges as detrimental to unity. His ego professes his need for unity together with despair about having lost any claim to being loved though his 'guilty' behaviour.

The manic believes all his wishes for unity fulfilled or believes he has the power to enforce their fulfilment. His elated ego has to deny all past and present experience of reality which would face him with all the difficulties which stand in the way of the desired agreement with everybody else.

In hysteria the needs of the self are not disallowed, only the responsibility for pursuing them. The attempt is made to have them gratified without guilt or responsibility by manipulating other people.

There are many more forms of narcissistic self-rejection in the service of remaining at one with others. I want to mention only three more.

The first is the need always to feel justified by convention, by what everybody does; with unwillingness ever to take a stand of one's own alone. This is so frequent an attitude that it is normal in the sense of average. Yet with advancing age it leads to an emptying of life, life becomes boring and discontent often seeks justification in some physical ailment.

In a second form general conventions are despised either because of a feeling of being incapable of consistently obeying them, or because of striving for a more individual gratification of a longing for unity. This seemingly leads to an emphasised individualism, but it in fact consists of a mixture of self-indulgence (the immediate gratification of every need, as a baby demands) and a standardised behaviour perfectly attractive according to the narcissist's own lights. The perfect dandy no longer asks what others find attractive; he has introjected the loving mother and is thus the sole arbiter of attractiveness. This produces a dandified conventionality from which every dispensation is allowed which self-indulgence may demand. Thus the dandy, as for example Oscar Wilde, is typically amoral.

Like the dandy the paranoiac no longer cares about the approval of others, not because he regards general conventions and morality as invalid, but because he is convinced he is the only perfect being who is still upholding them. He longs to be universally loved, but there are no worthy lovers except himself. Thus he isolates himself and no longer turns outward for love and approval. He is the perfect fulfiller of the paternal law but there are no loving fathers left in the world outside. Thus his longing for unity is seemingly absent because all the unity he regards as possible is perfected in his own identification with the *imago* of the perfect father.

The study of narcissism enables one to observe the various dimensions of the empirical ego, because they are either rejected or over-emphasised by the narcissist. To have wishes, urges and needs, to have any privacy, to be tolerant of aggressive destructive tendencies or of conflict, disapproval, guilt and responsibility; to have powers which however are limited: these are ego aspects which may be rejected in one or another form of narcissism. To be socially acceptable, to be conventional and thus uncriticisable, to attract attention and goodwill, are ego aims which may be over-emphasised. So may ego activities which appear innocuous with regard to perpetuating unity with others. Objective thinking is an example of this, that is, thinking which does not deal with one's personal needs and wishes, and which by its objective rightness and accuracy is beyond criticism. Artistic creation which does not seem to involve on in conflict with others (though unintentionally it may arouse a storm of controversy) is another example. Narcissism thus may have socially most valuable results.

The narcissist cultivates a well-defined image of himself. Even the hystrionic hysteric who plays a different role with every person he meets pretends to be totally identical with the role he is playing at the time. The narcissist is intolerant of the many-sidedness and unpredicatability of his being. This is true even of the amoral and self-indulgent dandy. He too strives to maintain and display a fixed style and image of himself. The self-indulgences which contradict this image are treated as being of no account and as something he can ignore. Oscar Wilde describes this well in *The Picture of Dorian Grey*.

Wilde's story illustrates too the deep split which typically exists in narcissistic cases between the ego and the material bodily aspect of the person. The corruptible aspects of the body — illness, ageing and death —frighten the narcissist. The unity he longs for is imagined as unchanging, timeless and unending. The ego should be above the body's natural fate, it should be unchanging, indestructible and deathless.

There is one further reason why the body, and urges which are commonly apperceived as originating in the body, are rejected by the narcissist. One of the earliest occasions when the infant becomes aware of selfhood is during the act of defaecation. We know that this act easily becomes linked to fantasies of destructive attacks on mother's power. It thus becomes symbolic for all ego activities which are destructive of the unity with mother, and which therefore are shunned and rejected by the narcissist. The body (the guts) contains the unity-destroying forces. The narcissistic ego wants to be superior to the body, purer, nobler, immaterial. The ego may be identified with the the soul, the spirit, or reason, while the material aspects and powers are regarded as foreign and hostile. The fact that the narcissist can be fascinated and preoccupied by nudity and by sex does not contradict this. He may delight in the beautiful youthful body without being able to identify with the corruptible, excreting body. Sex may be seen as unifying and, during the surrender of the climax of the sex act, as liberator from the awareness of selfhood. Yet just because the narcissist wants to cultivate only these two aspects of sex at the expense of its self-assertive aspects, narcissistic sex is so often frigid and impotent.

Consideration of narcissism also helps to clarify the vague concept of love. Narcissists aim at unity and in the service of this some of them develop great ability for empathetic understanding of others. This sensitive understanding is often regarded as 'feeling' and love. The narcissist looks for identification and amalgamation with the other. Narcissism therefore promotes homosexuality, where the tension of the differences of the two sexes is absent. It also promotes sado-masochistic relationships in which identification and complete containing of one by the other is aimed at. The love which is denied to the narcissist, in spite of sensitive empathy and striving for unity, is the love which promotes full self-acceptance and active self-realisation, and which delights in the active self-realisation of the other.

Is narcissism curable? This seems a nonsensical question. It is not an illness like measles, but a complex organisation of emotional tendencies and needs. In some cases it promotes a socially most effective and successful life. In adolescence narcissistic trends are frequent and lead to typical juvenile romanticism, juvenile dandyism, juvenile religion, and nowadays (1968) to the anarchism of youth, of the cult of the flower people, and the hippies' Eastern mysticisms and drug-taking. This juvenile narcissism is usually transient and is overcome under the influence of maturing experiences.

When narcissism causes suffering and calls for help, in some cases changes in the life situation can terminate narcissistic tendencies. To leave the shelter of the parental home, to terminate an over-dependent love relationship or marriage, to overcome a reluctance to train for or accept responsible work, may start a new and healthier development. Yet in most cases therapy has to try to bring about a slow transformation of emotional organisation. It is a useful but somewhat tantalising exercise to try to describe a man totally free from narcissism and this an be done only in evocative, symbolic terms such as 'individuation' (Jung), 'faith' (Karl Jaspers), 'Gelassenheit' (Heidegger) or 'love'.

It would be utopian to expect that therapy in each case would reach this 'healthy' goal. The patient in most cases will be satisfied (and the therapist has to be satisfied) with far less. Some greater freedom to become active in one's own name, some more tolerance for guilt, criticism, conflict and aggression, some added flexibility of the ego image, some more trust in others: these may alleviate the suffering of a patient and change his life though narcissistic features may persist.

To bring about these relatively slight changes the therapist may have to apply all his experience, skill and patience. There is no separate therapy for narcissism.

The narcissist often expects to be helped by getting from the therapist that love and attention which he has always craved in vain. Not only are these expectations insatiable, they are a distortion of the unity which originally was valued, namely the unquestioning unity of mother and infant. The narcissist usually cultivates peripheral aspects of childlikeness such as passivity, pleasing goodness, suppression of needs and demands which may be criticised, and so forth, and he craves for reassurance and shelter. In contrast, in the primary unity the infant experiences himself as accepted in whatever he spontaneously needs, feels or expresses. He is neither passive nor trying to be good, and he can trust he will be understood and will receive the appropriate response to his smiles as well as to his distressed or angry cries.

The therapist therefore helps the patient not by gratifying the distorted narcissistic demands but by offering a more genuine and comprehensive understanding and acceptance, given not as a reward for good behaviour, and with an aim going far beyond reassurance and immediate relief of anxiety.

The Heart of Man
(Erich Fromm)

Erich Fromm is a psychotherapist who started out as a pupil of Freud but came to feel Freud's natural-scientific approach to man unsatisfactory, and to believe that a humanistic idea of what man is must be made the basis of psychological theory and therapeutic practice.

In his book *The Heart of Man*, subtitled 'Its Genius for Good and Evil', he is attempting to take part in a welcome re-establishment of contact between ethics and psychology, a contact interrupted at a time when psychologists conceived as their aim to be pure natural scientists. The attempt at re-establishment of contact follows from a recognition that the dynamic and analytical psychologies are among the human studies, *Geisteswissenschaften*, and are not natural sciences.

The Heart of Man attempts to explain man's genius for good and for evil in psychological terms. Evil Fromm regards as the result of three basic human tendencies:

1. Love of death instead of love of life;

2. Narcissism or Self-love instead of love for all;

3. Symbiotic-incestuous fixation, which is to say a wish to be totally contained in a mothering figure.

These tendencies Fromm deems the more malignant the more regressive and archaic they are.

Psychological theories which relinquish the purely natural-scientific basis must establish their own basic concepts, the usefulness and validity of which remain dependent on the sensitive accuracy of their description of the psychological phenomena considered.

Fromm's basic concepts do not strike me as particularly helpful.

His concept of 'life' is obviously a validating one, and therefore it has more than the one opposite. People who in his sense of 'life' lack 'love of life' do not necessarily in consequence love death. Most of those who are not 'biophils'—in his sense of courageously and creatively facing the difficulties of life—do not love death but love rather a sheltered and secure life.

Only on the basis of his fallacious pairs of opposites is it possible to arrive at the patently wrong statement that it is because they love death that people do not protest more against nuclear war.

Fromm's two basic concepts of narcissism and incestuous symbiosis are equally superficial and untenable.

The essence of narcissism is not as Fromm thinks self-love, but the fear and destructive hatred of all that is not in conformity with the narcissist's narrow concept of what he or she is and ought to be.

The detrimental quality of the symbiosis is not its incestuousness but the reluctance involved to accept responsibility in one's own name.

It is therefore not at all surprising that the result of Fromm's discussion is so unsatisfactory, and that *The Heart of Man* presents the phenomenon of an extremely clever and learned work which persistently reaches to wrong conclusions.

If the most regressed person were the most evil, then the most evil person would be a schizophrenic who is paralysed by an intense wish to avoid all evil, and who has regressed at a time when under the circumstances he had no choice in the matter.

In contrast, Edmund in Shakespeare's *King Lear*, who is undoubtedly evil, yet has not at all regressed in any of the three directions identified by Fromm, would thus according to Fromm's discussion be good.

Shakespeare's Sonnets
120 and 121

That you were once unkind befriends me now,
And for that sorrow which I then did feel
Needs I must under my transgression bow,
Unless my nerves were brass and hammered steel.
For if you were by my unkindness shaken,
As I by yours, y'have pass'd a hell of time;
And I, a tyrant, have no leisure taken
To weigh how once I suffered in your crime.
O that our night of woe might have remembered
My deepest sense how hard true sorrow hits,
And soon to you, as you to me, then tend'red
The humble salve which wounded bosoms fits!
    But that your trespass now becomes a fee;
    Mine ransoms yours, and yours must ransom me.   (120)

'Tis better to be vile than vile esteemed,
When not to be receives reproach of being,
And the just pleasure lost, which is so deemed
Not by our feeling, but by others' seeing.
For why should others' false adulterate eyes
Give salutation to my sportive blood?
Or on my frailties why are frailer spies,
Which in their wills count bad what I think good?
No: I am that I am; and they that level
At my abuses reckon up their own.
I may be straight though they themselves be bevel;
By their rank thoughts my deeds must not be shown,
    Unless this general evil they maintain:
    All men are bad, and in their badness reign.   (121)

Shakespeare's sonnets are intriguing not only for their poetry but also because of the psychology of their content. Quite apart from the element in them of conventional duty offerings from the poet to his noble patron, they are the direct poetic expression of feelings about the two addressees, a psychologically consistent record of an emotional relationship with them. The order in which at least the first 126 poems were published appears meaningful psychologically and doubts as to whether it can be thus meaningful strike the psychologist as far-fetched. When I first read the poems from the point of view of a psychologist, I was struck by Sonnet 120, which seemed to me to represent the end point of a psychological development and the attainment of an emotional security superior to that expressed in all the other sonnets. This remains my opinion, and to explain this I have to describe my reading of the whole series of poems.

The poet was intensely in love with the addressee of the first 126 sonnets. His love was inspired by the beloved's physical beauty and the poet never tired of praising this beauty in every possible way. The beloved's beauty became the cipher for all that had ever stirred the poet's deepest feelings. As such it transcended the factual reality of the beloved's body. Yet this does not justify the denial that it is physical love. The Stoics separated spiritual love radically from physical love, but the Platonists of the Renaissance expressly objected to this because thus spiritual love was seen as cold. The Platonists admitted sensual physical attraction as an essential part of spiritual love, though sexual desire had to remain excluded. Edgar Wind in discussing Titian's famous picture 'Sacred and Profane Love' points out that the naked woman represents sacred love. She is very attractive physically, though sexual desire and possessiveness are strictly controlled. It seems most probable that Shakespeare's relationship with the young noble never led to physical intimacies. In Sonnet 20 the poet wittily distinguishes between love and the (sexual) use of love, and expressly renounces any claim to the latter:

> *And for a woman wert thou first created;*
> *Till nature, as she wrought thee, fell a-doting,*
> *And by addition me of thee defeated*
> *By adding one thing to my purpose nothing.*

> *But since she pricked thee out for woman's pleasure,*
> *Mine be thy love, and thy love's use their treasure.*

His love is Platonic but not Stoic. The poet is united with the beloved only by the two elements of 'slight air and purging fire' but not by the heavy elements of 'earth and water' (44); yet he remains concerned about the other's 'fair health', that is, his unimpaired physique (Sonnet 45) and he worries again and again about the damage to the beloved's beauty which ageing can bring about.

The beloved represents the vision of all that most deeply gratifies the poet, perfection seen in the image of perfect physical beauty. The image of the young nobleman has absorbed into itself all and everybody the poet ever loved, 'Their images I loved I view in thee' (Sonnet 31), and as such is visible only to the poet. It is the cipher and embodiment of the poet's total love potentiality, and of all his being longs for. The beloved's beauty is the ultimate truth, 'Both truth and beauty on my love depends . . .' (Sonnet 101). Thus what the poet sees in his friend is a projected image. It idealises the young noble and ignores his blemishes, for example when speaking about the young man's attitude to marriage. The poet clearly sees how Narcissus-like, selfish and self-centred the young man is (Sonnets 9,10), 'Grant, if thou wilt, thou art belov'd of many,/ But that thou none lov'st is most evident...' (10). Yet in praising his perfect truth and beauty the poet ignores this and does not foresee the disappointments later to follow for himself from the young man's selfishness.

Shakespeare experienced his vision as timeless and eternal, and he has to preserve this vision for all time in his poetry. It is for the subject-matter of his poems that Shakespeare claims perpetuity, and for his poetic art only because it reveals the beauty of the beloved, timeless as a Platonic idea.

Shakespeare's vision of the friend's beauty is the visible representation or symbol of his own love and of the core of his own self-awareness. Thus the centre of the poet's self-awareness and his vision of the friend are identical, the friend and he are one, they seem to be in the same image. This is described in a somewhat scurrilous sonnet (62) in which the poet imagines himself being as beautiful as he apperceives his friend to be, until a mirror shows him his real face, 'Beated and chopt with tanned antiquity'.

Sonnet 22 expresses the identity of the more powerful image that the poet's heart lives in the breast of the friend and the friend's heart in his own. Thus, wherever one lover is, the other is also present. I do not believe that the sonnet tells anything about whether in reality the young friend returned the poet's love. Even at the height of his love Shakespeare knows that in many ways he is different from his idealised friend; but these differences appear negligible, for the friend is 'all the better parts' (Sonnet 39) of him. By basing his sense of identity on an identification with the friend, and by neglecting all feelings and desires which are weaker than the love of the friend, Shakespeare becomes alienated from himself. His awareness of himself, as well as of his friend, is falsified by the illusion that each of them is identical with that perfect beauty which Shakespeare's love has conjured up.

Before discussing the development of Shakespeare's relationship with his male friend, we shall have to look at what he has to say about the woman to whom Sonnets 127-152 are devoted. The poet was involved with her simultaneously with his love of the young man, and this involvement was apperceived as a complementary opposite of his love of the man. Her darkness is seen throughout as a symbolic contrast to the young man's fairness. This correlation makes it probable that the poet's statements about the lady are as much influenced by projections of the poet's feelings and imaginings as are those about the male beloved.

His feelings about the lady are thoroughly ambivalent on two separate scores. His sexual desire makes him look for love as he experiences love with the man, namely for a deeply stirring beauty and for oneness. Yet he knows that the beauty he sees in the lady is illusion. All his five senses deceive him and he has to remind himself several times that he cannot compare her with the beauty he longs for, and that she falls short of it in respect of every sense (130, 131, 137, 141).

In faith I do not love thee with mine eyes,
For they in thee a thousand errors note ...
Nor are mine ears with thy tongue's tune delighted;
Nor tender feeling to base toouches prone,
Nor taste nor smell desire to be invited
To any sensual feast with thee alone; ...

Yet all of this is in vain. he has to go on to think her 'bright,/Who art as black as hell, as dark as night ...' against his better knowledge (147) or to compare her to the sun and the evening star (132).

He also longs for oneness with her, but in contrast to the male love this longing is entirely demanding. Total oneness is to be achieved not by identification, as in the homoerotic relationship, but by the demand that the woman should love the poet as a mother loves her babe (143); or at least she should attend to him out of pity (140, 142) and reassure him:

'I hate' she altered with an end
That followed it as gentle day
Doth follow night ...
    And sav'd my life, saying 'not you'.   *(145)*

He asks for declarations of love (145). Yet he knows that he is not loved like a child, and he has to share her favours with other men.

This brings into view the other ambivalence of the poet, about sex. The woman's unfaithfulness pains him. Yet he obviously overstates her wantonness. According to him she refuses no fair suitor; she is like a large and spacious store, so that it will not matter to her that she might add the poet to her abundance (135, 136). Shakespeare wants to see her as the Great Whore, the universal temptress. In Sonnet 150 he expressly states that it is her unworthiness which inspires love in him. Her betraying him rouses his desire, and against all better reason he reacts with physical desire, phallic erection and the urge to possess her, Sonnet 151:

... I do betray
My nobler part to my gross body's treason;
My soul doth tell my body that he may
Triumph in love; flesh stays no farther reason,
But, rising at thy name, doth point out thee
As his triumphant prize ...

Shakespeare can amuse himself with crude sexual *double-entendre* (135, 136, 150, 151), yet the famous Sonnet 129 has also to be taken seriously—as soon as his sexual desires are gratified, sex is hated and despised:

Th'expense of spirit in a waste of shame
Is lust in action; and till action lust
Is perjured, murd'rous ... full of blame ... usw.

He assures us that 'All this the world well knows' and in vain tries to get rid of the lure of sexual desire. Shakespeare's attitude to sex conforms to a conventional mediaeval Christian outlook. It is in this mood that Shakespeare can compare his two loves (Sonnet 144) and call his male lover an angel and a saint, whereas he sees the woman as an evil temptress who wants to corrupt the saintly male to be a devil.

Simultaneous involvement with two lovers, one representing purity, fairness and beauty and the other one sex and the dark sides of human nature is of course not unique. In German literature Gottfried Keller describes a simultaneous involvement with a fair and with a dark woman, in his autobiographical novel *Der Grüne Heinrich*. C. G. Jung has observed that it is not rare to find in the dreams of modern men the appearance of two *anima* figures, a fair and a dark. And Freud was able to trace back the origins of this split to the infant's early mother-*imago*, which may be split in two: one being the caring and loving mother with whom the infant is totally at one, the other the frustrating mother who represents powers which are in conflict with the infant's urges and demands. The latter *imago* in addition absorbs the child's own tendencies directed toward independence, thus creating conflict with the mother. Through this the image of the frustrating mother loses its purely negative connotation, and it also becomes attractive as image of selfish freedom from restraints, and image of selfish power. As the child first experiences these powers in the act of relieving himself, the *imago* of the frustrating mother becomes associated with gross bodily powers, with guts and dirt. She is seen as a chthonian force. In contrast the all-loving mother is then apperceived as a superior being who is pure; she is apperceived beautified. She and her substitutes may be experienced as sensually attractive, and even sexually desirable insofar as erotic feelings and sex are experienced as forces which intensify total union with her. Yet insofar as sex is predominantly seen as a gross bodily power it may be directed to women who are like the chthonian mother. The erotic tendencies may become split: the spiritualised and purified love may be directed to a person with whom one longs for total unity, while sex and intercourse are experienced as selfish exertions of power in a relationship of tension between two essentially different agents. In such a situation, longing for total union often becomes directed towards a being of the same sex, and in this an identity of sex facilitates identification of two lovers. Homoerotic love will then tend to be spiritualised and intensely aesthetic, culminating in the total identification of the lovers; while sex and intercourse will be desired with a woman who is treated with some hostility and disdain.

The love which aims at recreating that total unity which first is experienced between infant and loving mother is romantic love, and homoerotic love is often extremely romantic. Yet romantic love cannot have lasting gratification, because total identification of two grown-up beings is not possible for any length of time. Life forces us to be self-assertive and to gratify needs which may not coincide with the needs of the beloved one. Romantic love ends, therefore, with either the separation of the lovers or the premature death of one or both lovers (as in *Romeo and Juliet* or in

Keller's *Der Grüne Heinrich*), or the romantic love has to be transformed into a maturer kind of love and relationship.

It is a deeply moving aspect of Shakespeare's Sonnets that they show such a transformation of his love for the young man. Three crises in their relationship bring about this transformation.

The first crisis occurred when the young man became the lover of the dark lady. This upset and hurt Shakespeare deeply. Yet it affected his relationship with the young man less than might have been expected. The poet himself felt that this was peculiar and needed explanation. He proposed two such explanations. One (Sonnet 135) was that he was an accessory to the robbery the lady committed by stealing the young man from the poet. It was Shakespeare who brought them together (Sonnet 134) by asking the young man to write to the lady on his behalf and to promote his suit. In Sonnet 42 the poet explains that he is reconciled to his friend's intimacies with the dark lady because he and the friend are one, so that her love of the friend is also love of him. Though this sounds rather contrived it may all the same contain some truth. It is as if it gratified an unconscious archetypal wish that the fair and the dark *anima* become united. Such fantasies can ocasionally be observed in dreams: (*at the time of working on my first paper on the Sonnets I saw in an exhibition of Courbet in Zurich his life-size painting of two beautiful naked women, one dark-haired, one fair, resting in bed together obviously after lesbian love-making, a theme which may have attracted the painter for the same reason. The painting belongs to the collection of the Petit Palais, Paris*).

The second crisis was caused by the uncongenial behaviour of the young friend, by the attention he paid to another poet, and by Shakespeare's fear of the loss of his affection through his listening to untrue rumours about the poet.

At times (Sonnets 48, 49) Shakespeare sees clearly that he cannot count on the constancy of his friend's affection, and knows that the friend's love of him is not as great as his own for the friend. The friend's relationship with others, that he 'grows common' (Sonnet 69) disquietens the poet. Then (Sonnets 67, 68) new waves of gratitude and love reassure the poet again, until the nobleman's attention to a rival poet makes Shakespeare fear that this will take the friend away from him completely. His jealousy of the rival is usually explained by Shakespeare's anxiety lest the young noble withdraw his patronage from him and bestow it on the rival poet. A different interpretation is however possible if the assumption is correct that the nobleman is the Earl of Southampton and the rival poet Marlowe. Marlowe is known to have been homosexual, and Southampton was susceptible not only to praise but to homoerotic charm. His sins and vices mentioned in Sonnet 95 may already relate to homosexual activities and, according to A. L. Rowse, homosexual involvement is a known historical fact of Southampton's later life. Shakespeare's jealousy of the other poet is erotic, and this alone can explain the wild feelings of annihilation (Sonnets 89-94) which in Shakespeare resulted from the friend's real or suspected with-drawal of love.

> I *will acquaintance strangle and look strange* ...   (89)
> So *shall I live, supposing thou art true,*
> Like *a deceived husband* ...   (93)

Finally (Sonnets 95, 96) it is only anger about the friend's loose living which ends the poet's nearly suicidal depression.

All these upheavals force Shakespeare to face the young man's separate-ness and indifference towards him, and his vain superficiality and unprinci-pled living. Yet this does not destroy his loving vision of perfect beauty, projected on to the young man. He cannot abandon this vision because his very life depends on it. He is identified with it, and without this identity his life seems pointless (Sonnet 92). During his rivalry with the other poet he readily grants the competence of the other man's poetry and the flattering quality of his praises of the young man. Yet no-one but Shakespeare alone can truly see and praise the young man's beauty, for it is revealed only to his love.

Then after the angry sonnets 95, 96, Shakespeare's feelings for the young man are cool and wintry for a while (Sonnets 97-99): 'What freezings have I felt, what dark days seen?' (97). He turns to his Muse, the personifica-tion of his creative power, to occupy itself again with the one theme which is worthy of contemplation and praise, the beauty of the beloved and the revealing of its 'truth' by the poet's verse (Sonnets 100-103). The exaltation of the beloved's beauty now goes further than ever before. It transcends anything which can be said in words or poetry about it (Sonnet 103). The revelation of this transcendent value of beauty to the world happened only with the young man's birth (Sonnet 104) and all beauty which before this was seen and praised was only the prophecy of the revelation which was to come with the young man's birth (Sonnets 106, 107): 'all you prefiguring' (106). It is worthy of absorbing all the poetic powers of the poet.

A tendency to idolise and deify the homoerotically beloved has occurred again and again, for example in the love of the Emperor Hadrian for Antinous, or of Stefan George for Maximin. Shakespeare is aware that he is experiencing his love in quasi-religious terms, and feels the need to refute the doubt that he is indulging in idolatry; and this he does (Sonnet 105) with the assertion that his vision is 'fair, kind and true'. This most extreme quasi-religious exaltation of his love and vision immediately precedes the third and final crisis of the poet's relationship with the young man, which brings about its transformation.

Shakespeare is away from his friend. he makes new acquaintances, experiences success and enjoys the praise and flattery he receives; he gets involved with critics or succumbs to temptations. And through all this forgets his friend for long stretches of time and neglects him. He feels intensely guilty about this, how could he feel otherwise as long as (Sonnet 109) he sees in the friend the *summum bonum*, 'thy sum of good'. He tries to excuse himself with the standard excuse of all disloyalty in love, namely that the new experiences only make the merits of the beloved shine all the brighter, and that they renew and refresh the poet's ability to love.

Yet he knows himself that there is something dishonest in this excuse (Sonnet 115) and he has to admit that this way of intensifying his love only poisons it (Sonnet 118). Still less sincere is the excuse that his straying away from the young friend gives the friend the chance to prove the constancy of his love (Sonnet 117). No, it has to be admitted that the old love has been ruined. The one hope for the relationship between the poet and the young man lies only in a new and different love being built, Sonnet 119:

> . . . *Now I find true*
> *That better is by evil still made better;*
> *And ruined love, when it is built anew,*
> *Grows fairer than at first, more strong, far greater.*

The basis for such a new love is described in Sonnets 120 and 121. Shakespeare now feels free from guilt and self-rejection. He no longer feels the need for self-justification or excuses, nor for forgiveness by his friend. Neither does he any longer blame the friend for his shortcomings in comparison with the ideal picture he had projected on to him. He no longer identifies the friend himself with the ideal vision of perfection which his former love had made him see. Now he recognises that the various unkind-nesses of his friend which had made him suffer are part of the friend as much as those of his qualities which stimulated the vision of beauty. And in the same way he sees and accepts all his own interests, and now the friend is loved for his total humanity, and he is loved with all the poet's faculties alive, including the critical ones. The love is no longer one of perfection but of the common humanity which includes the differences and variances of interest of the two lovers. It accepts the uniqueness and individuality of each of the lovers, it emphasises the common humanity instead of the common supe-riority of the lovers. It creates existential acceptance of the self as well as of the other.

When I first read the sonnets I was struck by the first line of Sonnet 120 as meaning just this. It seemed to me that the acceptance of unkindness as a constituent part of love and befriending could not be expressed more strikingly than by the line, 'That you were once unkind befriends me now'. When later I read interpretations of the Sonnets by others I found that some who like myself did not speak English as their mother tongue understood this verse in the same way, while no English interpreter did. For example the Italian translator of the Sonnets, Alberto Rossi, gives the following translation:

> *Che ingiusto tu sia stato ora mi fa tuo amico*
> *(That you have been unjust makes me now your friend)*

English commentators do not regard 'unkind' and 'befriends' as opposites, and this drove me to consult dictionaries on the word 'befriend'. Modern dictionaries like *Chambers'* or the *Concise Oxford* justify Rossi's translation of 'befriends' as 'makes me your friend'. However the *O.E.D.* states that in Shakespeare's time 'befriend' meant 'to help', 'to favour', and the standard *Shakespeare Lexicon* by Alexander Schmidt quotes nine places where 'befriend' occurs in Shakespeare's writings always meaning 'to be kind to', 'to favour', 'to benefit', 'to be fortunate for'. I therefore do not doubt that the first verse of Sonnet 120 says that the former unkindness of the friend is favourable to the poet. Yet the meaning of the whole sonnet remains unchanged in the affirmation of the friendship of two men neither of whom is perfect and whose imperfections form a new link of mutual equality and love. A. L. Rowse says that in Sonnet 120 there is manifest on Shakespeare's part a feeling of independence, security and equality as never in any of the earlier Sonnets.

A relationship like Shakespeare's love of the young noble—which produced the experience of total at-one-ness in the vision of perfect beauty with which both the friend and the poet were identified—can represent a lasting enrichment of one's life and experience. It brings the lover into contact with the deepest, which is to say, earliest layer of his feelings and self-awareness. This is true of all experiences of total at-one-ness, whether the love of one other person or at-one-ness with nature, with works of art, or with God. This all-absorbing at-one-ness cannot last, because it alienates one from common reality. Yet one may be lastingly grateful for having had the experience in spite of pain and suffering caused by overcoming the all-absorbing exclusiveness of the experience, and by the inevitable return to being separate and alone. This lasting gratitude may also embrace the person who originally called up one's love, he may remain a cipher and symbol of the deep experience he stimulated, may become lastingly an image of the *anima* or the Self. And though a realistic relationship of two separate beings has replaced the former at-one-ness, the reality of the friend may still at times hint at the former vision of perfection, and one may be grateful for the reminder.

That is the lasting love of which Shakespeare speaks in the last four Sonnets addressed to his male friend. After this the series of Sonnets ends. Maybe the realities of life of the two friends, their differences of age, status, occupation, social qualities and interests separated their ways; or maybe their new realistic friendship did not demand or allow poetic expression. The Sonnets do not inform us about this.

The Problem of Individuation in the Writings of Friedrich Nietzsche

This is not a paper on Nietzsche in general, on his life, his philosophy, his psychology, or on the deep and varied influences which he exercised upon the history of human thought and, unfortunately, also upon political ideologies. It is a contribution, rather, to the study of the problem of individuation.

To make Nietzsche the subject of such a study is justified not only by the fact that Nietzsche had an extremely rich mind, the development of which can be clearly followed in his writings and in the rich biographical material which we possess, but also because individuation was one of the central problems of Nietzsche's own philosophical thinking, perhaps the most central of all.

Four periods are usually discerned in his philosophical development: the early one coinciding with his friendship with Wagner and characterised by the idealisation of genius, 1868-76; the positivistic period from 1876-1881; the period of his metaphysical discovery of the 'Eternal Recurrence' and its preaching in *Thus Spoke Zarathustra*, 1881-85; and the last period, which had already begun during intervals in writing the four parts of *Zarathustra*. and which is marked by a more systematic formulation of his philosophy of *The Will to Power* and by an autobiographical description of his own philosophical development, 1884-1888.

In all these periods there are sayings which emphasise the importance of individuation:

It is the task of a free man to live for his own sake and not others. (Aphorism 121, *'We Philologists'*).

The Greeks are interesting and infinitely important because they have such a plenitude of great individuals. (Aph. 200, *ibid.*).

I believe that everyone must have his own opinion about everything concerning which opinions are possible, because he is a unique individual who has to react in a new and individual way. (Aph. 286, *Human All Too Human*).

Active successful natures do not act according to the maxim: 'Know thyself', but as if always confronted with the command: 'Will a self, then thou wilt become a self.' (Aph.366, *Human All Too Human*, II)

We seek to become what we are—the new, the unique, the incomparable ones, making laws for ourselves and creating ourselves.' (Aph.335, *The Joyful Wisdom*).

One must learn to love oneself with a wholesome and healthy love that one may endure being with oneself and cease roving about . . . And verily, it is no commandment for to-day and to-morrow to *learn* to love oneself. Of all the arts it is the finest, subtlest, the last and most patient. ('The Spirit of Gravity', *Thus Spake Zarathustra*)

And Nietzsche's last book, *Ecce Homo*, has the subtitle 'How one becomes what one is'.

What is it that causes this high estimation of the individual and makes individuation such an urgent task for Nietzsche? To answer this question we have to consider some biographical facts of Nietzsche's personality and development.

He was born in 1844, the eldest son of a country parson. His father was a well-educated and gifted man, highly musical, delicate and lovable, and the child was very fond of him from his earliest youth. Yet this beloved father died suddenly when the boy was only four years old. This grievous loss led to an intense identification with the father image. We possess the record of a dream which the child dreamt at the age of five—some six months after his father's death—which runs as follows:

I heard the sound of the church organ playing a requiem. When I looked to see what was the cause, a grave suddenly opened and my father, in his shroud, arose from it. He hurried into the church and, in a moment or two, reappeared with a small child in his arms. The grave opened, he stepped into it, and the gravestone fell once more over the opening. The sound of the organ immediately ceased and I awoke.

When Nietzsche recorded this dream, at the age of fourteen, he interpreted it as a premonition of the death of his baby brother, unexpectedly from convulsions, a few months after the dream. One may however doubt whether this interpretation is correct. The dream may refer to Nietzsche himself. The child, which is to say Nietzsche himself, is taken out of the church, the mother symbol, and united with the father in his grave. Whether this guess is right or not, there can be no doubt about the fact of the boy's identification with his father. He needed it badly, to cope with a difficult life situation. After his father's and his baby brother's death he remained the only male in a household of six women: his grandmother, two aunts, his still very young mother, his sister and a maid. There was no male person present to help him in the task of breaking the original oneness with the mother and her substitutes, and to develop into a being different from the women amongst whom he lived.

Nietzsche tackled this difficulty by precociously emphasising his male independence and by identifying himself with his inner image of the father.

As a young boy he showed great independence of thinking; he displayed a precocious dignity and was somewhat priggish in his strict morality and his obedience to laws and regulations. He was gentle and considerate in his intercourse with others, but rather aloof; his schoolfriends found him slightly strange and unlike themselves. He shunned everything common and unclean, the world of the earth mother and of sex, particularly, were excluded. The father, whom Nietzsche remembered and whom he idealised, had been a richly emotional and artistic personality; therefore an identification with him had not the effect of thwarting all emotional development in the boy, as so often is the case; yet the emotions which developed were of a lofty, spiritualised and artistic type. Religion, music, poetry and asexual friendship were the boy's main interests.

Friendship with Wagner

Nietzsche, the young student of classics, is an unusually gifted scholar, industrious and painstaking, intuitive and full of ideas and artistic interests, yet emotionally somewhat young for his age. He is an idealist who is looking for personalities on to whom he can project his exalted image of the ideal father which is, at the same time, his own ego ideal. He found two such masters: Schopenhauer, who was already dead at that time and whom Nietzsche knew in his writings; and Richard Wagner, who became his intimate friend for the eight years between 1869 and 1876. This friendship was of the utmost importance to Nietzsche's development. Wagner lived in Triebschen near Lucerne, and when Nietzsche became professor of classics in Basle at the early age of 23 he became a frequent visitor in Wagner's house.

Wagner was 31 years older than Nietzsche. He was the independent genius who towered far above ordinary human beings and who, with his music and his books, showed his contemporaries the way out of their humdrum misery and philistine blindness to true values. At least, that is how Nietzsche saw him then. He became an ardent admirer of both Wagner's art and personality. At the same time this friendship inspired Nietzsche's own creativeness and, under its happy influence, he wrote his first philosophical book, *The Birth of Tragedy out of the Spirit of Music*. It is a philosophy of art, exemplified by the development of the Greek tragedy, but it is more than that. It is the description of Nietzsche's ideal of man at that time.

Already in his first philosophical book Nietzsche is dealing, therefore, with the main theme of all his philosophical efforts: what is man, how should he be and behave? Nietzsche's main interests throughout his life were the psychology and morals of man. In this first book he identifies three psychic principles, or functions, which he symbolises by the three Greek names of *Dionysos*, *Apollo*, and *Socrates*.

Dionysos, the chthonian God of orgiastic ecstasy, of lust and drunken raving, symbolises the unconscious and chaotic life impulses, the dark and inarticulate instincts. They form the basic motive forces of art, but can become art only through the interference and help of another principle which gives shape and measure to the formless Dionysian elements. This principle is symbolised by Apollo, the Sun God. He represents what, in Jung's terminology, we would call 'intuition' or 'imagination'.

Apollo produces the dreams which symbolise inarticulate, unconscious urges in well defined dream images and stories. He created the mythical stories which make the chaotic Dionysian urges visible and comprehensible. Similarly, the Greek tragedy transforms and makes articulate the Dionysian urges through the influence of Apollonian clarity and imagination. Apollo is called the *principium individuationis* which transforms the chaotic sea of Dionysian emotion into well defined visible forms. The Apollonian individuation rests, somewhat precariously, on the seething sea of collective and impersonal Dionysian emotions. On the other side it is endangered by deterioration into impersonal intellectuality. If Apollonian order and clarity goes too far, it results in the pure thinking which Nietzsche represents in the figure of Socrates. Socrates was the destroyer of Greek tragedy and the founder of scientific thinking, a form of thinking objective and impersonal. Nietzsche thought that Socrates was the ruler in Nietzsche's own day. Yet he believed that Wagner and the musical drama would restore, in modern times, the spirit of the Greek tragedy, that happy union of Dionysos and Apollo.

This is of course typical romantic philosophy, not only because Nietzsche finds the golden age in times long past, but also because the basis of personality is found in the dark region of the chaotic emotions. They are shaped into individual form and personality through the influence of imagination and intellect. Reason is valuable, as long as it co-operates with the emotions and shapes them. As isolated intellect it destroys personality and personal value and makes life impersonal and shallow. For the representative of the one function of imagination, Apollo, to be called the *principium individuationis*, corresponds with frequent experiences in the earlier stages of the process of individuation. There the development and inclusion in the ego of a so far undifferentiated function produces a heightened sense of individuality and of being personal. In later stages of the process of individuation it is no longer a single function but a symbol of the psychic totality, such as the Self or the Libido, that is experienced as the *principium individuationis*. We will see an example of this in Nietzsche's later writings. The dream theory Nietzsche develops in this book of 1872, *The Birth of Tragedy*, is akin to that of Jung. He does not like Freud believe that a definite thought is artfully disguised in the symbols of dream, but that dream is the expression of chaotic unconscious emotions and urges, and often the only form in which these urges can be comprehended and expressed. The three psychic functions which Nietzsche discerns in this book could be described in our language as thinking (Socrates), imagination (Apollo), and unconscious emotionality (Dionysos). We shall see how, in Nietzsche's further development, there always appears such a trinity and not a quaternity of mental functions and complexes.

The Positivistic Period

In order to understand the next step in Nietzsche's development we have to return to his biography. His friendship with Wagner had not only the exhilarating effect which resulted in the writing of the *Birth of Tragedy*, it also brought Nietzsche face to face with some problems which are inherent in an identification with the father image and in the projection of an idealised image on to another person. Every identification of this kind contains an element of submission, a longing to sacrifice and surrender the ego to the exalted image of the father and to the person on whom this image is projected. Nietzsche had extraordinarily strong tendencies towards sacrificing himself for his friend. Already the fact that he linked the final analysis of Greek tragedy in *The Birth of Tragedy* with his admiration for Wagner's music drama, was such an act of self-sacrifice, for it gave the book an ambiguous character and jeopardised the goodwill and interest of classical scholars. At another time Nietzsche offered to renounce his professorship in order to become a propagandist for Wagner's cause. He supported Wagner's plans for the Bayreuth Festspielhaus with considerable sums of money and, finally, wrote a paean on the occasion of its opening, at a time when he himself was already very doubtful about its success and value. Such a self-sacrificing love is, at the same time, very demanding, for self-surrender is bearable only as long as the idealised person does not disappoint the expectations which are projected on to him. This however has to happen sooner or later.

In Nietzsche's case the first Wagner festival in Bayreuth in 1876 brought about this disappointment. The people who gathered round Wagner on that occasion were not the spiritual leaders whom Nietzsche had expected to see, not men who were dissatisfied with the philistine mediocrity of their time, but idle rich and empty socialites. Nietzsche could not bear to see Wagner feted by them, and his own intimacy with Wagner destroyed by their demands on Wagner's time and attention. Nietzsche had to regain his independence.

Until now Wagner, the genius, had appeared to Nietzsche to be the embodiment of all the highest values. Now Nietzsche could no longer allow himself to find the embodiment of value mainly outside himself, for it created dependence and made him unfree. *Der Freigeist*—the Free Spirit—who recognised no authority outside himself and who followed his own inclinations, now became his ideal and goal. He turned against dependence in two ways: by fighting the emotions in himself which longed for shelter and consolation from outside, and by attacking the claims of everybody and everything which demanded dependence and submission. The means with which he attacked his fetters was positivist rationalism. Then Socrates, symbol of scientific thinking, who had before been rejected as destroyer of personal values, now became ruler. Scientific thinking which isolates, creates clear distinctions and destroys wishful illusions and the 'participation mystique' with fellow men and nature, appeared now as the *principium individuationis*. Ours, Nietzsche argued, is not a meaningful and humane world, well ordered by a kind God. All belief, whether in a God, in eternal values or eternal truth, rests on erroneous and unhistorical wishful thinking. Morals are rules which derive their validity only from their usefulness in a certain historical situation, but have no validity beyond that. Such criticism of religion and moral values in the name of pure thinking is, plainly, in danger of ending in cynical nihilism and leading to the development of libertinism instead of freedom of spirit. Nietzsche avoided this danger for several reasons.

First: no matter how radical his intellectual criticism of moral values, in practice he remained a believer and adherent of those values which were represented by the image of his late father. In his practical behaviour Nietzsche was, all his life, a moral perfectionist on conventional aristocratic lines. His criticism of religion and morals, when he broke away from Wagner, was only for the purpose of overcoming his feeling of dependence. Aristocratic ethics had become so much second nature to him that he could practise them without any awareness of dependence. (Theoretically, he justified his practical conventionality by a belief that ethical excellence was the result of breeding, and of inheritance from a long chain of ethical ancestors, such as he had himself.)

Second: His criticism of wishful emotional influences upon religious and moral thinking did not lead, as with so many other positivists, to a neglect of the value of emotion and feeling. He rebelled against the rational dogma of Christian religion, but knew that the logical refutation and destruction of the religious dogma left unaffected the emotional needs which created it. He had himself been a religious child, who knew and appreciated these needs, and loved the specific Christian feelings and virtues. (He once confessed that at the age of twelve he saw God in all His glory.) And he was far too much of a musician and poet to be able to overlook the importance of emotion and feeling. Religion may have come to an end as a teaching of dogmas about natural facts, but it will continue to be a problem of history and psychology, he expressly stated.

Third: Nietzsche's positivistic attacks on morals and religion are not nihilistic because they are made in the name of an ethical value, which is expressly acknowledged and in which Nietzsche believed passionately, namely *intellectuele Redlichkeit*—intellectual honesty. Nietzsche's positivism is more than mere ruthless logical thinking and impassioned observation of facts. An ethical fervour burns in it. Nietzsche himself realised that this was a remnant of and derivative from the religious attitude of his forebears, and says: 'The Christianity of my forebears reaches its logical conclusion in me: in a stern intellectual conscience . . .' His intellectual conscience rebels not only against intellectual fallacies and lazy contentment with intellectual prejudices, but it criticises, above all, spuriousness of feeling and faked sentimental beliefs. In the name of 'intellectual honesty' Nietzsche became the greatest critic of false sentiments, and of the spurious self-importance of man in the *fin de siècle* period. 'Intellectual honesty' is the great purifier of the emotional and moral atmosphere but is not, in itself, the basis for a new set of values. It is one of the preconditions for a more genuine and valid moral orientation, but this orientation has to come from other sources not clearly visible in Nietzsche's writings of that time. The following table of the four cardinal virtues to be found in the book *Dawn of Day* (Aph.556) is therefore peculiarly unsatisfactory:

> Honest (*redlich*) toward ourselves and all who are our friends; brave in the face of our enemies; magnanimous towards the vanquished; polite at all times: this is how the four cardinal virtues desire us to be.

The absence of the Christian virtues of charity and love from this list, and their substitution by politeness, produces an atmosphere of cold detachment characteristic of the tendencies which make the outcome of Nietzsche's positivistic period appear somewhat doubtful and unsatisfactory.

'Ubi pater sum ibi patria'

Nietzsche had taken abstract logical thinking seriously for the first time and realised it as a help in breaking away from dependence on parents and parent-substitutes. (Formerly he had avoided thinking where it threatened to divorce him from the emotional field. Thus this exceptionally gifted thinker had completely failed in mathematics in his school-leaving examination, and was granted his certificate only because of his excellence in languages, classics and Bible studies). He had gone through the pains and depressions of breaking away from his fatherly friend, Wagner, and was prepared to bless his suffering, no matter how bad it was, for the help it had given in finding himself. (During the period 1876-1883 he suffered from almost unbearable attacks of migraine which forced him to abandon his teaching job at the University of Basle and to restrict reading and writing to a minimum. Since vaso-motor disturbances such as migraine very frequently accompany attempts to break away from dependence on parental images, it is most probable that Nietzsche's migraine was psychologically conditioned or at least aggravated).

He had experienced loneliness, as it inevitably resulted from separation from his dearest friend, but he had become more lonely and aloof than this event, or his progress in individuation, warranted. This was due to the fact that his attempts to free himself from the influence of parental images, particularly the father image, had in some ways failed. He had succeeded in divorcing his longing for surrender and self-renunciation from the father image and in breaking his dependence on persons on whom he projected this image.

Yet this image remained as powerful and fascinating to him as ever. He had freed himself from every authority outside himself, only to establish the same paternal authority more firmly in his own personality. More than ever does he himself play the role of the father. In the book *Dawn of Day* he characteristically states (Aph.473), 'A powerful mildness like that of a father—wherever this feeling takes possession of you, there build your house ... *Ubi pater sum ibi patria'.*

All his efforts at overcoming the father went in the direction of becoming superior to him, more powerful, more spiritual, more learned. All his strivings go upwards, towards the regions of eternal snow and clear air, away from the common into the aristocratic world, away from the uncleanliness of the common ground into aesthetically purified regions, away from the earth into the airy spaces of the spirit, into spiritual freedom: that is, more exclusively into the fatherly world. The realm of the Earth-Mother remained as inaccessible to him as it had been during his early youth. The material world and sex were still outside his orbit. Thinking had become the dominant function, while intuition as well as feeling and emotion were distrusted and suspected of creating dependence and vassalage. However, the situation at the end of Nietzsche's positivist period is better described in terms which are nearer to Nietzsche's own experience and self-expression.

In one of the prefaces which he wrote in 1886 for books of the positivistic period, he calls his positivism an anti-romantic self-cure, because he was sick and nauseated by the feminine undisciplined nature of romanticism. In the name of virility and strength of intellect, he is now fighting against two big emotional complexes:

(1) against romantic longings to be contained in and sheltered by loving parents, and to surrender to them;

(2) against the Earth-Mother and everything which is common and which he has in common with every other human being, even with women.

Eternal Recurrence

The two succeeding periods of Nietzsche's writings are characterised by the re-emergence and glorification of those two complexes which were condemned during the positivistic period.

Re-emergence of the romantic longing for union with the parental image took the strangest form imaginable. Nietzsche was an extremely gentle and kind man in his daily life. He always said that sympathy and pity gave the greatest temptations to him to betray his philosophical principles. After his separation from Wagner he violently suppressed all longings for sympathy and union with a parental figure, but this longing remained one of his most basic urges. When such longings cannot find an outlet in the relationship with fellow men, they often lead to a mystical gratification. Yet, Nietzsche being an atheist, the *unio mystica* with God was out of the question.

The summer of 1881 Nietzsche spent in the Engadine. He was in a highly emotional and elated state. Suddenly, on a walk, it struck him that the Pythagorean idea of the Eternal Recurrence of everything that was happening, of all life, was an insight of the most stupendous importance, It was like a revelation, as if a star had risen before him, showing him the way of life.

He first tried to rationalise this overwhelming experience and to prove mathematically that every moment in life had existed many times before and would recur again, with all forces arranged exactly as at present.

It is easy to see that this mathematical reasoning is unsound. And Nietzsche's attempt to explain the ecstasy which this thought produced in him, by the moral impetus which he expected to result from it, was no better. He believed that every action became morally more important if one knew that Eternity was at stake. Now one was bound to live in a way which justified the desire to re-live every single moment, for that, inevitably, had to happen. Yet the mathematical inevitability of the Eternal Recurrence of all possible combinations of life circumstances is morally absolutely equivocal. However I act or do not act, both combinations will have to recur. The blatant fallacy of this reasoning proves, surely, that the idea of Eternal Recurrence received its emotional tone from non-rational sources. Nietzsche suddenly felt saved from his loneliness, he experienced himself no longer as an ephemeral spot, lost in a meaningless universe, but as a being with an infinite past and an eternal future. Life, which had lost all transcendent meaning when Nietzsche denied the existence of absolute and eternal values, regained such meaning again through the belief that our individual life will recur eternally.

Our individual life is eternal life and, therefore, infinitely important. The emotional meaning of the concept of Eternal Recurrence becomes still clearer in the chapter 'The Seven Seals' or 'The Song of Yea and Amen' in *Thus Spake Zarathustra*, where Nietzsche addresses Eternity as a woman he loves:

> Oh how could I not be ardent for eternity and for the marriage ring of rings—the ring of Eternal Recurrence?—Never yet found I the woman by whom I would have children, save it be by this woman that I love; for I love thee, O Eternity.

Eternity is the mother with whom he wants to be united in mystical marriage.

I am aware that all this seems extremely strange and almost incomprehensible either to reason or to empathy. So much, however, is clear: something of the greatest psychological importance must have happened, if a man of Nietzsche's energy and honesty of mind is beginning to address an abstract and remote idea like Eternity as a woman whom he loves and by whom he wishes to have children. In fact, we have reached a fateful turning point in Nietzsche's inner development. The positivistic over-emphasis on rational thinking and ego-independence and mastery is broken; and the longing for self-surrender and union with things symbolically feminine is again admitted.

The immediate result was a renewed contact with the unconscious, and Nietzsche's mind became literally overflooded with archetypal material. In this state he wrote his most famous book, *Thus Spake Zarathustra*, and I shall have to speak of this presently. First, however, I want to point to two other aspects of Nietzsche's mystical experience.

(1) By finding an entirely abstract representation of the mother image in the concept of Eternity, Nietzsche's separation from the material world became greatly increased and his urges for union were dissipated by an entirely abstract and immaterial idea.

(2) The concept of Eternity is wholly undynamic. In other mystical experiences the ego unites with a superior and more comprehensive power and dissolves in it. In Nietzsche's mystical experience the very opposite has happened.

An increased emphasis is laid upon the ego through the idea of Eternal Recurrence, and Eternity, whom he professes to love, remains a powerless abstraction. Nietzsche, in his love of Eternity, remains a lonely actor on a stage, without an active counterpart. In the previous positivistic period Nietzsche had eliminated the father and taken his place. Now he reduces the mother image to a mere abstraction. Nietzsche's own ego becomes more and more the only power that exists. The fatal development toward paranoic loneliness has proceeded a step further. From now onward Nietzsche's contact with his fellow men becomes more and more difficult and superficial. His mind is increasingly preoccupied with himself alone. Certainly he continues to argue against Socrates, St. Paul or Wagner, or to quote approvingly Zarathustra, Caesar, Goethe and Napoleon, but all these, and other historical figures he mentions, interest him only insofar as they represent qualities in himself. His arguments with them and against them are arguments with, or against, certain aspects and tendencies of his own soul. The world ceases to be an independent power, and all the powers in it are projections of the many facets of Nietzsche's own personality.

Zarathustra

I am however anticipating later stages of development. We have to return to *Thus Spake Zarathustra*, the book in which Nietzsche intended to reveal and teach in poetic form his new wisdom of the Eternal Recurrence. It is Nietzsche's most famous but also his most mysterious book.

Zarathustra the Persian sage and moralist returns from the dead and preaches Nietzsche's wisdom in sermons and parables. The first three of the four parts of the book were written in an ecstatic mental state, each within the short time of ten days. In his autobiography, *Ecce Homo*, Nietzsche describes this as follows:

> Has any one, at the end of the nineteenth century, a distinct notion of what poets of a stronger age understood by the word inspiration? If not, I will describe it. The slightest remnant of superstition in a man would make it almost impossible for him to escape from the idea of being a mere incarnation, a mere mouthpiece, a mere medium of superhuman powers. The concept of revelation—in the sense that suddenly and with indescribable certainty and subtlety, something becomes visible and audible, something that overwhelms one and shakes one to the very depths—is simply a description of facts. One hears—one does not seek; one takes—one does not ask who gives; a thought suddenly flashes up like lightning, it comes with utter necessity, without faltering—I have never had any choice in the matter ... Everything happens quite involuntarily, as if in a tempestuous outburst of freedom, of absoluteness, of power and divinity. The involuntary nature of the images and similes is the most remarkable thing; one no longer knows what is image and what simile; everything seems to present itself as the readiest, the truest and simplest means of expression.

C.G. Jung has made a study of these similes and images, and demonstrated their archetypal nature. Zarathustra is a representative of the archetype of the wise old man, and Nietzsche is identified with this archetype. He is also identified with the *anima*, whom he addresses in the two dancing songs as 'Life'. Speaking in the songs she calls herself 'The Profound One, the Loyal, the Eternal, the Mysterious One'. Zarathustra loves her, yet she is identical with his own wisdom and himself. What we observe here is a tremendous inflation which renders Nietzsche quite impersonal. He is speaking like God in the Bible, like the sole possessor of eternal truth. At this stage, the father image has lost all individual features and has become pure spirit. Nietzsche's development towards ever higher and airier regions has reached its culmination. Zarathustra himself is the superman whom he preaches. He has reached the summit of azure loneliness, a dead end above and outside the human world, where life and true communication are impossible. Nietzsche himself realised that an *enantiodroma,* a complete reversal of the values and accents of life, had to happen if life was to go on. Zarathustra ought to return to the Earth-Mother. In his autobiography Nietzsche says of *Zarathustra,*

> Nothing similar has ever been said, felt or suffered. The reply to such a dithyramb of loneliness in identification of the sun and light would be Ariadne. Yet who, apart from myself, knows who Ariadne is?

The mythical woman who showed Theseus how to find his way through the subterranean labyrinth of the Minotaur, and who later when abandoned by Theseus on the Isle of Naxos became the bride and companion of the god Dionysos, Ariadne is a representative of the archetype of the dark chthonian *anima*. In Zarathustra's 'Nightsong' Nietzsche writes:

> Light am I, oh, that I were night! But this is my loneliness to be begirt with light . . . I know not the happiness of the taker; oft have I dreamed that to steal must be yet sweeter than to take. It is my poverty that my hand never resteth from giving. Ah, ye alone, ye dark ones, ye of the night, that transform light into warmth, ye alone drink milk and solace from the udders of light. Alas, there is ice around me, my hand burneth touching iciness. Alas, a thirst is within me, that panteth for your thirst.

He longs to get away from the sun and light, into the motherly night, away from the icy heights to the warm earth, away from Dionysos and Zarathustra to Ariadne. In his last book before his collapse, the autobiography *Ecce Homo*, we find this cryptic saying: 'I have already died as the father and I am living on and am growing old as the mother.' Unfortunately this statement expresses more a longing than a reality. Nietzsche never quite recovered from the inflation and ecstasy of Zarathustra. He remained caught in the spirit, he could no longer relax enough to be really intimate with his fellow men. The nearer they were to him the more he expected the impossible from them, i.e. communication on the purely spiritual level of Zarathustra. He became hypersensitive and intolerant in his demands upon friends and, in these last few years of his sanity, lost all but one of his friends. Yet, in these same years, he developed the new philosophy which glorifies the supremacy of instinct, the *Will to Power*. Of this last transformation of his outlook I have to speak now.

The Will to Power

The books written in between and after the conception of Zarathustra reveal greater self-assurance than Nietzsche had ever shown before. His thinking is richer, clearer and of greater audacity. He tests the validity of every commonly accepted value, not only of religion and morals but also of truth, science and art. He asks which human need they have to satisfy, for their validity depends on whether or not they assist and strengthen the life of the total personality. There are no independent values irrespective of the part they have to play in the life of the individual. His thinking has now however lost a quality which had given it a peculiar fascination before. It no longer serves the purpose of finding a new attitude to life. Nietzsche has, now, a fixed standpoint outside and above the common human world; and he asserts again and again that he philosophises from above, from a superior spiritual level, from whence he looks down on the vicissitudes of life. His new audacity is an audacity of thinking, but his thinking no longer influences either his actual behaviour or the structure of his personality. His mind has gained, in this way, a peculiar freedom, the freedom of detachment. Yet even this freedom is not absolute. It is limited by his passionate need to justify and defend his spiritual isolation and superiority. This again and again hampers and distorts his intellectual findings and gives them an ambiguous character.

For instance, he realises the limitations of reason and of scientific thinking. He knows that often fear and emotional weakness are the cause of overdevelopment of the intellect. He asks why man becomes interested in truth; he sees truth and scientific insight as a preoccupation only of certain groups of people and not of the most vital, active and dynamic ones. He realises that science and thinking cannot produce a *Weltanschauung*, a guide for our outlook and behaviour. To live means to evaluate, to prefer or to reject, to desire, strive, will and command, all of which is beyond the confines of pure thinking and science. We are never able to see and comprehend the whole of life or of ourselves. We only see sections of the whole, and all philosophy and *Weltanschauung* is merely a doubtful interpretation of the whole, from the standpoint of our limited individual perspective. Who is it, then, that produces these interpretations? Not our conscious mind and intellect alone, but a life power which acts largely unconsciously, something instinctive, which Nietzsche calls the 'Will to Power'. The meaning of our life and action is largely unconscious. A life power, which aims not only at self-preservation but at self-realisation and expansion, expresses itself in all our actions, emotions and thought. Nietzsche's concept of the 'Will to Power' is akin to C.G. Carus's 'Unconscious' or Jung's 'Libido'. Like Carus and Jung he does not assume the existence of a number of definite, independent forces and instincts, as Freud does, but he sees, in all life, the expression of the one 'Will to Power'. Because it is one, it also aims at oneness and unification of our personality, of our outlook and of our concept of the world. The 'Will to Power' has now become the *principium individuationis*.

The 'Will to Power' gets its fullest expression, not in the instantaneous gratification of animal urges, but in the self-expression of the whole personality. Therefore, the 'Will to Power' may demand discipline, postponement and sacrifice of instinctual gratification and may even lead to the sacrifice of life itself. The 'Will to Power' finds its highest expression in the richest personality, in whom the most diverse mental forces are fully developed and co-operate freely; the man in whom spirit and senses are united; for whom even the most sensual experiences have become spiritual symbols and who feels nearest to the Divine when he most honours the body. Such a man accepts every aspect of life, even the most horrifying, and knows the truth of the inscription over the entrance to Dante's *Inferno*: 'That, too, has been created by Eternal Love.'

From the Jungian point of view one will readily agree with these ideas of Nietzsche's. Nietzsche's teaching about the 'Will to Power' has, however, some far less satisfactory aspects. They are based on Nietzsche's intense need for independence through superiority, a need which resulted in his identification with the archetype of the omniscient father and pure spirit. In order to justify these tendencies Nietzsche at times changes the 'Will to Power' from an instinct of self-realisation to a will to overpower others. The cruder and the more destructive this will to overpower is, the more fully it appears to Nietzsche to express the primal life instinct. He comes to admire the barbarian, '*die blonde Bestie*' (the blond beast) and the beast of prey in man. He becomes a romantic glorifier of war and of the enslavement of the working classes and of women.

Whoever like Nietzsche strives for freedom through spiritual superiority and through domination of the inferior world, has to develop and glorify forces exactly corresponding to those which he wants to subjugate as inferior. In the last analysis, the primitivity of Nietzsche's will to overpower, and of his glorification of the brute in man, mirrors the primitivity of Nietzsche's idea of the Earth mother whom he hates and tries to suppress. His glorification of brute force is not the genuine expression of crude vitality, it is the glorification of a protection of his spiritual isolation against the common and chthonian world.

Nietzsche's last ideas about morals are a similar mixture of deep insight and distorted evaluation. It has already been said that Nietzsche's criticism of moral values did not affect his own practical moral behaviour and his aristocratic perfectionism. Now he goes further and discriminates explicitly between two types of morals, those which are the expression of a negative attitude to life and those which express a positive, expansive attitude. If one is weak and tired, if one fears conflict and suffering, one will praise that behaviour as moral which promises to make life easier and less strenuous. Kindness and peace, pity and charity, are the highest values of such people; to be good and law-abiding is their ideal. The same ideals may result from the 'resentment' of oppressed social classes against their rulers. Classes who have no power of defending and asserting themselves, may still put their hope in the victory of morals which will oblige the rulers to be considerate, just and kind. They will, therefore, praise those who are weak and humble and abhor fighting and domination. They want equality. The oppressed classes, like the fox in the fable, vilify what they cannot get and try to produce a bad conscience in those who are free-er and who, of course, believe in strength and power and the joys of life.

The free ones, like the free born Greeks and Romans, value qualities exactly opposite to those praised by the weak. Their virtues are those of the '*vir*', the *man*: physical excellence, strong instincts, political power and all the discipline, hardness, cunning and unscrupulousness needed in political struggle. They hold that life means fighting and living dangerously, and appreciate most those qualities which equip man best for war and conflict.

Whatever the merits of such a differentiation between two types of morals may be, it becomes misleading if one type is regarded as valuable and the other type treated with contempt, as they are by Nietzsche. One type he calls the morals of masters, the other the morals of slaves and the human herd; one he calls 'yea saying' and the other 'nay saying' with regard to life; with one Nietzsche identifies himself, and the other he regards as far beneath himself.

Nietzsche is certainly right when he points out that the morals which stress the equality of men and praise charity and love are frequently abused as a screen for self-centred demands and hidden urges of domination, or for a lazy attempt to ignore the hard reality of conflict; but he attacks not only the abuse of valid morals but the morals themselves. Self-assertive tendencies, and tendencies which stress union with our fellow men and result in morals of charity, love and peace, develop side by side in every individual and remain necessary ingredients of the healthy personality. In his intolerance of dependence Nietzsche overstresses individuality and tries to eliminate everything collective. Such a hostile attitude to essential parts of human nature completely foils Nietzsche's longing for a 'yea saying' attitude to life. All his 'yea saying' sounds forced and spurious, and his last books leave one with the impression of a universal hatred of men and life.

He hates everybody decadent or weak because those are the people who depend on and produce the 'nay saying' morals. Weak, according to Nietzsche, are those who are ill; weak is the woman, this one half of humanity that is 'typically ill, changeable and inconsistent'; weak are the culturally sophisticated, the artists, the neurotics, the criminals; weak are the socially mixed types, the offspring of socially and racially mixed marriages. The pessimists and decadents ought to commit suicide. Another list of beings whom he despises consists of 'shopkeepers, Christians, cows, women, Englishmen and other democrats.' There is not one human quality which, at one time or other, is not torn to bits. Now he turns against consciousness and intellect, now against instincts and spontaneity, now against civilisation, and then against barbarism. At times he rejects every possible value because it can be abused.

Consistently he rejects women—feminine is, for him, synonymous with bad. He tries to write a kind of negative anthropology, analogous to the negative theology of old. Just as the theologians tried to describe God by showing that everything the human mind can imagine is not yet God, but Maya, so Nietzsche tries to describe the superman by showing the doubtful value of every imaginable human quality, hoping that, in the centre of all these negations, a valuable core may become visible. What does become visible, is a God, or an archetype, like Dionysos or Zarathustra, but not a human being. All attempts at finding incarnations of this God merely lead to romantic fantasies about the Greek past or to archetypal glorifications of men like Cesare Borgia, Don Juan, Caesar and Napoleon. And, above all, to a megalomaniac concept of Nietzsche himself.

Nietzsche's Complex Personality

Nietzsche's efforts to reach individuation end sadly in a paranoic attitude. His deep yearning for love, union and self-surrender finds expression only in some poems, 'The Dionysos Dithyrambs', where he movingly voices his longing for the peace of eventide and for death in unification with

Eternity. In his contact with fellow men he can no longer express and pursue these longings and he remains emotionally isolated and aloof. He is identified with the archetype of pure spirit, and his life consists of lonely thinking and writing. At the same time he hates 'thinking', and his attacks on Socrates, the thinker, are now more violent even than they were in his first book, *The Birth of Tragedy*. In vain does he seek contact with Dionysos, the chthonian god of instincts; his way is barred by his tragic dissociation from the Earth mother, as is evident, for instance, in his inability to enter into a creative relationship with women and with what they symbolically represent. He is compelled to remain independent and superior to everybody, at any cost. The more his contact with the mother image and the world in general is lost, the more Nietzsche becomes inflated and identified with all the archetypes. His life and his book *Thus Spake Zarathustra* mark—so he pronounces—the 'Great Noon' of human history, the beginning of a new epoch. He imagines himself as the Messiah and Dionysos in one.

It is futile to speculate whether Nietzsche could have reached a more successful solution of his inner conflicts if he had been spared the brain disease which caused his collapse in December 1888; and futile to speculate too whether the paranoic megalomania of the last period of his life was caused or influenced by the development of G.P.I. Unfortunately, and significantly, his most intense influence on posterity is based just on the paranoic element in his writings. It is easy to show that Nietzsche, had he lived to see it, would have been utterly disgusted by the Nazi movement. All his life he treated antisemites with the utmost contempt and was most intolerant of all histrionic pomposity, such as that of Hitler and men like him. Yet this cannot acquit Nietzsche of the charge that his ideas about the prerogative of the master-man and the master-race have inspired, and seemed to justify, the most dastardly actions of the Nazis.

However, one cannot simply dismiss Nietzsche for this reason. Quite irrespective of Nietzsche's importance in the field of philosophy and psychology in general, discussion of which was not the purpose of this paper, Nietzsche was one of the most impressive personalities of the nineteenth century because of his passionate struggle for individuation. With great strength and integrity of mind he strove for formulations of this age-old problem which were in keeping with modern consciousness and knowledge. With sincerity and courage he rejected all ready-made solutions and he refused to be content with easy self-deceptions. He faced with unfailing patience the sufferings and disappointments which lay on his way. He was always prepared to change and contradict earlier convictions when his inner development demanded that course, no matter what his critics might think or say. Therefore his development shows some of the basic problems of individuation with unusual clarity. He was aware of the manifold conflicts and contradictory tendencies in himself and did not try to make things smooth and simple by ignoring one side of the conflict. Even when, in the end, he became one-sidedly spiritual, his intellectual honesty prevented him

from overlooking the other side. His writings, therefore, depict faithfully
the paradoxical nature of the human mind, with all its contradictory tendencies and conflicts. He is one of the most stimulating and stirring authors for
everyone who does not look for ready-made solutions and results, but who,
like Nietzsche himself, is engaged in the quest of his own individuation and
of his individual formulation of this eternal problem.

*The assistance of Dr. Lotte Paulsen is acknowledged in reading the first
draft of this paper and making numerous helpful suggestions.-KMA*

Rilke and Nietzsche

Nietzsche's influence on German-speaking intellectuals during the first half of this century was so great, and obvious, as to be in danger of being overrated. As a man who published large volumes of aphorisms he often expressed thoughts which occurred also to others. Some of his ideas, particularly his attacks on religion, were so much in the air that they were voiced by various people: similarity of ideas should not necessarily be taken as evidence of Nietzsche's influence.

In his book *The Owl and the Nightingale* (Faber, 1960), Walter Kaufmann devotes a long chapter to 'Nietzsche and Rilke' in which he claims a close affinity of outlook between these two men. After mentioning Nietzsche's influence on Rilke's juvenilia, and the fact that Nietzsche and Rilke loved the same woman, Lou Andreas-Salomé (and after some rather wrong-headed interpretations of three early poems by Rilke, about which I shall say more later), Kaufmann develops four inter-related motifs which he regards as equally characteristic of. and central to, the work of both men. They are:

1. The same experience of their historical situation as being one of the disinherited ones to whom in a time of transition 'the past no longer belongs and not yet the future' (Rilke: *Duino Elegy* 7).
2. A rejection of all that has hardened into traditional stereotypes; the resolve each to be open for his own individual call. Both men want a new honesty as their kind of piety.
3. An acceptance of the terribleness of life and the realisation that terribleness and bliss are identical, the same face of the divine head looking in two directions. Only by facing up to the terribleness of life can one escape mediocrity and experience the bliss of life.
4. The rejection of otherworldliness; the resolve to remain faithful to the earth. 'His attributes are taken away from God and return to the creation' (Rilke).

Kaufmann regards Rilke's later poetry, and particularly the *Duino Elegies* and the *Sonnets to Orpheus* as truly Dionysian in Nietzsche's sense: as celebrating life with all its agonies. He sees of course that there are also striking differences between Nietzsche and Rilke, but belittles them, for example by interpreting the many references to angels in the *Elegies* as referring to something akin to Nietzsche's superman. Summing up, he says that both for Nietzsche and for Rilke there is nothing that gives our lives meaning from outside, but that a certain mode of experience makes life infinitely worthwhile, and to both 'the secret of the greatest fruitfulness and the greatest enjoyment of existence is: to live dangerously!'

Kaufmann's description of Rilke as a Nietzschean found followers immediately: and another American immigrant professor, Hans Cohn, has repeated this thesis extensively in his book *The Mind of Germany* (Macmillan, 1961). I regard Kaufmann's thesis as fallacious. It is true that many similarities exist between the personality of Nietzsche and that of Rilke, but it is all the more remarkable how different are the intentions embodied in their expressed statements.

Nietzsche rejected and was scornful of metaphysicians. He sometimes called them '*Hinterweltler*' because they were looking for a reality behind the natural reality of the world; and because this word is a pun with *Hinterwaeldler*: backwoodsmen. Rilke was decidedly a metaphysician to whom the true reality was behind and beyond the physical and material world. The whole of his late poetry is an attempt to approach this immaterial reality, which is at the same time experienced as mysterious, numinous, and often tremendous, *schrecklich's*. He conceived this reality as comprised by powers which transcend our conscious will and intentions. I shall illustrate this not by reference to Rilke's preoccupation with God in his early writings, or with angels in the *Elegies*: Professors Butler, Mason and others have tried to clarify what Rilke meant by angels, and whatever they are they transcend human possibilities, whereas the superman is a longed-for new type of man. What I shall do is discuss some more direct expressions of Rilke's spiritual aspirations in his late writings.

Let us start with the poem which, following Rilke's own instructions, is on his gravestone:

> *Rose, Oh reiner Widerspruch,*
> *Lust, Niemandes schlaf zu sein*
> *Unter so vielen Lidern.*

> *Rose, Oh pure contradiction,*
> *Joy, to be nobody's sleep*
> *Under so many eyelids.*

At first glance this 'pure contradiction looks like pure nonsense. Does Rilke say any more than that he likens the rose petals to eyelids? This would at best be a piece of the aesthetic ingenuity which Edwin Muir rightly described as Rilke's besetting sin. We will, however, have to regard 'nobody's sleep' as something more than just nothing. It is a kind of Cheshire Cat, a serious one, namely the state of sleeping without any physical substratum, an image of peace, undisturbed and undisturbable by the physical world. It is a *metaphysical* image in the original meaning of the word. And as we cannot imagine a sleep without a sleeper, 'nobody's sleep' leaves us bewildered and mystified just as does the grin of the Cheshire Cat.

It is a constantly repeated practice of Rilke's to call up images of material things, and then by use of negations to eliminate their material aspect so that something mysteriously immaterial becomes visible or is hinted at.

This immaterial, purely spiritual something is the true reality which matters. To Rilke *'Alles Vergängliche ist'* not *'nur ein Gleichnis'*, but everything finite and material becomes a way to the infinite and immaterial if one focusses it and then with the help of negations separates it from its material aspects. That is the 'pure contradiction' which Rilke is after.

I shall quote three more examples of this description by negatives of the reality which counts:

In *Sonnets to Orpheus* II:10 Rilke first describes the destructive powers of engines and technique, and contrasts this with the metaphysical true reality as follows:

> *Aber noch ist uns das Dasein verzaubert; an hundert*
> *Stellen ist es noch Ursprung. Ein Spielen von reinen*
> *Kräften, die keiner berührt, der nicht kniet und bewundert.*
>
> *Worte gehen noch zart am Unsäglichen aus . . .*
> *Und die Musik, immer neu, aus den bebendsten Steinen,*
> *baut im unbrauchbaren Raum ihr vergöttliches Haus.*

> > Yet being is still enchanted; at a hundred
> > places it is still pristine. A play of pure
> > forces which nobody touches who does not kneel
> > > and admire.
> >
> > Words still evaporate tenderly before the
> > > Unspeakable . . .
> > And the music, always new, builds from the
> > > quivering stones
> > its numinous house in unemployable space.

In Sonnet II:20 Rilke uses an almost absurd simile for the immaterial nature of true communications and at the same time indulges in extravagant mystification:

> *Sieh in der Schüssel . . .*
> *seltsam der Fische Gesicht.*
>
> *Fische sind stumm . . . meinte man einmal. Wer weiss?*
> *Aber ist nicht am Ende ein Ort, wo man das, was der Fische*
> *Sprache wäre, ohne sie spricht?*

> > See in the dish . . .
> > strangely the face of fishes.
> >
> > Fishes are mute . . . someone opined. Who knows?
> > Yet is there not in the end a place where that
> > which would be the fishes' language, is spoken
> > > without them?

Finally, here are the first four lines of sonnet II:12.

> *Wolle die Wandlung. O sei für die Flamme begeistert,*
> *drin sich ein Ding dir entzieht, das mit Verwandlungen prunkt;*
> *jener entwerfende Geist, welcher das Irdische meistert,*
> *liebt in dem Schwung der Figur nichts wie den wendenden Punkt.*

> *Will transformation, Oh, be enraptured by the flame*
> *which consumes that which would be proud of its*
> *changing forms;*
> *the designing Spirit who masters the world*
> *loves in the sweep of the figure only the turning*
> *point.*

The last line seems to be directly derived from Lao Tzu's symbol for the efficacy of the 'nothing' when he says that the usefulness of a cart rests on the empty point where the thirty spokes of the wheel meet. (Aphorism II of the *Tao Te Ching*).

Kaufmann, who also translated this poem, overlooks the fact that *'Wandlung'* and *'Verwandlung'* are concepts often used by Rilke both in the Elegies and the Sonnets, and that they nearly always refer to the transformation of something material into something immaterial and thus valid. These words are in general much more charged with meaning than is 'change', *'Veraenderung'*, which Kaufmann uses in his translation. Rilke, who came from the Roman Catholic tradition, certainly was aware that he was using what is also the German word for the transubstantiation. Kaufmann translates the second sentence as: 'Oh experience the rapture of the flames in which a life is concealed exulting in change as it burns'. This has nothing to do with Rilke's text but simply aims at transforming this poem into something similar to Nietzsche's poem:

> *Yes, I know from where I came!*
> *Ever hungry like a flame*
> *I consume myself and glow,*
> *Light grows all that I conceive*
> *Ashes everything I leave:*
> *Flame I am assuredly!*

Kaufmann ignores the difference between these poems, namely that Nietzsche is experiencing himself as a destructive fire, whereas Rilke is addressing the Spirit as master of all the world in one more of the eternal dematerialising symbols, the consuming flame.

There is another sonnet (I:12) in which Rilke addresses the Spirit directly, and this in terms which scarcely differ at all from the Christian tradition. The Spirit is the uniting agency. He is the source of the uniting

images and figures, in and through which we live without conscious awareness of our place in them, and He transcends us so that we depend on His
grace and munificence for our living:

> Heil dem Geist, der uns verbinden mag:
> denn wir leben uhrhaft in Figuren.
> Und mit kleinen Schritten gehn die Uhren
> neben unserm eigentlichen Tag.
>
> Ohne unsern wahren Platz zu kenne,
> handeln wir aus wirklichen Bezug.
> Die Antennen fühlen die Antennen,
> und die leere Ferne trug . . .
>
> Reine Spannung. O Musik der Kräfte!
> Ist nicht durch die lässlichen Geschäfte
> jede Störung von dir abgelenkt?
>
> Selbst wenn sich der bauer sorgt und handelt,
> wo die Saat in Sommer sich verwandelt,
> reicht er niemals hin. Die Erde schenkt.

> Hail the Spirit who unites all;
> for truly we live in images [figures].
> And the mechanical clocks are negligible
> beside our actual day [the 'temps veçu']
>
> Without knowledge of our true place
> we act in reference to it.
> The antennæ feel the antennæ
> [probably referring to the sense organs of insects]
> and empty space has transmitted . . .
>
> Pure tension. O music of forces!
> Are you not immune to all disturbances
> through our daily tasks?
>
> Even when the farmer cares and acts,
> where the seed ripens in summer
> he is never commensurate. The earth gives.

The Earth here is an example of the Spirit which transcends us, that is, it
is a *numen*, Mother Earth, and not a positivist concept of the ground. A
Christian probably would prefer to speak of the grace of God which gives us
our daily bread, but Rilke uses a feminine name for the *numen*, for personal
reasons which we shall discuss later. Such feminine aspects of the deity are

however also known to Christianity, particularly to the Catholic tradition.

Besides all the traditional images for the immaterial reality, such as wind, breath, space, the starry sky, timelessness, music, song, silence, dance, unity, *et cetera*, Rilke uses two which are specific to him and of peculiar importance in his poetry. One is the transformation of the outer reality into inner image, word and song. This removes the ephemeral quality of the things of this world by giving them lasting names; and gives the vocation of the poet a nearly priestlike quality, for he is an actor in the mystery of transubstantiation.

The other image which is of peculiar importance in Rilke's late poetry is that of the dead. The dead are those who are freed from material existence, from the needs, desires and unrest of our life. And they are the completed ones who have experienced all the bliss and all the pain of life to its very end. Thus they are nearer the true reality than we living ones who are still entangled in striving. In the tenth *Elegy* Rilke describes the transition of one recently dead into the more valid reality of the dead. Certainly thus his concept of the after-life is unlike that of Dante or Calderon, without resurrection and judgment. Death is the transition into an existence in timelessness, total stillness, freedom from all needs and therefore of accepted solitude. it is a return to an age-old land where in a grove in the valley the spring of joy wells up. It is the return to the primal unity with the mother-ground of all being.

It is wrong to impute to Rilke the maxim 'live dangerously' with its implied ignoring of death. He spurns any attempt to deny the pain and sorrows of living, and particularly spurns the attempt to ignore the most cruel fact of the finiteness of life. Death should be faced without negation or cheap consolations. Yet Rilke sees no merit in exuberant living and reckless exposing oneself to danger. Such life is no nearer the true spirituality than the contemplative life. On the contrary, Rilke lived a rather sheltered, contemplative life, and described this in his writings as most appropriate for the approach to that spiritual reality for which he longed.

Orpheus became important to Rilke both as the singer and as the one who had been in the underworld with the dead. Kaufmann points out that the features of Orpheus and Dionysos blend in the Greek legend and he thinks that Rilke's *Sonnets to Orpheus* and *Duino Elegies* are Dionysian poetry in Nietzsche's sense. Dionysos is to Nietzsche the chthonian God of orgiastic ecstasy, of lust and drunken ravings, of inarticulate instincts. Only through the Apollonian influence do the Dionysian urges receive form and achieve the ability to become articulate in images and art. If one wants to force Rilke's Orpheus into one of these two categories, he is certainly an Apollonian figure, a bringer of order and beauty whose song outlasts the destructiveness of the Dionysian Maenads (as expressly stated in *Sonnets* I:24 and II:24). He is not a chthonian figure but a dweller in both worlds, the underworld and the spiritual world of song (*Sonnets* I:6, 7, 9). Actually Rilke's own image of Orpheus has nothing to do with the Nietzschean opposites of Dionysian and Apollonian, but is clearly a hermetic image. In *Sonnet* I:7 he is expressly described as *'einer der bleibenden Boten'*, one of the eternal messengers, who has dwelled amongst and eaten with the dead ones, like Hermes, the psychopompos. He is an agent of the metamorphosis (I:5), a transformer and uniter of the opposites, a helper of the *mysterium coniunctionis*, the uniting image of the *'Doppelbereich'* (I:9).

Now all this has, of course, nothing whatsoever to do with Nietzsche, the positivist, or the preacher of God's death, or the destroyer of the old tables of values and morals, or the teacher of the universal will to power, or the admirer of the *'blonde Bestie'*. And the philosophy of the 'eternal return of the present moment' which Nietzsche adopted to express his radical acceptance of reality and his rejection of every form of flight from it, is the very antithesis of Rilke's attempt to transform the ephemeral outer world into lasting internal imagery and into a truer spiritual reality. The only feature common to both philosophies is that neither makes sense logically.

What both men had in common was an over-emphasised need in their childhood to find a separate identity from their mothers: Nietzsche because after the death of his father, that is from four years old onward, he lived as the only male in a household of six women; and Rilke because his mother was possessive and neurotic, and she called up expectations of intense mother love in her child, when she had nothing to offer but spurious feelings and fuss. Nietzsche grew up in identification with the idealised dead father, and longed for an idealisable father figure, which he finally found in Wagner. When he had to find the way back from this idealised relationship to the reality of the world, he did so with the help of rationalist positivism. Rilke could not identify with his father, who had separated from his wife when the boy was nine years old, leaving the child with her. The father wanted the child to become an officer like himself, which was deeply antipathetic to the weakly and spoiled boy. Rilke all his life was searching for women whom he could admire and trust, and who like an all-providing mother would make no demands upon him. His lasting preoccupation was with genuineness of feeling. He started out as an aesthetic romanticist. Under the influence of a pilgrimage to Tolstoy he came to a *muzhik*-like religiosity and childlike intimacy with God. Here is an example of this from the *Stundenbuch* (1899) written when Rilke was twenty-four years old.

> *You neighbour God, when sometimes I disturb you*
> *in those long nights with my knocking*
> *this is because I hear you breathe so rarely*
> *and know, you are alone in the hall.*
> *And if you need something then nobody will be there*
> *to put the drink into your groping hands.*
> *I listen constantly. Give me a sign.*
> *I am near you.*
> *Only a thin wall is between us*

by chance; for it could be
that one word from your mouth or mine
will break it down
silently and without noise.

This type of religion could not last in a man with Rilke's need for genuineness of feeling. His way out of this type of subjectivity into a more intimate contact with the objective world was not via positivist philosophy but via something which he called '*Anschauen*', empathetic observation of the greatest intensity. For weeks he might go the the Jardin des Plantes in Paris, or other places, and observe one animal or something else until he could reproduce empathetically the very essence of its being and feeling in a poem. He thus tried to equal the craftsmanlike accuracy and faithfulness of reproduction he admired in the work of Auguste Rodin, whose secretary he was for some time. Kaufmann misunderstands and also misrepresents Rilke's poetry of this period. He translates the most famous of these poems, 'The Panther', and rightly states that the poem asserts nothing, no belief, no truth, no philosophy. It only describes the panther going to and fro in his cage. Yet he seems to regard it as permissible to change this by adding the single additional line: 'This is a portrait of the human condition (namely a Kafkaesque portrait)'. Another poem of this period on a badly damaged 'Archaic Torso of Apollo' deals with the life which can still be felt in the relic, and with the impression that this truncated work of art still demands a response from the observer. The latter idea is expressed poetically, lamely, and rather pretentiously in the last five words of the sonnet: 'You must change your life'. Again Kaufmann wants to find here a philosophy 'no longer that of Kafka but of Sartre, no longer nihilism but a call for decision', (as if an abstract exhortation to change one's life was the meaning of existentialism). Kaufmann states that both these philosophies can be found in the work of Nietzsche, too, and in the same sequence as in Rilke. In this turgid way one can of course prove anything one likes. Let us just state that Rilke never held either of the philosophical beliefs which Kaufmann interpolates into two of his poems of empathic observation.

In a poem called '*Wendung*' ('Turning Point') of the year 1914 Rilke describes his struggle for the most intense empathy and observation, and the limitations of this approach to the world. He comes to the conclusion that it is not enough to observe, what really is wanted is love of the world. Empathy produces images in which the world is imprisoned and violated, but beings need to flourish freely in and through love. It remains doubtful whether Rilke ever succeeded in becoming a lover like this. True love is active and self-assertive in all its openness towards the loved ones. Rilke remains the passive receiving one '*ausgesetzt dem Übermaas von Einfluss*', 'exposed to the excess of influence' as he described himself in the 'Spanish Trilogy'. He remains the '*Schauende*', the admiring visionary of that which transcends him. Only his visions in the *Elegies* and *Sonnets* are those of the whole of existence, and no longer merely of single objects. And in this vision of the whole, pain, cruelty and death must find their place as well if this vision is to be true and genuine and not romantically falsified. Thus in *Sonnet* II:9 Rilke states that lenient judgments are no nearer the true divine mildness than the torture and frequent death sentences of former judicial procedure. And in *Sonnet* II:11 he even justifies the sport of pigeon shooting for 'To kill is one form of our errant sadness' (*'Töten ist eine Gestalt unseres wandernden Trauerns'*). This sentence is printed large in the original. 'To the serene spirit all is pure which also happens to us ourselves.' Again Kaufmann mistakes these statements as being Nietzschean, which they are not. Nietzsche at times saw in cruelty the most direct and unbroken expression of that will to power which he regarded as the basic motivating force of all existence: he therefore praises men like Cesare Borgia. Nothing is further from Rilke's intention. In the sonnet about judges he debunks our pride in the progress of humanitarian leniency, because it is equally as bad as the torture of olden times. Both are equally unlike God's graciousness. And whilst Nietzsche at times could see in killing the exuberant assertion of the sovereign will to power, Rilke regards it as a form of our errant sadness. It is to him nothing meritorious but he knows that to the Spirit death and killing are not unclean. He says no more than what was often expressed in the *Totentanz* speculations of the Middle Ages; or than what Goethe says of the Mothers in the second part of *Faust*. In general, Kaufmann ignores the extent to which Rilke's ideas and imagery follow Christian traditions. Even Rilke's emphasis on the fact that the spiritual vision of the whole has to embrace also the underworld, the realm of the shadows and the dead, has antecedents in St Hildegard's address to the Holy Spirit:

> *In altissimis*
> *Et in*
> *terrenis*
> *Et in omnibus abyssis*
> *Tu omnes compones et colligis.*

One may also think of Dante's inscription over the entrance to the Inferno, that this space also was shaped by God's Love and Light.

Not one of the four motifs which Kaufmann enumerates as identical in Nietzsche's and Rilke's ideas can stand up to any critical scrutiny.

1. Nietzsche wrote his main works after the Franco-Prussian War, when Germany was on the crest of a wave of confidence, the so-called *Gründerjahre*. Nietzsche saw through the hollowness of this confidence and foresaw the future, namely the coming nihilism, with unique clear-sightedness. Rilke is by nature an outsider in any society. In his longing for genuineness of feeling and expression he would have found any possible society spurious and lacking in genuineness. He had little historical or political sense. When he wrote the seventh *Elegy* in 1922 he saw that the times were out of joint, but this was an insight he shared

with all German-speaking people. He had no foresight of the future; and, oriented as he was towards the timeless spiritual reality, the future was not his concern. After Mussolini's seizure of power he corresponded with an Italian noblewoman, the Duchess Gallarati Scotti, on the subject of Fascism. He approached it as he approached all life: as an aesthetic impressionist. He displayed no more insight than the English travellers, when they found Fascism all right because the railway trains were cleaner and more punctual. The only poetry referring to political events is in five songs written in August 19, when Rilke was infected by the general elation about the war, an elation which swept Europe and turned out to be without insight and validity. These songs are awkward products and best forgotten. Historically Rilke's introversive spirituality was of importance because it satisfied needs of German intellectuals who could agree neither with the hollow pomp of William II nor with the official German war propaganda; and who retreated from this and from the fratricidal hatred of the 1920s into introverted subjectivity. With the coming of Hitler, Rilke's passive contemplation became outdated. One was forced to act: to submit, or flee, or fight.

2.   Nietzsche experienced himself as a destroyer of the old table of values, as an unmasker and destroyer of false morals. Rilke is as little concerned with morals as he is with action or with will. Will, desire, craving. appeal, are all forces which hinder man's approach to the spiritual reality: this approach happens in a passive, silent, receptive way (Cf. *Elegy* 7). In a letter of 20th September 1910 Max Weber discussed Rilke and called him a mystic not of the ecstatic (eroticised) type, but of the type of Tauler (the supposed disciple of Meister Eckhart who preached the transcendent reality without having had an ecstatic encounter with it). This description of Rilke remained true also with regard to his later writings. Rilke's deepest concern was a longing for total spiritual union as it ideally exists between mother and infant. Lovers may experience it for short moments by the grace of the Gods, for it cannot be produced intentionally (see *Elegy* 2). Nothing could better bring into focus the difference between Nietzsche and Rilke than a comparison of Nietzsche's poem quoted above (where he sees himself as a consuming fire), with Rilke's 'Die spanische Trilogie'. The first part of it is a fervent prayer that the Lord may make *one* thing of the poet, and a long catalogue of impressions.

> *Aus dieser Wolke, siehe: die den Stern*
> *so wild verdeckt, der eben war – (und mir),*
> *aus diesen Bergland drueben, das jetzt Nacht,*
> *Nachtwinde hat für eine Zeit – (und mir).*
> . . . *usw. usw.*
>
> > *aus vielen Ungenaun und immer mir,*
> > *aus nichts als mir and dem, was ich nicht kenn,*

> *das Ding zu machen, Herr Herr Herr, das Ding,*
> *das welthaft irdisch wie ein Meteor*
> *in seiner Schwere nur die Summe Flugs*
> *zusammennimmt: nichst wiegend als die Ankunft.*

> *From this cloud, see: which hides the star*
> *so wildly, which has been there just now–(and me),*
> *from these hills opposite which have now night,*
> *night winds for some time–(and me),*

. . . etc. etc. [Here follow six more such impressions]

> *from lots of vague impressions and always me,*
> *and from that which I do not know,*
> *to make the one thing, Lord Lord Lord, the thing*
> *which cosmic-earthly like a meteor*
> *extracts from its weight only the sum of its flying*
> *not weighing anything but the arrival.*

This certainly is longing for mystical union with everything, and for transformation into something immaterial and purely spiritual. The elements which should be united in this one thing are all passive impressions. It is a purely aesthetic universe free from all moral and active components.

Honesty was described by Nietzsche in his early writings as one of the four cardinal virtues. He tried to live up to this moral value by intellectual honesty and rational positivism. Later on he aimed at honesty of existence, a type of honesty which allowed and justified every kind of dishonesty and deceit by the individual in his struggle for powerful living. Rilke aims at genuineness of feeling and sensation and accuracy in their verbal expression. He is not a theoretical thinker. And with his fervent longing for a transcendent spiritual reality he is a dualist and a deeply split personality. Lou Andreas-Salomé described him once as follows:

> The tendency to dematerialise everything, the incongruity between his physical and his spiritual being, both of which seemed to try to be the whole, this affected even his physical appearance. His face showed no sign of ageing though this would have been natural, his features were not lined or moulded by his years but they stopped being really his own. Too large and anxious, the eyes stood above his face as if they knew that something had happened to the face, as if they asked whether a strange power, and if so, what, had illegitimately taken possession of it.

Rilke always experienced himself as a double being, 'Rainer' and 'the Other', and he has described this split between his physical and spiritual being vividly in the fourth *Elegy*, in the image of the angel moving the puppets in the puppet-theatre; and in *Sonnet* I:11 in the image of rider and horse, who are at one only for short moments, for already table and pasture separate them.

3. The acceptance of suffering and pain, and the realisation that without this acceptance our outlook becomes childish and shallow, is old Christian wisdom. Rilke strives towards this acceptance in the name of genuineness of being. Unlike Nietzsche he is not concerned with flight from mediocrity and longing to be a superior being. He has no superman aspirations and, insofar as they are genuine, the simplest man or woman is as welcome to him as any genius or supposed superman.

4. Rilke's metaphysical longing was not 'otherworldly' in the sense that certain mediaeval Christians rejected this world for the world to come, but in this sense no nineteenth or twentieth century German writer of any consequence was otherworldly. Rilke was a believer in a superior or spiritual reality to the end of his life, and his remark that attributes of God were taken away from Him and returned to the creation, could have been made and has similarly been made by a great number of Protestant theologians. One could even argue that this is the very meaning of the Incarnation.

Rilke had some deep insight into the fact that we live by belief, and I want to finish with a few remarks about this. In our time of demythologising, the concept of faith is often reduced to mean simply trust in oneself and in God. That it also means faith in merely believed facts is awkward to us. We think that the world of facts is to be left to science, which can prove or debunk them. Rilke however knows that 'we in truth live in images', *'wir leben wahrhaft in Figuren'* (*Sonnet* I:12). Our world in which we actually live is an imaginary world, a believed world just as is the world of primitives who know no modern science. Our dreams, and all the imaginations which regulate our life, and also our language, are animistic in nature. Normally we do not reflect upon this, but naively regard these beliefs as the undoubted reality. Jung told once how he came to an African village and asked the inhabitants about their beliefs. They emphatically denied that they had any. When walking around Jung saw small huts in the fields and was told that these were the dwelling places of the dead ancestors. This was not regarded as a belief but simply as fact. In the same way, we regard as fact what really we only believe. Rilke has described this way of being in *Sonnet* II:4. This sonnet deals with the Unicorn, but what he says there of the Unicorn is applicable to all our beliefs and the most basic 'facts' of our life:

> *dieses ist das Tier, das es nicht gibt.*
> *Sie wusstens nicht und habens jeden Falls*
> *−sein Wandeln, seine haltung, seinen Hals,*
> *bis in des stillen Blickes Licht−geliebt.*
>
> *Zwar war es nicht. Doch weil sie's liebten, ward*
> *ein reines Tier. Sie liessen immer Raum.*

Und in dem Raume, klar und ausgespart,
erhob es leicht sein haupt und brauchte kaum
zu sein. Sie nährten es mit keinem Korn,
nur immer mit der Möglichkeit, es sei.

Und die gab solche Stärke an das Tier,
dass es aus sich ein Stirnhorn trieb. Ein Horn.
Zu einer Jungfrau kam es weiss herbei—
und war im Silber-Spiegel und in ihr.

      Behold the beast that never was.
      They did not know its non-existence and thus they
                                   loved it
      —its gait, its pose, its neck,
      Up to the still light of its eyes.

      Though it was not. Yet as they loved it
      It rose as a pure being. They always spared it space.
      And in this clear, delineated space
      It lightly raised its head and scarcely needed
      To exist. They did not nourish it with corn
      But only with the steady supposition of its being,
      Which gave such strength unto the beast
      That from its forehead grew a horn. A horn.
      White, it drew near to the pure maid,
      And was both in the silver mirror and in her.

Some Answers to Nihilism

I shall base my discussion of the problems of nihilism, and the answers to it, on two German novels which I regard as not only the most important German literary publications of the 1940s but also the most impressive contemporary attempts to grapple with our questions: Thomas Mann's *Doktor Faustus* and Robert Musil's *The Man Without Qualities*. Both books have been influenced intensely by Friedrich Nietzsche. The life story of Mann's hero, Leverkuhn, reproduces many salient features of Nietzsche's biography. Of Musil's hero, Ulrich, it is stated that Nietzsche was his teacher.

Nietzsche was the philosopher who forced us to see the variety of tendencies in modern European civilisation which lead to nihilism and the precariousness of all moral and ethical attitudes which try to stand up against it. He was able to predict the nihilistic tendencies in modern authoritarianism as well as in modern individualism and democracy. The two books I am going to speak about were written under the influence of the collapse of Germany and Austria-Hungary in the First World War and the subsequent developments which verified so strikingly Nietzsche's predictions.

The centre of Mann's book is the discussion between Leverkuhn and the Devil which results in the Faustian pact between them. Unlike the Satan of the Old Testament and particularly of the Book of Job, who is one of the *bene'ha elohim*, one of the sons of God, and unlike Mephistopheles in Goethe's *Faust* ('part of that power which wills always the evil and creates *always* the good'), Mann's Devil is the absolute nihilist. He comes from an Inferno which is not created by the love of God but lies beyond the region of any love. Therefore when he appears the most terrifying, all-pervading coldness radiates from him; and the price man has to pay for the pact with him is to renounce all love. This seems to be the basic precondition of all nihilism: all love is denied, ignored or debunked.

Mann's Devil appears during the interview in a variety of guises. First he is a rake and pimp, the most primitive and the oldest form of nihilist. The values of society mean nothing to him and he is too weak or lazy to look for a substitute for them. Thus he lives only for the satisfaction of the most primitive and ephemeral pleasures. His belief is 'All is vanity'. Such a cynic may be a personal misfit, or he may belong to a social group whose standards are collapsing or have collapsed, as in a plague-ridden town, or in pre-Reformation Germany with its political and religious unrest, or in a community after a devastating war and defeat. Or he may be a social pariah, say a travelling ham-actor, whose features Mann's Devil also has. He is actor through and through, totally spurious and insincere, with reference not only to the world but also to himself, protean in his appearance, everything and nothing, belonging to no period and no society.

The Devil explains to Leverkuhn that he has singled him out for special attention because of his high intelligence and his vocation as a musician who works irrationally by inspiration in solitary creativeness. For high intelligence, solitude, and the solitary expression of emotion in music, all are factors predisposing to nihilism. While discussing this the Devil suddenly changes his appearance to that of an intellectual aesthete. That the aesthetic attitude and the ethical are opposites, and that the first is often ethically nihilistic, is familiar to us from Kierkegaard's *Either-Or*. In his lecture on Nietzsche Thomas Mann's main criticism of Nietzsche was that he was in the last analysis an aesthete and not unlike Oscar Wilde, if one ignores the differences in their intellectual interests and capabilities. The aesthete doubts the possibility of consistently loving or of consistently being loved; his destructive urges seem to exclude this possibility. He shuns feeling because with him love is so inseparably linked with hate and destruction. He assumes that aesthetic sensation can take the place of feeling. Therefore the aesthete is a detached observer of life who avoids 'engagement'. This he has in common with certain types of scholar.

The next guise into which the Devil changes is that of a scholar, a theologian. In his detachment the scholar may see more clearly and deeply than the ordinary man the things of which he has special knowledge, which breeds a feeling of superiority and intellectual pride. This superiority and sense of singularity is the other recurring feature, besides lovelessness, of all original nihilists. Leverkuhn is driven ahead on his path to hell by the need and urge to be superior and out of the ordinary.

The figure who represents Thomas Mann's answer to Leverkuhn's nihilism, Dr. phil. Serenus Zeitblom, appears mediocre and ordinary to the point of dullness compared with his friend the composer. He is the man of the middle of the road, the man who leads the ordinary bourgeois married life, who does an ordinary job as a schoolteacher and belongs to a well-defined group in the Civil Service with clear-cut professional ethics. More important still, he is a humanist and a Catholic and is embedded in the two strongest and richest historical traditions in our time; he is limited but also supported by them. Yet how strong is this support, how fit are these traditions to resist the undermining effect of nihilism? Do they give clear and convincing guidance to the man of our time as to how to behave, and do they give answers which convince the ordinary man as well as the intellectual? Thomas Mann believes in humanism but his confidence in it as an effective answer to nihilism is weak, for he himself cannot escape the fascination of the Faustian nihilists who dare to transgress healthy human limits and by questioning everything hinder traditions from becoming stifling and barren. The nihilist pays with his humanity and his mental balance for his prophetic insights. His is a fate not to be envied and still less to be desired, but neither is it to be despised. His creativeness cannot be denied though the greatness of his creations does not justify regarding the creator as great and exemplary. The man of the middle road, the humanist, remains moderate and relatively weak, even when he attacks his most radical opponent, the nihilist. His gentlemanly fight with the Devil seems bound to be lost and every other form of fighting seems to end in driving out the Devil by Beelzebub. Is there a way out of this dilemma? Mann does not show one.

Robert Musil is not slow to point out the inherent weakness of Mann's bourgeois and humanistic answer to nihilism. Musil does not write as a biographer of Nietzsche but as his disciple. Musil's book seems to me to be the most original and radical continuation of Nietzsche's criticism of morals. The basic question around which this very long book revolves is a moral one.

Robert Edler von Musil was born in 1880 in Klagenfurt in Austria, the only child of a university professor. He went to an officers' training school but left before finishing there to study engineering. After having been assistant lecturer at the Technical High School at Stuttgart for a while he turned his interest to philosophy and experimental psychology and became a Dr. phil. of Berlin in 1908. I mention all these details because Ulrich, the man without qualities of the book's title, had a similar career to that of Musil, except that he ended up with pure mathematics instead of philosophy. In his later life Musil devoted himself to writing and the work of a librarian. In 1930 the first volume of *The Man Without Qualities* was published and in 1932 a part of the second volume appeared. Then the Nazis banned the book, and the author emigrated to Switzerland, where he died suddenly in 1942 leaving unfinished the book on which he had worked for twenty years. It was practically forgotten in Germany and completely unknown abroad when on 28th. October 1949 the *Times Literary Supplement* published a front page article [unsigned, as was customary, but later identified as by Musil's English translators Ernst Kaiser and Eithne Wilkins].

In that article Musil was praised as 'the most important novelist writing in German in this half-century', who could be compared in range and intelligence only with Proust and Joyce. The writing is praised for its ease, restraint and understatement, and the book is called 'extraordinarily amusing and extraordinarily difficult'. All this is true. I have, however, grave doubts, which I shall explain later, as to whether the TLS article is right in describing Musil's writing as not exclusive and not bitter, and above all as not sick. Other critics have praised the great precision of Musil's narrative, though some have doubted whether the book is rightly described as a novel. Thomas Mann says it remains suspended between essay and sparkling epic comedy. With the additional material published there the 'complete' edition of 1952 confirms Mann's impression.

The core and centre of the book is not an epic situation but a precisely formulated moral question which could be stated as follows: Assume that there is a mature man in his early thirties, bodily healthy and strong, highly intelligent and conversant with all the ideas of his time and experienced in many fields of human activity, free from bonds of marriage, of independent means and master of his time because he has granted himself a year's holiday from all occupational obligations. Assume further that he is sexually neither inhibited nor frustrated nor dependent on parental figures but independent in outlook and fearless in thought and action. How would such a free man behave, what would be the values and motives which would inform his actions, after all the necessities which rule the actions of ordinary men, all the economic, occupational and emotional pressures, have been taken from him?

Such a man may perhaps get his directives from a religious belief, but Ulrich rejects religion as too easy a way out of his dilemma. He wants no easy escape and consolation.

Here we come across something which might paradoxically be called the heroic ethos of nihilism. To want to see the truth no matter how bitter it is, and to reject every easing of the situation which cannot stand up to the strictest rational criticism — this gives Nietzsche as well as Freud the sense of ethical justification for his attack on all the accepted beliefs. And every common-or-garden nihilist nowadays feels superior to and more heroic than all believers because he rejects every escape from the only true insight that all is vanity. There is a stoic streak in Ulrich as in so many highly intelligent nihilists, a conscious acceptance of utter loneliness without relief. In spite of his varied male and female contacts Ulrich remains alone (during the first half of the book) and so much so that often his remarks to people seem inappropriate to the personality of the addressee, and as if they were part of a soliloquy unconcerned whether it is, or can be, understood rightly by the person in whose presence it is spoken (or for that matter by the reader).

Now, how about social ethics, aims and standards, can they not provide directions for Ulrich's behaviour? A very large part of the narrative of the book has been devised for the purpose of discussing this question and answering it in the negative.

The story takes us to Vienna in 1913, the critical year before the outbreak of the First World War. (We are however told that every year is a critical one.) Vienna is the capital of a multi-national State where the most diverse cultural and national influences meet. But as the Austrian-Hungarian double monarchy has lost belief in its own task and meaning within a divine order nobody dares to co-ordinate these cultural tendencies. One 'wurstelte sich durch', muddled along.

In this town a group of people are trying to prepare for a nation-wide celebration of the seventieth anniversary of the Peace-Emperor Franz Joseph's accession to the throne, due in December 1918. The author of the book is in league with the reader in knowing that within a year there will be no peace; that before the end of 1918 the Emperor will be dead; that in December 1918 there will no longer be any Austrian monarchy; and the multinational state will have disintegrated. Thus we are made aware that everything which seems indisputable reality to every person in the book (except Ulrich himself) is unreliable and not fit to serve as a guide for practical orientation. Reality is debunked as no more than a set of erroneous beliefs.

There is a search for a suitable general idea for the celebrations, one which would have a moral appeal to the public, and this gives the author the opportunity to discuss a great variety of moral ideas in detail. He debunks them all with that brilliance of epigrammatic formulation in which Nietzsche was his teacher. It is beyond me to reproduce these arguments as to why each one of these ideas must seem nonsensical, absurd or paradoxical. The author however also mentions some general principles as to why social morals have lost their power to convince and guide the individual. Perhaps the most general reason for this is that capitalist, bourgeois society is the heir of the morals of so many classes, of so many national groups, of so many religious and so many different historical periods, that each moral norm immediately brings to mind a contradictory one of equal power of conviction. Nobody bothers to think and to feel with any clarity and accuracy about all these norms. Ulrich on one occasion proposes the setting up of a Ministry of Accuracy in moral matters and matters of the Soul before there can be any hope of tackling the moral chaos.

The moral chaos of course results in the victory of the most primitive and narrowly egotistical power aims, as they become evident in the war of 1914. In a world of such chaotic moral orientation it becomes impossible to attribute any historical event to one or another cause and reason, and to hold anything or anybody responsible for events. History becomes meaningless and is replaced by a narrative of incoherent happenings. 'Such things do now happen' is all that can be stated, and this phrase is actually the sub-title of the first half of Musil's book.

Musil's irony and sharp wit is aroused not only by the half-baked social morals but still more by the spurious and impotent ways in which people try to deal with the moral chaos. All those insincere answers to and camouflages of nihilism which have become the substitute of effective morals are ruthlessly unmasked and debunked. Ulrich has at one stage a division of them into two groups, those which look for salvation by the advice of 'Back to', say 'religion' or 'simplicity' or 'nature' or what not. And the other group hopes for everything from 'Forward to', say, 'vegetarianism', or 'Esperanto' or 'a pure Aryan race' or any other such aim which may provide a moral principle for some questions but claims to answer all.

Now what are Ulrich's own conclusions from the state of affairs in which he finds himself? He cultivates (during the first half of the story) an attitude of what he calls active passivity. As he knows no meaningful aims for action he refrains from taking the lead, from offering advice as to how to improve matters, from becoming a reformer himself. He is in consequence infinitely tolerant toward others and he dislikes coercion not on principle but because nobody is in possession of worthy aims of coercion. He behaves like a liberal individualist but without a positive belief either in liberalism or in individualism. He believes that most of our activities are idle fuss and that even the most gifted man has no more original ideas during his lifetime than could be fully expressed in about three essays. We should all be better off if we confined ourselves to these three essays and kept our mouths shut and our pens dry for the rest.

Ulrich does not however become a hermit, because this too would be a meaningless decision. He partakes in ordinary life, although he drifts into the various happenings without a purpose or inner necessity of his own. He remains detached from others because he cannot take seriously the reality in which the others believe. The debunking of reality brings Ulrich near to the world of the insane, and Musil introduces two insane figures into the narrative, Moosbrugger and Clarisse, to act as foil for Ulrich. He differs from them in that his rejection of the accepted reality is not compulsive; and in that it is not only one subjective potentiality replacing the generally accepted reality: it is a multitude of subjective potentialities among which Ulrich moves in freedom, obeying only the demands of honesty of spirit. Ulrich appears eminently sane in the first half of the book because he is unselfconscious, bodily healthy and intellectually vital, and because his nihilism is not yet actively destructive; for he regards the nihilism still as something which *can* be overcome if he waits until the spirit moves him to a fuller and more positive insight.

So far Ulrich's awareness of the living spirit as the supreme value has only increased his world rejection, because it has only served as an ideal in comparison with which everything has been found wanting and unsatisfactory. In each situation he sees many potentialities of interpretation and evaluation apart from those which people take so seriously. He wants to invent what could have happened and not only what has happened. He cultivates a sense of potentiality in place of the 'sense of reality' because he hopes to approximate to true reality more closely than we do through blind belief in one generally accepted reality. He does not doubt that his year's holiday from all obligations of work will end with his finding compelling aims and values, that is to say a positive and not only critical expression of the living spirit.

That these aims and values must be of a highly subjective nature is a foregone conclusion. The second half of the book deals with the love between Ulrich and his sister Agathe. Their love should end their despair as ordinary beings and transform them into beings who can permanently live the life of the spirit through the autonomy and self-evidence of these feelings. The natural affinity of brother and sister increases the degree of their unity with one another beyond all ordinary love. The dissolution of their individual beings in a new united existence reaches such an extent that only sayings of the great mystics seem adequate to describe this ecstatic relationship. Yet it belongs also to the peculiarity of incestuous love that

awareness of the world in general, or more precisely the emotional importance of the world, gets lost to a still greater degree than in any other love.
The beloved one represents all there is outside the self, as the mother does to
the very young child.

There follows an imperviousness to the rules of the world, they are
disregarded to such an extent that it is of no account whether or not one
becomes criminal. There is experience of the beatific illusion that none of
the problems of the world matters any more, and of once again approaching
the paradisal state. This is romanticism in its purest form, liberation from
the sufferings and meaninglessness of life through reunion with the earliest
love-objects, the mother or sister. That romanticism can offer an answer to
nihilism only for short ecstatic moments, and that in the end, in its inevitable failure, it only intensifies the nihilism, is one of the most frequently
and most clearly explored sides of emotional life. It suffices to mention Anna
Karenina among innumerable other figures in literature. Thus it seems on
the whole incredible that an intellectual like Ulrich should have believed his
incestuous love could open the road into the Millennium. Yet the second half
of the book is actually called *Into the Millennium, or The Criminals*. It is at
this point that Ulrich ceases to be sane. He expects from his love not only
momentary ecstasy but permanent salvation, the permanent spiritual
vivification.

As early as in her discussions with the chiliastic heretics of the 11th and
12th centuries the mediaeval Church already recognised clearly that the
attempt to perpetuate mystical union and thus to start the Millennium is the
essence of what separates heretic and insane self-deification from truly
religious mysticism. It comes therefore as a surprise only to Ulrich and
Agathe, and not to the reader, that this answer to nihilism has to fail and
that it results in the nihilism now becoming openly destructive. The 'Journey into Paradise' is followed by a real witches' sabbath of universal destruction, with adultery, rape, murder and so forth. For example Ulrich, at the
instigation of the schizophrenic Clarisse, liberates the prisoner Moosbrugger, who promptly repeats his previous crime of sexual assault and murder,
as Ulrich clearly had anticipated. Nothing matters, all is vanity. This cannot
all be described in detail here, but there is some point in dwelling a bit longer
on the connections between nihilism and romantic love.

Romantic love seems to be an answer to nihilism, for into the nihilist's
life, from which it has been so characteristically absent, it reintroduces love.
Why does it then so often increase nihilism, as illustrated by Ulrich's
development, or by Anna Karenina's drug addiction and final suicide?

Romantic love tries to re-establish the most complete love and unity
which the child experiences at the beginning of his life in relation with his
mother. Everything which could disturb this unity is pushed aside and
ignored. Romantic love removes the lover not only right out of the world but
out of himself as well. It is the love of a part personality for a part personality
where every force which could disturb the harmony of the two is ignored and

made unreal. The paradoxical result of this is that an experience which first appears as an infinite enrichment of the personality turns out to be unbearable as utter impoverishment. There remains only the one relationship, that with the beloved: all other relationships stop. Both Anna Karenina's relationship with her lover and Ulrich's with his sister break down because the loss of contact with the world becomes insufferable; and Ulrich and Agathe return from their journey into Paradise poorer in relationship than when they set out on it.

Because romantic love is the love of a part personality for a part personality, projection plays a prominent role in it. Both Ulrich and Agathe are peculiarly one-sided people, he lives mainly by his intellect and imagination, and she is a remarkable study of a predominantly feeling type. When discussing love of one's neighbour Ulrich states that he has little or no love of self, something typical of the nihilist. He describes his sister as his self-love, and the same is true *vice versa*. Anything that each of them really values is only to be found in the other; the usual overvaluation of the love object at the expense of all love of self reaches an extreme degree in this incestuous relationship. When the relationship breaks down all values are lost. Ulrich and Agathe actually intended to commit suicide if their bid for the Millennium failed, but then even suicide appeared meaningless because all was vanity.

The fundamental split between thinking and feeling is typical of the paranoid and nihilistic personality. Ulrich before meeting Agathe is identified with an archetypal male figure characterised by intellectual superiority and detachment. This identification breaks down in romantic love and identification with a paternal *imago* is replaced by identification with a feminine and maternal archetype of all-feeling. Ulrich experiences these two states as irreconcilable, as if he had two completely separate personalities who alternated in ascendency. When Ulrich changes from the father identification to the feminine state the validity of law and moral norms disappears, for it is part of the paternal archetype. Lawlessness increases nihilism.

Recognition of transcendent supra-individual laws and norms seems to be as fundamental to being human as love and relationship are. It is an ontological aspect of being human, a fact which has found only scant recognition in some of the psychological literature.

Nietzsche was aware of his father identification and once said '*ubi pater sum ibi patria*', where I am the father there I am at home. As Zarathustra he yearned for Ariadne, who would lead him down from the icy heights of mental superiority and identification with the father, but she never came. In Musil's book the hero finds Ariadne, with the result that he loses his last homeland. After the breakdown of his and Agathe's love he is left in a complete void.

Musil had planned not to end the book with this all-pervading nihilism but to strive for some positive answers to it. However we have only sketchy hints of how this was to be achieved. He thought of three answers to nihilism which were to supplement one another. This is remarkable of itself, for considering the complexity of our own being and of our life it may be true that we need a whole battery of answers to fortify and guide us. Musil called his three answers utopian because they are at variance with what science would call reality and with the naive reality of the ordinary man. Two of these utopias we know already. They are the two attitudes which Musil described at length in the first and second halves of his book. One is the active passivity resulting from the awareness that the reality which people naively accept is only one of a great variety of possible interpretations of experience, and is not the true spiritual reality. The other utopia is produced by ecstatic states of the type of Ulrich's and Agathe's love. The third utopia which Musil introduces at the end of his book he calls 'the utopia of the positive outlook' or 'of the given social conditions', and he means by this the recognition of the drives which result from the nearest and most pressing necessities of life such as the need for food, protection, order and so forth.

In other words Musil reintroduces into Ulrich's world all those motives which in the beginning of the book he had carefully eliminated in order to explore how a man would act if he were set free from all everyday needs. These daily necessities are a matter of course to the ordinary man but, according to Musil, they are utopia to the genius who accepts them with the mental reservation that they do not belong to the true reality of the spirit, a mental reservation which is meant to preserve the genius's freedom of and superiority to the humdrum necessities of life. All this sounds somewhat unsatisfactory, for all these answers confirm nihilism more than they fortify against it.

For example, Musil as nihilist cannot discern between the ecstatic states which are inspired by God and those inspired by the Devil, as theology does; or between healthy and pathological (maniacal) ecstasy. By treating all these experiences as equally valid he exposes them all to the suspicion of being cheap self-deceptions and escapist arrangements, a suspicion which is so obviously justified with regard to pathological ecstasies. Or by claiming that the genius ought to recognise our common human needs only as a utopia and with the mental reservation of being superior to them, Musil postulates exactly that superiority to human fate which is essentially nihilistic. Musil's teaching of the genius is the very opposite of the Christian teaching of the God-man who accepts his human fate without any reservation.

The two books I have been discussing look for two diametrically different answers to nihilism. Musil wants to answer the question of how one can live though all the propositions of nihilism are true. Like the existentialists he starts from nothingness and tries to find ways of living in spite of the basic nothingness. In such an approach it seems inevitable that the nihilism appears more impressive, convincing and genuine than do the answers to it. That is true of Koheleth, the Preacher, as well as of the existentialism of Sartre or of Musil's attempt to find a positive ending to his book.

Thomas Mann, on the other hand, criticises the presuppositions of nihilism itself through his narrator Zeitblom. His type of answer to nihilism denies that nihilism asks the right questions. The nihilist arrives at nothingness because he wants to do so and because he formulates his questions in a prejudiced form. He aims at all or nothing, which always results in nothing or in the all *and* nothing of being superman *and* nihilist. Our due is the something, the part and not the whole, the segment and not the whole circle. This the nihilist rejects out of hand.

Answers which criticise the presuppositions of nihilism have however to beware of one highly tempting fallacy. I have tried to show that nihilism is characterised and constituted by a great variety of mental attitudes and tendencies. I have described the lovelessness of the nihilist; his sense of superiority, and mental pride, together with a marked lack of love of self; his intellectual or aesthetic loneliness and his separation from feeling; his asocial and antisocial tendencies, his stoicism, his occasional romanticism, and so on. It is tempting to isolate any one of these tendencies and direct the attack against nihilism against this isolated trend. There may then be a fight against science and rationalism, a burning of books, an attack on individualism which fails to see that the isolation of the nihilist is only misunderstood individualism. The nihilist aims to be different and out of the ordinary, while true individuation aims at wholeness including ordinariness and collectivity. Alternatively, introversion may be regarded as the arch sin which produces nihilism.

All these attacks overlook the fact that the many disparate and even contradictory tendencies of nihilism enumerated above are interlinked and form part of one coherent syndrome, the separate symptoms of which cannot be effectively changed in isolation. Earlier on I called this syndrome paranoid. Schematically its origin could be described as follows:

When the primal trust and loving unity of child and mother proves to be not a permanent and imperturbable state, some individuals feel unable to accept any less complete love and support, and after many vain attempts to establish the relationship of primal love with people other than the mother they resign themselves to live without love. They isolate themselves in the role of a superior being who needs no support or true relationship whatsoever, usually the role of the omnipotent, all controlling, spiritual father *imago*. They reject the mother who disappointed, the *imago* of the earth mother, and the common reality of man. Yet as everybody is aware that he too partakes in that common reality the rejection affects also the love of self. Self-rejection goes together with the striving for superiority and singularity. Intensively romantic love is no cure for the paranoid attitude, it constitutes only a belated attempt to reproduce the primal oneness with the mother *imago* as a permanent state.

This invariably has to fail. Only those who can achieve a reconciliation between love and self-reliant and self-assertive strength and who therefore also tolerate the same amalgamation in others, will be free from the longing for the paradise here and now; or from the need to be supermen in utter isolation and singularity. I have the impression that this maturity is to be found more frequently in people who tackle life courageously without writing about it than amongst the producers of literature. On the other hand the great living examples of mature freedom from paranoid tendencies and the great teachings of that freedom are persistently misunderstood and misapplied by the immature. It would need a great deal of convincing proof to support a contention that this is worse today than at any other time. At all times it has been the personal fate and venture of a limited number of individuals to have had to acquire this maturity, this positive humility, the hard way. And I see no reason to assume that it will ever be otherwise. I have the optimistic belief that the potentiality of mature humanity is imperishable, no matter what the political, economic or other social conditions are. It is an ontological potentiality which can end only with the end of mankind.

This optimism is not however intended as an invitation to complacency. On the contrary, the insight that the paranoid personality structure is the basis of nihilism seems to provide us with a more articulate guide for what we have to attack or support when asking for valid answers to nihilism. Everything which in the personal life, in education, social organisation, politics, in philosophy and religion, strengthens paranoid trends represents a negative value; and everything is welcome which enables man to tolerate the fact that both his strength and his love are limited.

Report of a Discussion:
Abenheimer, Penry Jones, R.D. Laing. Joseph Schorstein

Shortly after we started our discussion on nihilism we ran into difficulties with regard to what was meant by this term. These difficulties stemmed from three points:

(1) If nihilism were the denial of all values it would be an impossible attitude. No matter how futile or inconsistent or temporally limited valuating is, nobody can live and act without wanting and valuating something. We found particularly that the philosophers of nihilism rejected all human values because they compared them with superhuman values and found ordinary human values wanting. They rejected man for superman; society for total individual liberty; feeling and imagination in the name of intellectual honesty; ordinary human relationship for perfect love, and so forth. Thus the discussion of nihilism becomes a discussion of the luciferic sin of aiming at godlikeness, or a discussion of *hybris*. And the doubt arises, when we criticise nihilism, whether like Nietzsche's last man in *Also Sprach Zarathustra* we are only shirking intellectual adventure, want to remain undisturbed, and are vilifying a great light because it throws intense shadows. Have we a right to criticise the nihilist, is the critic not the arch-nihilist who denies the nihilist the freedom of his existential choice? Should we not accompany the nihilist in his intellectual adventure and be taken out of our smugness by his radicalism? These questions do not put the problem fairly. Criticism of the nihilist is not identical with smugly ignoring his attacks

on specific values. And if I regard a man's attitude as luciferic I do not deny him his freedom but implicitly accuse him of acting unfreely, of being under the influence of forces which are incompatible with human freedom. In other words to criticise nihilism seems to uphold an idea of human values and the human situation which condemn the nihilist's position as Luciferic and sinful. If we defend him in the name of freedom, then we treat freedom as an empty idea unrelated to value, a sheer nihilistic negation of all belief. Criticism of nihilism criticises this concept of freedom.

(2) The nihilist is often most impressive from the fearlessness and audacity of his thinking, the importance of some of his ideas, and the importance of his thinking for a certain historical situation. He breaks through antiquated and obsolete prejudices and we owe him gratitude and respect for this, particularly if he has paid for it all a price of suffering we would be loth to pay ourselves. We may therefore feel reluctant to criticise the nihilist, but that would lead to romantic ideas of the genius who owing to his achievement is one who cannot be regarded as an ordinary human being; and who is not to be evaluated on the basis of the criteria which are valid for others. I regard this as a dangerous belief which fits well into a nihilistic outlook.

I prefer greatly the opposite view that the greatness of a man becomes the more obvious the more we remain aware of his common humanity. Then we also see the price of distortion which has to be paid for greatness, and we do not relinquish our regard for the dignity of man in face of the creative genius. Thomas Mann is the outstanding critic of romantic ideas about the genius, in the name of humanism.

(3) In the course of the Group's discussion of the main paper, R.D. Laing drew the distinction between explicit and implicit nihilism. He pointed out that discussion becomes obscured if one speaks about both indiscriminately. The example of implicit nihilism which continually cropped up in the discussion was science. The scientist usually is not aware of being a nihilist and has usually no intention of being one. However by approaching the world objectively in the sense of eliminating subjective wishes, emotions, feelings and valuations he cultivates an outlook which is essentially nihilistic. The individual scientist may reject nihilism by differentiating between his scientific professional thinking and his personal life, but science, scientific thinking, too easily claims to be the only way of true thinking and becomes a *Weltanschauung*. This is the case for example in Communism. We who are all professionally concerned with man are faced with decisions as to how far we want to admit a scientific, loveless, and impersonal approach to man and how we can avoid it without sacrificing those benefits we all receive and want to have from science. I do not know a general answer to this question. Mere hostility to science does not seem a workable solution. Better and more critical scientific thinking helps sometimes to eliminate destructive trends of so-called scientific approaches to man. This is the case with those changes in outlook in analytic psychology in which the psychiatrists and psychologists among us are interested. Yet even if one strengthens non-scientific approaches to life by consciously focussing attention on the fundamental prescientific apperception by which we actually live, the relationship between this and objective impersonal science remains problematic and disquieting.

II

Our general theme was 'answers to Nihilism'. Penry Jones approached it in the good British way of empiricism, finding that even in people who have lost their contact with the church and who would be hard pressed if asked to formulate their beliefs explicitly there is a fund of beliefs implicitly present which act as guide for their behaviour and as a bulwark against nihilism. Thus seen from the British setting Nietzsche with his prophecies of an inevitable European nihilism seems alarmist. The world wars, however, the atomic bombs. the growing influence of soul- and mind-destroying agencies such as horror comics, cinema, television, sensational press, *et cetera*, leave us with doubts whether nihilism is not progressing and will overrun our insular idyll.

Joseph Schorstein seems to feel that answers to nihilism can only be found after having gone through nihilism, and that guided by Nietzsche and similar thinkers we have first fully to realise the precariousness of the cultural valuations on which our behaviour is based. That we have to face this precariousness is my conviction as well. For this reason for example I regard easy revivalism like Billy Graham's as of no real importance. The question which matters is what follows after one has realised the precariousness of traditional values.

I discussed Musil's abortive attempt to find a romantic solution in the experience of sexual love, which he described as an attempted journey into paradise. By describing it thus, love becomes an escape from and a rejection of the world, and this too is nihilistic though it involves two instead of only one individual. It is a different non-romantic love which can claim to be an answer to nihilism, a love which sees in the loved one not all and everything but a bridge to the world and to fellow beings, a love which through the loved one loves man as such, which increases and does not weaken our *Beheimstetsein* in the world, our at-homeness in the world. It is a love which is not ecstasy and self-estrangement, but increased humble self-acceptance together with the realistic and loving acceptance of the loved one.

This humble self-acceptance seems to me one of the necessary conditions of overcoming nihilism. It seems to me that all nihilism develops out of paranoid self-rejection and the overcoming of paranoid trends is necessary for all answers to nihilism. All answers to nihilism must contain an idea of what man is, what his status and place is, and how far the actual attitudes of an individual approximate to this idea, i.e. how mature these attitudes are. Dynamic psychology has such an idea at least in the negative form of knowing what deviates from the idea of man. Nihilism comes in low on the scale of maturity no matter how high the individual nihilist may range on the scale of intellectual insight, idealism, personal courage and intellectual honesty.

In our discussion Laing tried to give a more positive formulation of the idea of man by mentioning the need to have regard for the spiritual aspect of man. The spirit is certainly an important and pregnant concept and full of historical association. Yet just for this reason it is a most ambiguous idea which needs further clarification and discussion before one can feel at ease about its use in our connection.

The Individualistic Ego

In the following I intend to discuss some aspects of what we mean by the 'ego' or 'I', and this by way of criticism of Freud's theory of the ego and the individualistic philosophy implicit in it. I see Freud's lasting achievement and merit not in his theory but in his having created a new empirical science of man's motivation, having found new methods for studying it, and having explored large fields of experience which had been neglected though of basic importance for the understanding of motivation. Nevertheless I feel very critical of Freud's theory of his new science, and of the philosophy which it expresses.

Freud believed he was creating a new natural science dealing with natural energies, instincts and substantial structures. Certainly much of human motivation is like that of other animals; yet more important for this understanding of human motivation is that man not only reacts to stimuli and impulses like an animal, but forms concepts, images, feelings of his experiences which can be mentally reproduced and which allow man to discover ever new interconnections between the items of experience. Man lives in an interpreted world; he spontaneously and prescientifically finds meaning in his experiences. The new science of dynamic psychology which Freud discovered is the study of how man spontaneously and prescientifically apperceives (i.e. meaningfully experiences) himself and his world. These apperceptions may be conscious or may go on unconsciously. They affect all human behaviour. In particular behaviour is apperceived as motivated by motivating energies which originate in centres, the subjects of actions and wills (in the widest sense of 'will', including urges, desires, impulses, emotions, fears and the rest).

The dynamic psychologies deal predominantly with these energies and their subjects. The energies they discuss are unlike the energies of natural science; they are purposive and not quantifiable. And the subjects in which these energies originate are not natural objects but something immaterial even if they are perceived as hypostasised or are represented by substantial symbols. The ego for example may be symbolised by the body, yet one is usually aware that it is not identical with the body and is really insubstantial. Behaviourists have tried to debunk these concepts of insubstantial subjects as unscientific and as 'ghost(s) in the machine', yet these prescientific apperceptions are all the same so important that a man will not experience himself as alive unless he can experience himself as an active subject of wills. He will be a schizophrenic who acts only as an automaton or a zombie. The aim of Eastern philosophies to get rid of the ego and of will does not go against these findings: such philosophies are wise enough to teach that no-one should embark on the way of overcoming the ego until he or she has fulfilled his or her *karma* and has become a fully effective ego; for whoever fears this and tries to avoid it from the start becomes psychotic.

In addition, it is not merely one's own ego which one experiences as a living subject of action, we experience other human beings in the same way. Also, Piaget has shown that the young child may apperceive every object, in particular any moving object, as an active subject. We may regard strong emotions as active subjects and express this semantically in terms such as 'rage overcame me', 'love blinded me'. We prescientifically apperceive subjective immaterial powers who (not 'which') influence our actions. The Homeric heroes felt motivations instigated directly by gods.

In Christian thought the Holy Spirit, as well as the Devil and evil spirits, may actively inspire or possess us, and even pantheistic philosophers and psychologists of the 18th and 19th centuries reckon with such immaterial powers (i.e. 'meta-physical' powers in the literal sense of the word). For example, Carl Gustav Carus, who starts his 1848 book on psychology with the sentence: 'The key to the comprehension of conscious psychology lies in the region of the unconscious', means by the unsconscious a transcendental power which realises itself (*lebt sich dar*) in our physical as well as mental being.

Jung devoted a large part of his research to the description of the autonomous forces and subjects which modern man apperceives as affecting his behaviour. Autonomous complexes have their own psychic energies, they may possess one and hinder the ego from realising and expressing its own knowledge and aims. Archetypes like the shadow, the *anima* and the *animus* are autonomous complexes and subjects which in addition usually are personified or projected on to other human beings. And the Self is experienced as the origin and centre of all mental energy, its source and plenitude.

I. The Mature Ego as the Only Subject

Freud the natural scientist avoids the concept of 'subject' as unscientific. The scientist is interested only in what is objective, and the subject is to be eliminated. Yet no more than Gilbert Ryle in *The Concept of Mind* can Freud entirely avoid some use of our common language reckoning with subjects. Freud teaches for example that the ego is faced with the conflicting 'demands' of the id, the superego and reality. 'Demands' usually originate in demanding subjects, yet when speaking of the demands of reality Freud seems to have in mind only objective necessities.

The demands of the id are the demands of the instincts. These Freud originally regarded as objective energies like those of natural science. He believed them to be quantifiable and independent of purpose. Sex can be desexualised and aggression be de-aggressivised and then be stored up as neutral energy in a reservoir as electricity can be stored in a battery. Even when Freud later called the instincts mythological he meant by this only that they were necessary but unprovable hypotheses. That the instincts as energies are prescientific apperceptions of hypostatised and subjectivised motive forces, he nowhere states.

Other people were usually described by Freud as objects, love objects or objects of aggression, though most neurotic difficulties stem from their being subjects with wills and feelings of their own, or from an expectation that they will have such wills and feelings. In the paper 'Mass Psychology and Ego Analysis' Freud discusses relationship with other people in crowds, in organisations such as the Church or the army, the relationship of lovers, that between the hypnotist and the hypnotised person. Love, brotherliness, identification, submission, infectious imitation of the behaviour of others: all these are seen as regressions to infantile forms of behaviour. Man either makes the other his ego ideal or with others shares being the love object of an authoritative figure. In his mature state man frees himself from all this.

The super-ego and ego-ideal are split-off parts of the ego which like parental authorities make demands upon the ego; that is, they are apperceived as autonomous subjects. Yet it is the aim of maturation to get rid of these subjects: to the mature man morals are a matter of course, which is to say an integral part of the ego itself, not demands of a separate authority. Therefore only the ego of the mature man remains as possible subject. Freud tries to describe the ego too in objective terms, as we shall discuss later. Yet he cannot avoid admitting that it has at its disposal energies of its own, namely a reservoir of neutralised sex and aggression; and the ego can use its reason and thinking as an active subject. Ideally the mature man is the only subject in a totally objective world. He meets other people objectively as part of the objective reality outside. In himself he has to deal with the objective forces of the instincts but with no subjectivised agents. This is of course no longer a science of psychology but a description of a therapeutic and philosophical aim of the most individualistic nature.

II. The Origin and Function of the Ego

Freud had various ideas about the origin of the ego. At one time he postulated that it was present at birth and contained all the libido prior to libido being invested in objects outside the ego. This was one of those scholastic consequences of the dogma that the libido was a substantial energy which like other substances existed continually (i.e. not only intermittently) from birth, and therefore must have a place prior to being directed outward. The theory that the ego was this place was later abandoned, and substituted by the notion of the id as the original home of the libido.

Now a theory was proposed that the ego gradually develops out of the id.

This too was more an appendix to the libido theory than a seriously held and explored hypothesis on the origin and nature of the ego.

The final theory about the origin of the ego appeared in the book *The Ego and the Id*, and was formulated in Freud's last paper (*An Outline of Psychoanalysis*) as follows:

> From what was originally a cortical layer provided with organs for receiving stimuli and with apparatus for protection against excessive stimulation a special organisation has arisen which henceforward acts as an intermediary between the id and the external world. The ego is in control of voluntary movement. It has the task of self-preservation. It stores experience in memory. It adapts to the external world and modifies it through activity. It interposes between the demands of the instincts and their satisfaction an intellective activity which calculates the consequences of a proposed line of conduct, tests reality and thus introduces the reality principle as the opposite of the id, which is ruled exclusively by the pleasure principle.

The ego is a topographical concept, a spatial not a dynamic one. This topographical division between ego and id exists according to Freud not in man alone but equally in the higher animals.

I find this a most amazing description of the ego. No mention is made of how a man apperceives himself, to which the personal pronoun of the first person obviously refers. Instead of psychology we get a piece of anatomical, neurological brain mythology of Wernicke's type, combined with some phylogenetic musings. Problems of aiming at being or not being a self, or of overemphasising uniqueness, of self-regard or self-rejection, of ego boundaries, of identity, of the various forms of ego integration (and so forth) which constantly turn up in psychological practice cannot be discussed on the basis of this metapsychological concept. In consequence, if analytical clinicians discuss ego problems one always has first to discover what they actually mean by 'ego', for only one thing is certain: they are not referring to that spatial entity which originally was a cortical layer.

According to Heinz Hartmann, Freud's ego concept is meant to be not anthropomorphic or human-like at all; and if one wants to speak about the ordinary apperceptions of oneself one is advised to use a different term, namely the self. Yet the self is hardly anywhere mentioned by Freud. What is therefore the purpose of the Freudian definition of the ego? At first glance it seems to be as unindividualistic as possible. It is said to be the same in every physically healthy body and even to exist in animals. It is described as being of the same nature as any other body organ. Anna Freud calls it a territory. It is unhistorical, Freud states expressly. According to him the id is the representative of the phylogenetic past while the superego, as the derivative of parental influences, represents the individual past. Yet the ego is supposed to be all present actuality and nothing else. In this sense it is as lonely and individualistic as possible. It is the lone arbiter: it knows the present reality and it judges which demands from the phylogenetic and ontogenetic past can be pursued without danger from factual conditions. Its function is intellective.

Language is seen as nothing more than a receptacle of memories—that it shapes and articulates values and aims is not mentioned. Nor is there mention of any relationship of the ego to the future, though normally the ego is experienced not only as actuality but also as potentiality, as the unity of capabilities, values and aims directed to the future. Similarly we apperceive our fellow-men and relate in love and hate to their potentialities. Awareness of self and others as potentiality, is a source of experiencing the ego as related and interlinked with others. To ignore this makes the individualistic isolation of the ego appear even more pronounced. Freud described the ego of the lone thinker. According to Anna Freud it is 'independent of the emotions, and functions as accurate and reliable as a mechanical apparatus.'

That apperception of ourselves by ourselves to which the personal pronoun of the first person normally refers is neither present at birth nor does it develop out of the id. It develops out of the relationship with the mother, or her substitute, with whom the infant at first experiences himself as being one. She is apperceived as the gratifier of all his needs and his needs are experienced only in the image of the gratifying mother. His hunger is one and the same as the absence of the feeding mother. Only in conflicts with her does awareness arise of being a separate being and ego. Even after a separate ego has been apperceived, part of our striving is in the direction of re-establishing unity with the mother, or establishing a unity with an increasing circle of other beings. Also, the unity of the ego and the outer world is in another respect never broken. The outer world is experienced as wish-fulfilling or hostile; a landscape is experienced as peaceful or majestic, the house as homely, some food as tempting, excreta or spittle as disgusting, et cetera.

In emotional apperception of the outside world we concurrently apperceive ourselves. And we find ourselves above all through our contact with other human beings. In our feelings about another person we can become aware as much of ourselves as of the other. Yet all these forms of being interlinked with the world and with others are excluded from Freud's ego concept. What remains is a concept of self of exceptional individual isolation. The ego is the thinker, and Freud describes it as the 'clearing house' of the demands of reality, the id and the superego (like the clearing houses in banking transactions). The id as the opposite of the ego is described as 'the realm of the illogical': wherever thought is found, be it in dreams or any other unconscious activity, the ego is at work. By thinking and logic Freud means exclusively rational thinking free from emotional interference.

It is on this point that Freud differs from the frequently held philosophical belief that thinking is the specific human faculty which differentiates man from other mammals. For here thinking means the apperception of meaningful links and connections between our experiences. The links and connections which are thus spontaneously apperceived are predominantly purposive and emotional, and the logics of emotional thinking are not rational in Freud's sense. They are the logics of animistic anthropomorphic thinking and of normative thinking. The ego concept itself is not a scientific one but an apperception of this type of emotional thinking. It is the responsible subject of action and wills; and in it many tendencies, wills, desires, purposes, etc., are meaningfully organised.

III. The Will

In spite of the theory that the ego is a topographical concept, Freud could not ignore the fact that we experience it as an active agent. With regard to the immature ego he could explain this by a theory that the ego becomes the heir to 'object cathexes of the id'. The id, from where according to Freud all psychic energy comes, endows objects in the world with love and hate; and the ego inherits these energies either by direct identification with these love and hate objects or by identification with the super-ego or ego ideal which in turn has been the heir of the loved and/or hated father.

Within Freud's theoretical framework this may explain self-love and self-hate, but it cannot explain how the mature ego becomes the subject of wills and the active agent of a great variety of activities. Freud therefore assumes that the ego has access to a reservoir of neutral psychic energy, namely desexualised sex and de-aggressified aggression. This however explains nothing and only confuses the issue a great deal more. We are not told how we should imagine a 'reservoir' of psychic energy and where it is supposed to be.

And what is desexualised sex apart from a *contradictio in adjectu*? It is obviously not the same as sublimated sex, otherwise we would have been told so. And what is the empirical evidence that the neutral energy of will is derived from sex and aggression by neutralisation? We are faced here with one of those statements which have nothing to do with empiricism, but which in a scholastic way fits the will into Freud's instinct theory. This again emphasises the individualistic isolation of the ego. Every will, like all active forces, has an aim and purpose which links the ego as its subject with something else. Neutral energy just does not do this.

In order to study empirically the prescientific apperception of 'will', 'will-power', 'pure will', it is necessary to start with the fact that the will connects two poles, the subject of the will (the ego), and the purpose or aim of the will. Usually the emphasis is on the aim if one says 'I want to go to London' or 'I want to write'. The motive force and the aim are identical and it is a matter of course that it is 'I' who want the aim. This however changes in a situation of conflict if for example a friend says, 'no, let's go north to the

Highlands'. The answer '*I* want to go to London' now emphasises my will in contrast with that of the friend. An impression of more emphasis on the ego's will power does not arise from some access the ego has to neutralised energy, the original aim of going to London has been strengthened by new motive forces and aims. I may for example find the weather in the High-lands too uncertain, or I may find it difficult to give in in a situation of conflict. There are other instances in which the impression of pure wi l or pure will power arises, for instance:

(a) *Where the conflict is internal.* I want to finish this paper but am tired or am tempted by the weather to go for a walk. By sheer will power I go on writing. Here one can easily discover that ordinary motive forces are helping me to persevere, for instance a satisfaction I receive from not giving in, a hate I have of starting writing again on the day after, and so on. These motives may remain unconscious, and thus the impression of a pure will power of the ego arises.

(b) *If I resist some temptation by 'sheer will power'* I may be acting in accordance with moral principles of mine. It was Freud's merit that he showed that moral principles are purposeful motive forces like all others. They serve aims of remaining acceptable or lovable by parents, substitutes for parents, society at large. Yet these aims may remain unconscious. The ego is identified with one's moral principles and the whole emphasis rests on the subject of the aim, namely 'the pure will power of the ego', and the aim of the will is ignored.

(c) *One is in a dilemma and has considered the pros and cons of both sides without coming to a decision. Finally one decides 'by sheer will power'.* One may choose arbitrarily, strengthening the motives for one side of the dilemma by the motive that some decision, no matter which, is better than none. Or the dilemma is lifted on to a new level as may be the case in what existentialists call existential decisions. Instead of choosing between the conflicting aims which constitute the dilemma one chooses the self one wants to be and which is defined by the choice one makes in the dilemma. Here no single motive force may be adequate to make the decision under-standable. The ego in Freudian terms comes to a decision by identification with a highly complex and rich ego ideal; in Jungian terms it does so by identification with that plenitude of all motive forces which Jung calls the Self. This displaces the emphasis of the motivation from the aim to the subject of the will. Yet no neutral energy out of a reservoir is activated in any of these cases.

IV. The Organisation of the Ego (and the Total Personality)

According to Freud, integration of the personality is the function of the ego. The creation of order comes about through thinking, and according to Freud thinking is always an ego activity. Freud's therapeutic aim, 'where id was should ego be' means that ever larger parts of the personality should be under the control of rational thinking, which would be the essence of integration. What this would look like if taken seriously was described in Philip Rieff's book *The Triumph of the Therapeutic*.

There we read that the leisured rich of the United States are the cultured elite who represent 'psychological man' and Freud's individualistic ego and personality organisation. Religion has been abolished for it is the symptom of needs which can be gratified only by illusion and the rich need no such illusions. Culture so far has developed at an extortionate price in the shape of heavy loads of guilt and tensions which psychological man feels no need to pay. He wants self-fulfilment, 'Comfort is the great social tranquilliser', as opposed to high moral demands. If religion is redundant, so is any authority which makes absolute demands. Freud showed that all beliefs in absolute authority are derivatives of the illusion of the father's omnipotence, which psychological man no longer regards as valid.

Western culture is changing into a symbol system unprecedented in its plasticity and absorptive capacity. Nothing much can oppose it really for, in a sense, it stands for nothing, neither for the binding power of any faith, any tradition or custom, nor for any absolute commitment such as love or marriage. Let's have 'well-tempered love' and treat first marriages as 'trial runs' and periods of learning. We need cool democratic families. Crowded more and more together in the urban settings we are learning to live more distantly from one another, in strategically varied and numerous contacts rather than in the oppressive warmth of family and a few friends.

Even the social value of justice is redundant; everything is just which secures the 'consoling plenitude of option in which modern satisfaction really consists'. We no longer bother our heads about 'ultimate concerns'. they are 'for mystics who cannot otherwise enjoy their leisure'. In both American and Soviet cultures wealth has become the functional equivalent of a high civilisation. Social reformers no longer desire to improve the quality of life by irrelevant ascetic standards of conduct, they ask only 'for more goods, more housing, more leisure, in short, more life'. 'An elaborate and infinite sense of personal need proclaims the superiority of all that money can buy, technology can make, and science can conceive'. And 'there are no positive communities any longer within which the individual can merge himself therapeutically'.

Rieff describes all this without criticism or alarm. It is simply an aspect of the affluent society with which we have to live. He goes further and welcomes the new anti-culture. He is not afraid that it will lead to an unprecedented increase of asocial behaviour or to indifference to all concerns other than strictly self-centred ones. The reason for his optimism is that he puts his hope in 'vitality' and in 'prudence' resulting from the self-knowledge which psycho-analysis is to produce. In place of the 'symbolic impoverishment' of this anti-culture, the rich American elite have found functional equivalents for a system of moral demands in analysis and art.

> Freud has systematised our unbelief; his is the most inspiring anti-creed yet offered a post-religious culture ... What hope there is derives from Freud's assumption that human nature is not so much a hierarchy of high-low, and good-bad, but rather a jostling democracy of contending predispositions of roughly equal intensities ... Despite the near equality of our warring emotions, Freud hoped that somehow reason would cleverly manage to reassert itself (so that clarity) about oneself could supersede devotion to an ideal as the model of right conduct ... A man can be made healthier without being made better—rather morally worse. Not the good life but better living is the therapeutic standard ... the Americans were the first to realise that this popular standard is not difficult to follow.

This is certainly one possible interpretation of Freud's teaching on the ego, though not the one Freud applied to his own personal life. The man who produced that vast body of work to the very end of his long life, the man who in spite of this never became rich, the man who lived all his married life in Vienna in the same house was scarcely motivated by asking only 'for more goods, more housing, more leisure'. And the man who regarded morals as a matter of course believed in the good life more than in better living. Nor does Rieff's description of his American elite correspond to any of my acquaintances here in Scotland, perhaps because they are neither rich, leisured nor psychoanalysed enough.

If the ego were a 'territory' and a topographical concept it would have no place in dynamic psychology. Only if the ego is a truly dynamic concept, namely the subject and starting point of wills and other motivations, can one ask which motivating energies are attributed to the ego; how they are organised and interlinked; how stable and how strong this organisation is; how this organisation can be altered. Only when the ego is not seen as a natural-scientific entity can one realise that cultural and social conditions determine which motivations have to be attributed to the ego and which are apperceived as originating in autonomous subjects and forces. Irregularities in ego boundaries and multiplicity of personality become comprehensible, and the interconnection of the ego with the other autonomous subjects and forces which are apperceived becomes visible; for the first subject which is apperceived by the infant is the mother and not the ego, and the ego grows in content and power at the expense of and in conflict with the other subjects, often by way of symbolic murders of these.

Jung realised the dynamic nature of the ego by calling it a complex and he concurrently emphasised that it was only one of a multiplicity of similar complexes though it might be a *primus inter pares*. The organisation and unification of these complexes is apperceived largely as autonomous and not an ego activity. One finds or discovers one's true self and does not create it by thinking alone. The organisation of the complexes and their symbolic representation is based not on the logics of factual sciences but on purposive thinking. For example, the most important complex apart from the ego, the mother complex, represents needs and desires of the child. Symbols of the mother complex, such as the night or nature, gratify some needs which are part of the mother complex: they embrace, contain and shelter, they have need-fulfilling qualities in common with the mother *imago* but no factual features. From the point of view of factual thinking these identifications are irrational. The same applies to all the other complexes including the ego as it is pre-scientifically apperceived. In it opposites are united and contradictory tendencies have to be tolerated. And because the organisation and unity of the ego is irrational it can be apperceived only in imagery, the most important image being the body image.

Freud's topographical concept of the ego correlates with his fundamental dogma that all basic dynamism originates in sex and aggression and that these instincts belong to the id. One needs to free oneself from this dogma if one wants to study empirically what is meant by the (pre-scientific) concept of the ego. Two semantic ambiguities influenced Freud's teaching. There are two meanings to the word 'energy', the older one which relates to motivating forces, the other the modern scientific concept of physical energy. By falsely assuming that the motivating energies are of the same nature as the physical energies Freud claims not only that they are quantifiable, but also that they are constant and exist also when not visibly activated in outgoing love and hate. They then exist invisibly in the totally unknown id.

The term 'instinct' or *'Trieb'* is equally ambiguous. The Latin word *instingere* refers to motivation by forces outside the ego, such as the prompting by gods or by rage or by influences of the masses, e.g. through battle cries and songs. Today we still use the word instinctive in this sense when we say, for example, 'I distrusted him instinctively', 'instinctively I looked round and saw you'. In all these phrases 'instinctive' means that one acted for reasons for which the ego cannot account, one was guided by autonomous motives other than the ego's deliberate will. In this usage 'instincts' by definition do not belong to the ego and this is their only characteristic. They are defined by their autonomy but not by the content of the motivation. The German word *'Trieb'* which Freud uses emphasises this original meaning of 'instinct' still more strongly. The 'I' is the passive subject of the *'Trieb'*: 'I am driven' by a force outside the ego in contrast to 'I will' or 'I act' or 'I desire' when the ego is the active subject.

A second concept of 'instinct' compares animal and human behaviour. Animals behave instinctively while man can act consciously and rationally. Here 'instinctive' again does not relate to the content of animal action nor to what modern biology describes as 'instinctive behaviour patterns'. It emphasises that animals react to their experiences immediately, whereas man can stand back, apperceive what he experiences in symbols (either the symbols of language or of other symbolic forms) and is thus able to apply reason to his reactions. This differentiation played a large part in Neoplatonic philosophy. Plotinus is said to have been the first to describe the ego as only a part of the whole psyche, namely the part which is in contact with reason.

In Christian thinking these ideas united with the Biblical teaching that only man was given a Divine soul. He had to care for this Divine part by controlling his animalic tendencies. Now the instincts became urges characterised by content. In particular, sex was apperceived as animalic and as an instinct outside human morality. This hybrid of prescientific philosophical ideas Freud took over; and he added the equally non-scientific idea that the instincts are equivalents of physical energies. Now instincts were defined as quantifiable energies of specific content (sex and aggression) which did not belong to the potentially reasonable ego. According to Anna Freud the instincts on their way to gratification pass through the ego as through alien territory. This not only perpetuates Neoplatonic and Christian prejudices against the passions and against sex, but is also totally out of touch with all empirical observations about how man apperceives himself and the world.

Most people regard both their erotic activities and their hate or aggression as ego activities, and are prepared to accept full responsibility for them except when the erotic or aggressive urges are of of such strength or suddenness that they are beyond ego control. Yet this is quite a different question. If the ego is faced with uncontrollable urges or emotions it is inclined to reject responsibility for them irrespective of whether they are sex or rage or fear or sudden shock or overwhelming aesthetic impressions. The ego then feels overcome irrespective of whether or not the forces which are overcoming it are instincts in Freud's sense. It is necessary to get his dogma out of the way, that Eros and aggression belong to the id, if one wants to study empirically how one apperceives oneself as a dynamic subject.

V. The Therapeutic Aim

Freud's therapeutic aim is to increase rational ego control by wider consciousness of the demands of the id and the superego. Knowledge of what is going on unconsciously gives the ego the chance to decide rationally about whether or not to give in to the tendencies of the id and superego. Whether the ego wants to make use of its chance to act rationally is left to the ego to decide.

Jung too aims at increased consciousness, but what he means by this is not defined simply. In the definitions at the end of his *Psychological Types* he describes 'consciousness' as the relatedness of psychic contents to the ego. Consciousness is the function or activity which sustains this relatedness. The ego is defined as a complex which is the centre of the field of consciousness and which is of high continuity or identity. It both represents the content of consciousness and is one of the conditions which makes consciousness possible by relating the psychic content to the ego. Consciousness and ego are interlinked corollaries. Additional knowledge of what was previously unconscious is not enough to increase consciousness; the new knowledge has also to be related to the ego complex. Increased consciousness therefore means to Jung a variety of different things:

(1) *It means widening the ego complex by integrating into it motive forces which previously were integrated in other autonomous complexes.* The ego becomes aware of and takes responsibility for new contents of which formerly the ego was either unaware (unconscious) or of which it was aware as something alien to itself.

(2) One may be aware of certain urges such as sexual desires, but the ego may regard them as totally foreign to itself and be compelled to defend itself against them in every way. *Increasing consciousness may mean a change of the ego to a maturer state in which the ego can realise its power to deal with these desires other than by regarding them as totally alien.* An example of this would be the case of a physiotherapist who after treating attractive women usually developed irrational fears that he had made sexual advances toward them. His immature ego was afraid of all sexual desire both as overpowering and guilty. Realisation of the grown-up ego's greater powers of self-control allowed him to admit to his desires without fear of being overpowered, and therefore without guilt or need to punish himself with remorse for purely imaginary transgressions.

(3) *The ego may regard actions or other behaviour as ego activity when in fact motivation comes from other autonomous complexes. Increased consciousness clarifies this.* For example, the ego may regard blushing as ego activity and try in vain to control it consciously. Increased consciousness brings it home that the blushing is caused by other autonomous complexes. Then one might be kind to someone, regarding that as genuine feeling of the ego, but in fact rather acting out the role of good parent, or using the kindness to camouflage a most unkind 'shadow' complex. Recognition of the autonomous complex may be followed by its integration into the ego (as for example in the case of the unkind shadow) or a lasting conscious relationship may be established between the ego and the autonomous complex, freeing the ego from compulsion to play the role of this complex. This would for example be the case were a place found for the complex of the good parent in 'Nature' or the Godhead.

(4) An autonomous complex may be projected on to another person so that one cannot be aware of the reality of that person but only of one's projected image. *Here becoming conscious means becoming aware of the projection with the result that the reality which was hidden by the projection becomes visible.* The ego then has to come to terms with the projected complex in the ways described under (2), either by integrating it into the ego or by establishing a complex relationship with the complex, which then retains its separate identity but without projection taking place.

The ego is experienced as centre and subject of motivations. Through its feelings, needs and fears the ego is interlinked with other persons, things and autonomous complexes. Therapy aims at changing ego motives and the apperception of the wish-fulfilling or fear-inspiring quality of what is not ego. It does not aim at replacing the emotive ego with a detached rational thinker, nor the dissolution and eradication of all autonomous complexes, archetypes or every apperceived subject other than the ego. Therefore knowledge and rational control are neither enough nor the most essential part of therapy.

Dynamic Psychology and Truth

Dynamic psychology studies the prescientific apperceptions of self and the world which have influenced our behaviour. It deals with subjective modes of experiencing, with the subjective interpretation of all our experiences. It is a worthwhile study both because of the influence these apperceptions have upon all our behaviour, and because a regularity of these apperceptions and their interconnections can be found which helps to understand them. The aim of dynamic psychology differs from that of the natural sciences, insofar as in them every attempt is made to get away from subjective interpretations and reach findings which are objective in the sense of factual and irrespective of the wishes, fears or preconceived ideas of the individual. Many people today regard this type of objectivity as the only possible aim of an empirical study, and many dynamic psychologists, above all Freud, have believed that psychology could claim to be scientific only if an objective basis for it could be found.

Thus the physical basis of instincts was looked for in erotogenic zones, and that of the ego in a cortical layer. The assumption that everything psychic must originate in the *soma* may be right, but verification of that can be made only through the research methods of the physical sciences and not with the methods of dynamic psychology. What Freud did show was not that the so-called life instinct originates in the region of the mouth, anus or genitals, but that all kinds of emotive and motivational apperceptions become related to early instinctive behaviour patterns of sucking or defæcation or genital sensations.

Another attempt to create an objective science of dynamic psychology was made by looking for basic drives and impulses which were supposed to explain all subjective apperceptions and the behaviour resulting from them. The search for the basic biological motives should establish dynamic psychology as a branch of biology. Yet dynamic psychology does not search for biological facts but treats them as a matter of course, as every science does with regard to findings of other sciences which it has to take into account though unable to verify them with the research methods it itself applies. That the human baby is born with the instinctive behaviour pattern of sucking is taken for granted. That this behaviour pattern serves the biological purpose of nourishment is so much a matter of course to the dynamic psychologist that he may justifiably ignore it over the various other needs which the infant apperceives as being satisfied by his oral activities: such as the longing for care, unity, trust, freedom from responsibility, reassurance against anxiety, et cetera. It is these last-mentioned needs which later motivate significant oral activities, whilst the universal need for nourishment is without particular interest in this context.

'Basic motivation' can of course also be understood as referring to the earliest motivations which are apperceived and which are most important for psychic development. Yet here we are no longer speaking of objective biology but of subjective apperceptions of subjective needs and gratifying agents (which is to say, active subjects).

In recent years animal ethology has revived the hope that dynamic psychology could become a branch of objective biology, because some animal behaviour resembles in a rudimentary way human motivation. Yet if a dragonfly or a bird defends its territory it does this for the purpose of excluding competition in its hunting area, or for breeding purposes. These purposes play nearly no role if the Englishman regards his home as his castle. His children are born in a nursing home and are sent to a boarding school and business is not mentioned at home. He may invite guests, have servants or boarders and may permit the police to search the home if they have a valid warrant. None of this can a dragonfly do, nor has it any inkling of what man means by privacy. Such crude resemblances between animal and human behaviour add little if anything to our understanding of human motivation (though our knowledge of human motivation may sometimes help us understand animal behaviour).

The truth which dynamic psychology wants to discover is, what subjectively motivates a man's behaviour; which forces and agents he subjectively apperceives as being at work. This search is made difficult because one is not conscious of many of the forces and agents which are active. The unconscious forces and agents which we discover by the various methods of analysis are however of the same nature as the motivating forces and agents of which we are conscious. They too are subjective apperceptions, most often fantastic interpretations of the infant's or young child's experiences, or equally fantastic apperceptions of his own powers and of the powers outside himself. In other words dynamic psychology looks for links between subjective apperceptions. And because the subjective apperceptions are interlinked it is possible to verify the findings of dynamic psychology.

It is the context which justifies a psychological interpretation. If someone is not punctual for a meeting, he may be hostile to the other person whom he is meeting; he may have been detained by an important phone call; he may have a psychological block about being punctual which has nothing to do with the specific person he is meeting. Only the context of the person's other behaviour allows a statement about what has motivated the delay. Therefore verification of motives is done with the help of the hermeneutic circle in which all the particular observations interpret the general statements and the general interprets the meaning of the particulars.

The generalia which are used in dynamic psychology are mainly of three types.

(a) They either are general aims or general origins of motivating forces, or are both. Examples of general aims are in Freud's terms conscious control of the ego, in Jung's individuation. Examples of general origins of motivation are Freud's 'instincts' or Jung's 'archetypes'. An example of both general origin and general aim is Jung's concept of the Self which is apperceived as the alpha and omega of psychological development.

(b) They are descriptions of apperceptions and of connections of apperceptions which are sufficiently clear to be of help in the understanding of a great number of cases. In other words they are ideotypal descriptions. Myths and folklore may serve as such descriptions, as for example the Oedipus myth or Jung's reference to the night sea journey of the hero. Or they may be individual case histories which are particularly well studied and show relatively clear connections between relatively clearly described apperceptions. I am emphasising the aspect of 'relatively clearly' for none of the concepts used by dynamic psychology is free from ambiguity. We have to be satisfied if the descriptions evoke in the listener relatively clear ideas which are within his own emotive grasp. Some apperceptions appear together so frequently that we have to assume that an emotive connection exists between them, as for example between paranoiac delusions and homosexuality, or between obsessional doubting and orderliness. Yet we are not interested in statistical findings about the frequency of such coincidences: this is not only because most of the emotive concepts of dynamic psychology are not clear enough for statistical purposes, but also because the discovery of the emotive connections between the apperceptions does not depend on statistical verification. Neither statistics nor experiments help us understand the subjective apperceptions which concern the dynamic psychologist. Both these methods lead away from the individual subjectivity fo the phenomena we are interested in.

(c) Most people, and certainly dynamic psychologists, have some general ideas about what man is and about his place in the whole of existence. These ideas are usually clearly recognised as philosophical or religious beliefs and are helpful for orientation as long as one does not regard them as objective scientific truth; and as long as one remains aware that they are beliefs which are held in spite of doubt and uncertainty.

The concept of the ego is a general concept in each of the three senses I have just described. It is the origin (subject) of motivating forces and we therapeutically aim at ego development and ego strength. We can describe the ego only in ideotypal ways. And the apperception of oneself as ego is influenced by what one regards as human, and (which also influences these beliefs) what the place of the individual and of each sex is in society, and what the place of man is in the whole of being.

Reflections on Gunter Grass's Novel *Die Blechtrommel*: 'The Tin Drum'

Man is a vain creature. When we reflect about man we usually think of what we regard as the true man, that is, we think of an ideal. The truly human being is a gentleman to the English, *ein Gebildete* to the Germans, a nobleman to the Chinese, a *talmid chacham* (a Talmud scholar) to the orthodox Jew; and every other civilisation has similar ideal concepts of man. As long as the civilisation is strong and its valuations are generally accepted these concepts are not experienced as idealisations, but, to be a gentleman is natural to the extent that nobody but a gentleman counts. Everybody is naively expected to be a gentleman even if he has been brought up in an entirely different civilisation. If he is not a gentleman he is not worth bothering about and can usually can be ignored.

Certainly there is in all civilisations too an awareness of the non-civilised ordinary man or foreign outsider, but the names by which he is known bring home the disdain with which he is regarded. Thus the Greeks called him idiot, the Jews *am ha-aretz* (country yokel), we call him boor, boorish, or one of the wogs who begin at Calais. The concept of the ordinary man has usually been, in a negative sense, no less unrealistic and idealistic than the image of the true man. He has been just the opposite of the true ideal man. The Greeks regarded the ability to be reasonable as one of the characteristics of being truly human. The ordinary man was therefore regarded as stupid and idiotic.

A poetic description of the uncivilised man of the late Middle Ages is Caliban in Shakespeare's *The Tempest*. He is a direct descendant of the so-called Wild Men of the Middle Ages, hairy beast-like creatures, the mediaeval image of the natural man outside Christian civilisation. Caliban is characterised mainly by the absence of all the qualities of a true gentleman. He is ruled exclusively by the base primitive urges over which he has no control. He is unfaithful, disloyal, ungrateful, lecherous, a lump of brute strength who needs a stern master. Yet this uncivilised inhuman creature has also positive qualities which civilised man lacks, he is nearer nature and knows where there are fresh springs and fertile ground, and Prospero depends on his help in finding them. In spite of this Prospero's attitude to Caliban is totally negative, he treats him as a slave who has to be kept in constant fear.

This negative attitude toward the natural man changes usually only in times of cultural crisis, when old values come into doubt and are attacked by revolutionary forces. Then people turn to the natural man, uncorrupted by civilisation, who makes established values appear unnatural, questionable and invalid. The natural man is then seen as a being of pristine innocence, of uncorrupted naturalness, a being who has remained in touch with the primal concerns of living and existence. Therefore a return to a state of nature should cure the dying civilisation. In the French Revolution Rousseau's ideas inspired the revolutionaries. In the two big revolutions in our century, the Communists and the Fascists also rebelled in the name of the common man against the establishment. All the valuations of the bourgeois were regarded as corrupted by his striving for possessions and capital. The proletarian alone was still in touch with the values which really mattered, collective solidarity and co-operation, concern with the essential needs of life, realism and simplicity. This was the original Communist belief.

The German Nazi revolution too took place in the name of the common man and his contact with the primal values of *Blut und Boden*, blood and soil, against the sophisticated bourgeoisie and their supposed corrupters, the Jews. To understand the appeal of the Nazi ideology one has to consider the values of the establishment against which it rebelled. *Bildung* was the distinction of true humanity according to German ideas of the nineteenth and the beginning of the twentieth century. It meant to be educated and formed by German and world literature, to have an educated taste in the arts and music, to be interested in the philosophical ideas of Kant and his followers, and to have a fine introverted and individual sense of ethics. To feel justified before one's own conscience was more important than to have the approval of society. Social responsibility towards the community and the church played only a negligible role in *Bildung* and *Bildung* was quite non-political.

The ideal of other nations, for instance the English gentleman, originated in the style of life of the ruling classes, as progressively adopted by the whole nation. In contrast to this the German ruling classes, the princes and nobility, had no specific style of life of their own which could be communicated to the nation; and *Bildung* was the ideal of a bourgeoisie excluded from participation in political power. It was an ideal of the non-political *Untertan* or subject, with the help of which he upheld his dignity and self-esteem, in spite of being politically powerless. He himself did not of course realise this. The *Gebildete* regarded himself as the truly human being, and as such destined to rule. He believed *Bildung* was power, a belief also shared by the labour movement in the form of believing that education was power. This belief was extraordinarily strong and resistant to correction. The defeat of the revolution of the educated bourgeoisie against the absolute power of the princes in 1848 affected it as little as Nietzsche's ridicule of it.

Nietzsche saw from the start that in the *Kaiserreich* it was the army and the big industrialists who ruled, not the *Gebildeten*; but the *Bildungsphilis-*

ter, the educated philistines, dismissed this as one of those outrageous overstatements of his which could be ignored. When in 1918 the German ruling classes collapsed, political power fell into the hands of a bourgeoisie and a labour movement which were equally unprepared for it. They were unaware what political power was, how it was to be maintained, unaware of how to create leaders and how to be led. It was in this atmosphere that the Nazi movement grew up. Nazism preached the return to the will to power which according to Nietzsche was the basic urge of all beings. The old Teutons were supposed to have had it in its natural strength, but Christian teachings and bourgeois morals had corrupted it and produced slave morals instead.

The end of Hitler greatly weakened the Nazi movement but it did not strengthen correspondingly the position of the former establishment in Germany. In wide circles of the younger generation the traditional values were felt to be not so much corrupt as inadequate in the new situation in which they found themselves. Symptoms of this discontent of youth were manifold. Where it found literary expression it was mainly nihilistic, all the known values were criticised and no new valid ideals were discovered. All ended in alcoholic and sexual debauchery.

Where a new beginning was looked for, the eternal recipe of searching for a return to a state of innocence was applied. As all conscious thinking and intention had become suspect, natural innocence had to be sought in a time prior to the development of modern thought or outside of consciousness altogether. Heidegger went back to the pre-Socratic thinkers and interpreted them as if they had an immediacy of knowledge about man in the world which had been lost since their time. Others hoped to find a new basis of life in Jung's Collective Unconscious. American beatniks were influenced by teachings of Zen Buddhism with a total rejection of the ego and will, concepts which were fundamental to the whole of European thought. All these attempts to find a new starting point had in common that they were political only in their rejection of all political parties and aims; they all wanted to contact the regenerating basic forces not by collective social action but only individually.

Gunter Grass's 1959 novel *Die Blechtrommel* (*The Tin Drum*) belongs to this literature which rejects the whole of present civilisation and looks for a cure of our discontent in a return to a state of innocence. It is distinguished by a new and remarkable vision of the state of innocence, and it is about that vision that I want to speak. I am not going to discuss Grass's art in general, his considerable narrative and linguistic gifts, his bawdy humour, his style, the much criticised length of the novel (it runs to 734 pages) unless that helps describe his vision of the innocent today.

The style of this, Grass's first novel, is obviously influenced by the theories of German expressionism. Like most works of art the book is full of symbolism, but in order to give the symbols full expressive power and intensity the author feels free to distort reality and to deviate from it in the most fantastic way. In Britain we know this expressionist symbolism less from modern than from mediaeval art, where the artist represented Jesus as much bigger than the tormenting soldiers, thus translating His spiritual importance into visible superior physical size.

Grass uses a similar method to characterise the fictitious autobiographer of his book, Oskar. All ordinary people seem to Grass inflated and over-grown, and therefore his hero decides at birth to stop growing at the age of three, when he is just a yard high. And he stays like this until the end of the war, when he is twenty-one. Even after this he grows only one foot more. Thus he is not only an outsider in the world of grown-ups, he also retains the advantages of the three-year-old's mentality.

Three years is the age when the child explores the world on his own. He is not yet influenced by the cultural traditions and demands which create the grown-up world, and he has outgrown the total dependence of the infant. In Freudian parlance it is the height of the anal aggressive period, the child is unsentimentally selfish and self-assertive. In ordinary language it is the age of the *enfant terrible*, the three-year-old child is unsentimental, he will not express feelings which are not actually present, nor is he bound by tradi-tions, their pretences and illusions. His outlook therefore seems coldly realistic. He is highly sensitive to all falseness of feeling and all make-believe. He does not yet know the stage conventions of the plays grown-ups play, and therefore takes the world at its face value.

For example, when he sees the lovemaking of grown-ups he sees nothing of the exalted meaning it is supposed to have, his observations are simply factual and strike us as at the same time bawdy and innocent. He sees what is conventionally ignored, but sees that with an objectivity which is erotically not stimulating or exciting. Oskar's ability to see through and smash all pretences is represented by a fantastic expressionist symbol: he has the ability to sing in such a way that any glass he wishes to smash will crack and burst into pieces. Nothing as brittle and pretentious as glass is, can withstand him. Thus in the surgery of a pretentious doctor, consulted about the stoppage of Oskar's growth and not admitting to his ignorance of the condition, the boy smashes all the specimen bottles. In another scene Oskar smashes the glass dome of the theatre, this grand purveyor of pretentiousness.

The vehicle and perpetuator of all social make-believe is of course our language. So Oskar for the first twenty-one years of his life falls in with the suggestions of the grown-ups that he has remained in a baby state, and he finds it convenient to speak only baby-talk though perfectly capable of not only speech but writing and reading as well. Instead of speaking he makes noises on the tin drum of the book's title. The drum is his faithful and essential companion in his loneliness, his consolation when he is afraid, maltreated or embarrassed. Again, just as with the glass, Grass makes use here of a symbolism of noise-making and drumming well known in anthropology as well as in psychiatry. Making noise fills the empty world with one's own creation, it keeps evil spirits at bay and reassures: that is exactly what noisy maniacs in hospital experience. It is also the meaning of the drummer procesion round the precincts of the town, staged yearly before Lent in the Swiss town of Basle. In Oskar's case his drumming becomes more and more expressive, so that in the end it communicates feelings and mental images more effectively than any language could do. Simply by drumming, Oskar can transform at will his listeners into babies who wet their pants, or into little children who are afraid of such bogeys as the *Schwarze Köchin*, the black cook figure from a German nursery rhyme.

Oskar the three-year-old is of course amoral because no tradition means anything to him. He is not however evil or callous as mediaeval thinkers, and even Shakespeare, thought the uncivilised man must be. Grass even makes the point that the amoral Oskar is no worse than anybody else. For a while Oskar amuses himself by singing a hole into shop windows whenever he sees a passer-by looking covetously at some exhibit. Rarely does anybody miss the chance to steal the object. Even the chief public prosecutor cannot withstand the temptation. Grass's point seems to be that if one strips man of his pretences and social make-believe, he does not act much different from a three-year-old who follows immediate impulses only, and has little foresight and even less lasting remorse or regret for the past. It would even be better if grown-ups realised this.

Yet the bulk of Grass's criticism is reserved not for social customs and morals, but for the political activity of man. Here Grass supports the detached objectivity of the three-year-old Oskar by two other devices which show up the pretentiousness and futility of political ideas. Firstly the story up to the end of the war takes place in Danzig and West Prussia, which is to say a region where Polish and German civilisation meet and clash, a district which has constantly changed hands from one to the other through the last thousand years. In consequence the nationalism of the one is constantly made to appear futile, ridiculous or callously destructive by the nationalism of the other; and *vice versa*. To make the mix-up complete, Oskar's grand-mother belongs neither to the Poles nor to the Germans, but to one of those small Slavonic groups which have retained a language of their own and are the butts of both Germans and Poles. So Oskar's mother is half-Kashubic like his grandmother, half-Polish like his grandfather. And when Oskar is born it is never quite clear whether his father was the Rhineland German Mazerath, who had come to Danzig during the First World War, and whom Oskar's mother married; or whether it was her Polish cousin Jan Bronski, her lover before her marriage and thereafter until her death in 1938, when expecting another child by Bronski she tried to abort it, with fatal consequences.

The second device for debunking political ideas is in Grass's beginning the story not with Oskar's birth in 1924 but on the day his mother was conceived in 1899. On that day his Kashubic grandmother was working in the potato fields, when a Pole in flight from the Prussian police found no other place to hide from the pursuing gendarmes save the four wide skirts of Oskar's granny. He hid under them and thus escaped the police. The same evening he married Oskar's grandmother.

Political changes since that time in Germany, more particularly in Danzig, have been so radical and so various that anybody who has not lived there will find it difficult to to understand the effect that that has had on the people and their ideas. Certainly Britain today is also different from Britain in the late Victorian period, or even from the Britain of the 'twenties and 'thirties; yet with all this there is a strongly-felt continuity of existence and of ideas and beliefs. Not so in Germany and Poland. Under the *Kaiserreich* Poles were second-class citizens and Poland as a political power did not exist. Germany and in particular the East Prussian provinces were a military state. In 1918 that state collapsed, the princes abdicated, the army was dissolved, Poland was re-created and Danzig became a free city with a Polish harbour. Less than ten years later German irredentism began, it was stepped up when the Nazis came to power, and in 1939 Danzig was reoccupied by the Germans. Poland was overrun and in 1940 and for the fifth or sixth time in 200 years divided up again between Germany and Russia. Six years later Danzig was burnt down and occupied by the Russians, and returned again to the newly created Communist Poland. Germany was beaten and disorganised and became a black market paradise. And five years after this its industry was booming again.

Each succeeding period made the previous one meaningless and absurd. It is the natural conclusion from all these radical changes that all political systems and aims, even the present one, are absurd. No continuity exists. I experienced this feeling when I visited Baden-Baden after the war. When I lived there in the 'twenties the castle belonged to the pre-republican time, still vividly remembered, and an old dowager grand-duchess still lived in it. When I visited this castle a few years ago it belonged nowhere, not to the present, to the immediate past of the Nazis, or to their predecessors. With its nineteenth-century imitations of Versailles it was too new to be a worthwhile museum piece, while it was too unconnected with present life to be anything else. Grass reflects that when Danzig was burnt down at the end of the war, this was not the first time: it had been successively burnt down by the Pomerells, the Brandenburgians, the German Knights, the Poles, the Swedes, again by the Swedes, the French, the Russians, the people of Saxony. The present burning by the combined efforts of Russians, Poles, Germans and British was just a normal occurrence in an entirely meaningless sequence.

Grass however does not normally think of politics in such historical perspective, but simply from the point of view of the ordinary citizen, and then the business becomes still more fatuous. Bronski, who has been a secretary in the postal service, joins the Polish post office in Danzig after the First World War for no other reason than that that is opportune. Mazerath joins the Nazis in 1934 for no better reason. Neither has particularly strong nationalist feelings, yet both are killed in consequence of their decisions. Bronski is in the Polish post office when the Germans attack it on the first day of the war, and he and all other survivors are court-martialled and executed as *franc-tireurs* by the Germans. Mazerath dies when the Russians occupy Danzig: he wants to hide his party badge by swallowing it, and the open pin gets stuck in his throat.

The war comes into the life of ordinary people first when they get postcards from members of the family who are with the occupying army in Paris, then at the Eastern Front. Then news of the death of family members starts to become more frequent, food becomes scarce, black market deals more rewarding, war news more obviously false. Finally the ordinary fabric of life starts to break up. Young teenagers form secret societies with no other aim than to express their nihilism and with the realisation that the whole of political life is meaningless. One group of such high school boys makes Oskar their leader when he demonstrates to them his ability to break glass by singing. They do not realise that his destructiveness has a meaning totally different from theirs. They are disappointed by the failure of the Nazis to implement their boasts. Oskar is not disappointed, for he never believed any boast of the grown-ups. They were never anything but pretences to him. He is destructive against everything false and spurious, and not because he is disappointed.

It is however in this gang of nihilist youngsters that Oskar for the first time gets the idea that he in his childlike realism and objectivity may be the saviour who ought to gather disciples around him. This motif is fully developed only at the end of the book, for Oskar's leadership of the gang of youngsters is short-lived. After a few months the gang is caught by the police in the act of stealing holy images from a Catholic church, and the youngsters are executed by the Nazis. Oskar is regarded as an irresponsible imbecile, and the Nazis urge his father to consent to his annihilation. Before this can happen, however, the Russians overrun the town and Oskar remains alive.

The collapse and dissolution of the whole social fabric of Germany brings about a deep crisis in Oskar's life. Though he is now twenty-one years old he has not developed. His personality has remained that of a three-year-old who has had a great variety of experiences, but these have remained a chain of isolated events. They have not produced the unified whole of a matured personality. He has matured physically, but his sexual maturity is no more than a new appetite, and the addition of sex experiences to the chain of other experiences. A *Bildung*, whereby every present moment in a personality's life would inherently contain the whole history of that personality, has not occurred for him. The past exists only as a row of memories which again and again have to be enumerated and retold to give them presence at all. Oskar is a striking example of Hume's theory of personality which regarded the existence of a unified self as an illusion, for nothing more exists than a chain of memories.

The collapse of Germany destroyed the world of cultural pretence and of political make-believe and ideology. Now man had to be concerned only with the immediate task of survival and in consequence had become real. Oskar's voice lost, therefore, its power to destroy glass, for all the sterile pretences had collapsed. He stopped drumming and began to grow and to become more like other grown-ups. He grew into a hunchback four feet tall.

He is evacuated from Danzig together with his stepmother Maria and her son Kurt, whose paternity is again as doubtful as Oskar's own—for Maria was intimate with Oskar when an adolescent girl, and when she subsequently married Mazerath she may or may not already gave been pregnant by Oskar. They go to Dusseldorf, where Maria has a married sister. There Oskar finds work as a mason in a gravestone yard.

The period proved, however, short-lived, when people were real because they were concerned with their essential needs. It ended with the currency reform and the new prosperity in Germany.

Oskar drifts away from ordinary life again into outsider jobs, first becoming a model in the art school. Later, having resumed his drumming, he becomes a professional drummer. The new world of make-believe is different from the pre-war period, though no less spurious. Grass calls it the new *Biedermeyer*.

Biedermeyer was a style of life of the non-political German bourgeoisie of the middle nineteenth century; a smug, self-centred and self-satisfied way of caring for one's own well-being and for nothing else. The *Biedermeyer* world is an entirely private world; politics play no role in it. Yet the new *Biedermeyer* differs from that of a century earlier in that it is self-consciously uneasy about its self-satisfaction and knows that its feelings are false. Grass again invents striking expressionist symbols for this.

There is for example an institute where pets can be hired, such as a dog to take out for an afternoon. Even the love of a pet is a make-believe and should be free from the need to care for the pet. Still more grisly and funny is the Onion Cellar, an expensive night club where at a certain time of night onions, chopping boards and knives are distributed to the guests. They by chopping the onions produce a common orgy of crying; these people could only get in touch with any feeling with such help.

In this new *Biedermeyer* Oskar is somewhat more at home than in the pre-war world, for he too is non-political and believes that we should care for our nearest interests; politics usually is a megalomaniac flight from the human-sized world into superhuman pretences. His drumming is just that small-sized and primitive music which fits this new world, and he becomes a world celebrity. Yet he knows that he is superior to his audiences, for he has preserved genuineness of feeling and thus immediacy of contact with the urges and emotions of the child. So the idea of being the Saviour grows in him again, and the book ends with Oskar staging a repetition of Jesus' Passion. With his connivance a friend denounces him to the authorities, and he is found guilty of murdering a hospital nurse though in fact innocent of the crime. Because he is considered insane he is buried in a mental hospital for three years—as Christ was in the tomb for three days. Then the real culprit is discovered and we leave Oskar just about to be released or resurrected, and contemplating whether he should go into the world to look for disciples.

This is the barest outline of a story bursting with bizarre, horrific and funny events and people, and told with a lightness and ease which is rare in German. That it is more than just a jolly good tale can be seen in Oskar's doubt whether he is Jesus. This is more than blasphemous madness. Though as funnily critical of modern church decorations and art in Catholic churches, and the clergy, as he is of other aspects of our civilisation, Grass respects what is genuine in the Catholic faith. We get an indication of this when, before the war, Oskar tries to smash with his voice a stained-glass window which has in it the dove as symbol of the Holy Ghost. For the first time his voice is powerless. This window was obviously not sterile and brittle, it still contained life which could resist Oskar's destructive singing. Oskar's mother, and later Maria, his stepmother, who is reconverted to Roman Catholicism, get some genuine help and strength from going to church. Grass restrains his withering criticism when describing this.

The importance of the book I see in its not being nihilistic though as critical of the establishment and of our civilisation as any book I know. It contains a vision of the return to innocence and health which is entirely novel. Nihilists are disappointed men, having longed originally for an all-good all-loving, all-wise world. In not getting it their longing for perfection has turned into disappointed and destructive nothingness. Oskar the three-year-old is not disappointed. He turns to the world with a curious and inquiring mind, and if he finds most of the behaviour of grown-ups phoney he simply registers that fact; he has not expected anything otherwise. He only wants to discover the reality, he does not judge and still less does he condemn. The political ideas and philosophies and the other aspects of our civilisation which he sees, condemn themselves by their objective insincerity and contradictions, and by their senselessly destructive results.

And just because Oskar expects nothing he is also safeguarded against the other common dangers of disappointed men. They may try to represent what they longed for outside and could not find there. They try to be the all-loving ones and produce only faked sentimentality; or they try to be the all-knowing ones and become intolerant controllers and censorious superiors, or they replace the all-powerful father and become destructive dictators. They all become supermen and magicians or sentimentalists, and it is here that Oskar's refusal to grow big coincides with one of the basic aims of the Christian religion, namely to teach man humbly to accept that his strength is 'most faint' (as Shakespeare says in *The Tempest*). Oskar can believe that he has a message even for the Churches and their members, because so much of what they teach gives the impression that the ideals of goodness and love can be got for the mere wishing and pretending; and thus Church life is pervaded by sentimentality. The Christian injunction that we should become like children is usually understood to mean that we should be trusting, nice and obedient as grown-ups wish children to be (so that they may cause them no trouble). This is a sentimental view of childhood. Grass asks the question, which seems obvious and yet is entirely new, whether we should not be as children really are, instead of as grown-ups wish them to be. Oskar is as innocent as man can be, but he is also free from spurious goodness and sentimental love. He is actively interested in the real world which he explores, and therefore not vacantly obedient to spurious grown-ups. With all this he is more genuinely humble than children who submit to the pretences of grown-ups and help them perpetuate their illusions.

Most present-day literature is markedly anti-romantic, yet most frequently what has become bitter or cynical derives from the disappointments of the writers. Oskar the autobiographer is objective not cynical, and innocent not bitter. He does not praise cruelty as Nietzsche and Rilke do in order to ward off their own romantic longings. Oskar simply registers cruelty as part of objective reality. He is more genuinely non-romantic than those who have violently to fight Romanticism. And just for this reason love and sex find a more natural place in Oskar's life than in the ideas of so many anti-Romantic writers. He can acknowledge his longing for protective mother love without being consumed by this longing and deflected from his acceptance of the cold reality. All his life Oskar is attracted to the clean hospital nurses as the caring, mothering helpers. When he once mistakes his regard for them for sexual love he finds himself impotent. Love of mothering helpers is not sexual love. On the other hand sexual love is not debunked or devalued because it is unlike the mother-child relationship. Oskar has a deep regard for the essential decency of his former mistress and later stepmother, Maria, and at the end of the book he contemplates whether he should marry her as an alternative to going into the world and gathering disciples.

In general Grass's women are healthier, more down to earth and concerned with concrete, immediate tasks than men are. Some of them have quite clearly a mythical and timeless character, like the grandmother as the great earth mother, the hospital nurses as the angelic mothers, and the *Schwarze Köchin* as the destructive aspect of Mother Nature. Women are nearer nature than men, and far less exposed to the distortion and corruption of civilisation unless as its victims.

It is the men who represent civilisation and who lose their support and direction if the civilisation is rotten. There is not one man in the book who is not affected by this, none has really found his place, all are somehow funny, queer, ineffectual and to a degree lost. It is the world of the father which is in disorder and has collapsed. Grass symbolises this by the fact that the paternity of Oskar and Maria's son Kurt is doubtful; and by Oskar being partially responsible for the death of both his potential fathers, Bronski and Mazerath.

This decline and eclipse of the male principle is something frightening and new to us in the remembered part of our own history. The people of the East with their much longer memory of cultural changes within their own civilisation know of this in the form of typical situations in social and individual history. The Chinese *I Ching*, a Taoist oracle book at least 2300 years old, but probably much older, describes this as one of the typical situations in both human and social life. It discusses sixty-four typical human and social situations and the last of these is actually called 'the exhaustion of the male principle.' Nothing in this situation is in its rightful place, all is in disorder. This is an alarming state of transition when all can be lost if one impatiently insists on improving the situation quickly; but it can be the prelude to a new beginning if one has the endurance to wait until new life, and with it new orientation, grows again. Grass's own attitude seems to harmonise with this Chinese wisdom. Within the political field he wants to instil a healthy distrust of all political philosophies. This is important not only for the Germans, who through the past 150 years have again and again got intoxicated by such general political philosophies, with the most catastrophic results; and who at the same time neglected to cultivate a neighbourly regard for their fellow men. It is good advice for all.

The democratic influence of the individual on our political fate is minimal particularly in Europe, where political events depend more on what America and Russia will do, than on what we do ourselves. We intoxicate ourselves with the daily political news in newspapers, radio and television, and allow that to distract our attention from our nearest concerns which we can actively and effectively influence. The political control of the individual today is mainly a negative one, of being on guard against being carried away by high-sounding slogans and idelogies, and against their purveyors, the ambitious men who become politicians.

For the rest, let's live our private lives not as a romantic idyll, a *'stiller Garten,'* the peaceful garden of the Biedermeyer, nor as an exotic Zen Buddhistic abdication of all will, but love with the keen curiosity and awareness of the three-year-old Oskar, with his courageous objectivity and freedom from illusions, in the humility of knowing the limitations of his strength and stature. Grass's fantastic and humorous story contains a message which is worthy of being taken seriously.

Patrick White's *Voss*

On its most superficial level this is a historical novel about Australia in 1845, when a German explorer undertook an expedition into the still unexplored interior of the continent. White depicts the society of Sydney and other parts of the country convincingly. Some scenes, such as Mrs. Pringle's picnic at Point Piper, or the harbour scene on the day when the expedition embarks, become as vividly visual as a period film by Jean Renoir. However, in his choice of the historical setting White is already more than a historian. His book deals not only with the Australia of a bygone period, but with colonial life in general. How is it possible to go to a strange country as a colonial and be at home there? One can even go two steps further: how is it possible to emigrate to anywhere, as has been the fate of unnumbered millions of people in our day? And how is it possible to be at home anywhere, even for people who live where they are born and where their ancestors lived?

White describes three groups of settlers who are all in different ways not at home in and with Australia.

There are settlers who come to the country as greenfly to roses. They want to earn a living, to get rich quickly, and nothing else matters. Their lives must be conducted in some form, so they bring with them a convention of social behaviour, of church affiliation and of education; but all this is unoriginal, unrelated to their real concerns and unrelated to the country where they are. Certainly they have their well-built houses and well cared-for gardens, and they go to beauty spots for picnics; but all this could be anywhere in the world. The houses and gardens are just means of asserting their affluence, and of protecting themselves against dealing with their human reality by displaying economic superiority and security. At the picnic the men soon settle down to discussing the only thing which is real, namely business; while the women and the young folk are engaged in catering, in their superficial vanities, and in matchmaking. The paradox of the life of these people is that they belong nowhere and yet are totally creatures of their period, because related to no transcending values.

Settlers of a different type are the Sandersons in Rhine Towers. It is said of Mr Sanderson that in other times and circumstances he might have been a monk. What makes him monk-like is that he is not of this world but brings his own world with him wherever he goes. It is a dignified world with a rich and varied heritage, a tradition of respect for other people, from the natives and emancipated convicts up to the people of his own class. In the same way the land is treated respectfully, yet only so that people and land willingly contribute in recreating the world of the English gentry. Rhine Towers is a well run English estate and nothing there is indigenous to Australia.

Finally there is Boyle, the man who emigrated because he did not want to be at home anywhere, not even in his new country. He is 'of that order of males who will destroy any distinction with which they have been born because it accuses them'. He has done well for himself in Australia, but lives in a disgusting hovel. He has to display indifference to possessions and is interested only in himself, but negatively, 'to explore the depths of his own repulsive nature'.

Now why is White so interested in the question of being related to the country? Is this simply the romantic longing for being rooted and at home somewhere? White is not afraid of Romanticism (as I shall have to discuss later) but his insistence on at-homeness in the country has a deeper meaning. To be at home in the place where I live is an aspect of what the Germans with one of their vague but widely suggestive terms call *'Dasein'*. It is a dimension of existence. In an exalted moment Voss at one point says, 'I begin to receive proof of existence, Brother Mueller. I can feel the shape of the earth'. White regards lack of relatedness to the land as one of the main causes of the shallowness of Australian life and by making this one of the themes of his book he deals with one of the central difficulties of Australian existence.

In this sense *Voss* is an Australian novel tackling a burning Australian problem. In Australia the immigrant was not as in other countries faced with getting adjusted to an indigenous population and civilisation. He simply had to deal with the strange land. It is not enough to visit and admire beauty spots, or to have a house and garden somewhere, or even to farm there. Acquaintaince with a country grows only slowly; she wants to be courted, lived and struggled with, 'one has to be suffered in and by it'. It is a task for which even 'eternity is not too long'.

The man who goes out to explore Australia is the German, Voss. Certainly he has diverse motives for this enterprise, but one of the deepest is *'ein Land mit der Seele suchen'*, to search for a land with his soul. Voss says of himself, 'I will cross the continent from one end to the other. I have every intention to know it *with my heart*. Why am I pursued by this necessity it is not possible for me to tell".

This is typically German, Voss like so many Germans is awkward in his relationship with his fellow-men: stiff, formal, detached. The corollary of this social awkwardness is the specific German concern with nature and the land. Wherever one meets Germans, they are inveterate walkers because of their longing for contact with the land. Voss is not very much interested in geographical problems or geological or biological sciences; he makes observations about them dutifully but, so to speak, with his left hand. There is no regret when all the notes and specimens get lost. But repeatedly he wishes he were alone in the strange country, he and the land alone; and in the final consummation there is nobody with him but natives, who are part of the land.

No-one else in the expeditionary company is concerned with the country to the same extent as Voss. This company is the most incongruous collection of men, differing in race, social class, education, intelligence and interests. Their diversity already indicates that they have been brought together not to carry on exploration of historical conditions or Australian colonialism, but the human condition in general. At first no pattern can be discovered in this, only people, apparently combined only by chance. Only when it comes to the climax of the story, with its re-enactment of Christ's passion, does it become clear that they have been chosen for their ability to fill the roles in this drama.

To start at the bottom: the thieves at the Cross have their equivalents in Turner and Ralph Angus. Both perish, not even like beasts but unreconciled, unredeemed and lost. White describes them, particularly Angus, with a savage contempt. Turner is the spiv who wants to swindle his way through life, shirking work, exploiting others and trying to gain advantage by making mischief. Ralph Angus lives the mask which his education and the traditions of his class have produced; but he is nothing by himself, therefore he tends to gravitate towards the lowest whenever he finds himself in situations for which his education did not prepare him. He lives in 'hand-me-downs' and has nothing of himself. Here is an example from among White's cutting remarks about him:

> Finally Ralph Angus read the service, correcting himself time and again, for the meaning of the words was too great for him to grasp; he had been brought up a gentleman!

Such savage attacks have to do with the Australian contempt for privilege, but may also reflect White's personal reaction to his own unhappy public schooldays in Cheltenham.

At the other end of the scale are the two who accompany Voss to the end, Le Mesurier and the boy Harry Roberts. From their very first meeting Voss has been aware of a deep kinship with Le Mesurier. Both are men possessed but not knowing 'whither they are going', which Cromwell regarded as the mark of the man who goeth furthest. There is a dark foreboding in each man that he may reach his goal only by sacrificing his life. Le Mesurier is a poet and craves a vision of truth. And this vision and the poetic expression of it come to him on the expedition into the interior, and fulfil his life in the senses both of fulfilling its meaning, and of ending it physically. It is not the communication of his poems to others (for what can be communicated? Voss, the only one who reads them, sees only madness in them and does not want to comprehend); nor is it the fame which will survive him which consoles and reconciles him to life: but the creative vision as such.

The man of the atomic age can no longer hope that he may at least live on in the effect he has on others, for he and everybody he could have affected might disappear as radically as Le Mesurier, who destroys his poems before killing himself. His reconciliation must rest on something other than fame, memory or lament. Like the 'pre-historic' man he has no hope for historic survival. Thus Le Mesurier's 'beatific vision' combines in a curious way Christian elements and Australian aborigine religious ideas. His visions and poetry are not concerned with God in his glory, but with man's estate in the world. The two poems of which we know (through Voss's treachery) deal with childhood, its honesty, perspicacity, the immediacy of its perception and the convincing truth of its imagination; but also with its perversion through misunderstanding by grown-ups. The second poem deals with the collapse of the illusory kingship of man, the growth of humility which spares a space for God, Whose throne man is inclined to usurp in his flight from suffering and from his own shortcomings. Man who has been above himself needs to be incarnated again so that he can die like any other creature and his spirit be united with the Creator and the whole of creation, 'the rocks, the empty waterholes and the true love of all men, and you, O God'. We shall see that Le Mesurier's visions coincide with what Voss has to experience in his actual transformation and death during his expedition.

Harry Roberts is blessed as one who is poor in spirit (*geistlich arm*), blessed because he is capable of a simple complete commitment. It is to White's credit that he has created a figure who so much adored a fellow man that it amounted to deification; and yet whose life and death appear fully justified in spite of the general philosophy of the novel, its commendation of the humble renunciation of human self-deification. In a youth absolute commitment to an older fellow-man may be the appropriate expression of his love of man; and Harry's death together with Voss apears no less authentic than Eros' death together with Antony in Shakespeare's *Antony and Cleopatra*.

Of Voss's two remaining white companions, Palfreyman represents the Church. The Church of course ought to be present at a re-enactment of the Passion, yet does not quite manage it: Palfreyman dies prematurely. Palfreyman is treated with respect in the novel, though what he represents is ruthlessly criticised. That he is an ornithologist can already be read symbolically as signifying that the church concerns itself with what happens in the sky instead of with the human estate. Palfreyman is not married, nor has he ever as a man loved a woman: when at home he lived with his uncle, a clergyman.

His house is dilapidated, inside it is filled with glass objects, very fine and musical but dead and absolutely sterile, bought with money which the clergyman inherited from a distant cousin. The house, which may collapse any day and shatter the glass, is looked after by an old maid, Palfreyman's sister. She is neat and clean herself, but allows the house and the glass objects in it to become covered with dust. Her real interests are wild flowers, and she ventures out in all weathers to return, say, with an armful of common cow-parsley. Her uncle, the parson, has similar tastes and always brings in mosses to dry and plants to press. The rest of his time he spends in working out a key to the book of Revelation, oblivious of all and everything around him, and neglecting his parish most shockingly. In spite of all these weaknesses, and actually because of them, his parishioners love him and accept the reversal of roles that they, the sheep, look after their shepherd and protect him.

Palfreyman's sister is a hunchback who hates herself for the fact, to the extent of despairing of redemption because she so visibly bears the signs of God's disapproval. She is of a passionate, most erratic temperament: one day when her brother had surprised her looking at herself in a looking-glass, she became so irate she pushed him through the open window, only to be seized immediately by remorse. Then when she found he was not really hurt, she became resentful; for she would have liked to keep him in her own deformed image so that he would become completely hers. He in turn is touched by this perverted love, and wants to return her love, but always feels guilty because his love can never satisfy her needs. In the end he can tolerate his sense of failure only by flight as far away as possible from his sister. Yet his sense of guilt goes with him, and he feels responsible for every mishap. In his constant practice of self-denying love he increasingly mistakes self-denial for love. He practises humility, but knows nothing about the fundamental difference between the humility of self-negation and the humility of self-acceptance. In the end he sacrifices his life indecisively and uselessly, even to the detriment and embarrassment of his companions. All this has to be read metaphorically as describing the life of the Church; and terribly poignant these metaphors are.

When Palfreyman wants to meet the natives in an attitude comprehensible maybe to an English village gathering, but insipid in the eyes of Australian aborigines, one of them reacts by transfixing him with a spear. Judd's taking a gun and shooting the aborigine brings the situation temporarily under control, but makes the tragic end of the expedition finally inevitable. This action is very typical of Judd. In the hard life of a deported convict he has learned that survival is everything, and he has only had himself on whom to rely for this. That has made him the most useful and resourceful member of the expedition. Certainly he has had in himself also a vague longing for some higher aim and meaning in life, strong enough to induce him to join Voss's expedition. The instinct for survival has however remained his basic concern, which accounts for the earthbound heaviness of his character.

Judd is both intelligent and active; he is powerful, controlled, self-possessed, and yet like a dumb creature, imprisoned by the most profound and all-powerful need to preserve life. He thus becomes the Judas in the re-enactment of the Passion. He is also the first Adam, the unregenerate man and the Pharisee who is so absorbed in preserving life that he cannot grasp that one may have to lose it in order to gain it. Thus Judd has a rock-like steadiness and endurance which Voss envies. Voss's attitude to him is highly ambivalent, hostile, admiring, envious and respectful by turns. He promotes Judd's defection by predicting it when Judd himself has not yet clearly conceived the idea of returning home; and he lets him depart finally without reproach. When we meet Judd again as an old man he is like the Wandering Jew, homeless, surviving everybody, knowing of Christ but not comprehending him. He gets muddled and mixes up his memory of Voss with that of Palfreyman, thus mistaking Palfreyman's self-negating charity and his useless death for the fulfilment of the incarnation in Voss's death. He makes the mistake which will always be made by the unregenerated man who has no access to the inner direction of behaviour.

Judd's independence goes together with loyal service to the leader of the expedition, and he is even ready to accept insult and treachery from him as long as survival is not made impossible by Voss's demands and orders. Voss's own independence is of a quite different nature, for it upholds different values. He has to be the leader and dominant one. I have called Voss's world paranoid because I thus can see order in this highly complex and seemingly inconsistent character. His early childhood we have to imagine as Le Mesurier describes it, a childhood where the hearts of the children are taken out of their chests by silly, misunderstanding and respectless grown-ups; where children are not expected to think but are allowed to suffer; and where true closeness with beloved figures happens only in dreams. These experiences have left him with a frustrated longing for that love which is expressed in genuineness, honesty, understanding and helpfulness; and with the conviction that that love cannot be found. Therefore the only one he has been able to trust has been himself. We see him as a young boy, son of a timber merchant in a small north German town, tramping the heath in any weather, at any time of day or night, to escape from the oppressive safety and virtue of the home.

Then we meet him as the over-ambitious and over-correct student who gives up the study of medicine for botany because he is revolted by the bodies of men. He has had few friends and has found it desirable to be misunderstood by them.

> Finally he knew he must tread with his boot upon the trusting face of his father. He was forced to many measures of brutality in defence of himself ... Then when he had wrung freedom out of his protesting parents ... he did wonder at the purpose and nature of that freedom ... But the purpose and nature are never clearly revealed.

His aims as far as he sees them himself are described as follows:

> He did not expect much of love for all that is soft and yielding is easily hurt. He suspected it, but the mineral forms were an everlasting source of wonder; feldspar for instance was admirable and his own name a crystal in his mouth. If he were to leave that name on the land, irrevocably his material body swallowed by what it had named, it would

be rather on some desert place, a perfect abstraction, that would rouse no feeling of tenderness in posterity. He had no more need for sentimental admiration than he had for love. He was complete.

He needs nothing because he aims at self-sufficiency, indestructible, god-like. This however leads into endless paradoxes. He wants love but fears it, not only because it has always been disappointing, but because it undermines his self-sufficiency and control; it is soft and womanish. He wants to be a better lover than those he has found wanting, but is again and again brutal and treacherous in his need to secure his own completeness. He longs for honesty but cannot be honest with himself, for only thus can he uphold his illusion of being god-like. He wants to be complete, but has to be ruthless towards everything in himself which limits the omnipotence of his will, such as the instincts, feelings, and the life of the body. He has regard only for the manly will, everything else is rejected as womanish and soft. All these paradoxes transform his strivings for completeness and godlike perfection into something Luciferic and diabolically destructive. Yet his longings for a better life remain strong enough to become a vehicle for his conversion and change, a change which is simultaneously the failure of the Luciferic godlikeness and the fulfilment of a Christlike and therefore godlike humanity.

This change comes about through Voss's meeting Laura. The immediate impact this has on each of them derives from their each representing the other's unlived potentiality, pre-existent in him, and in her, prior to their meeting. Stendhal's simile for falling in love comes to mind: the saturated solution of salt which looks like pure water, in which the salt remains invisible until it crystallises round a thread of yarn immersed in it.

Laura has developed an unconventional and independent mind while living the most conventional of lives. She is fascinated by the daring man able to live, and not merely able to think, unconventionally. Contact with Voss liberates her too to live unconventionally, for example as a single woman to adopt the child of an emancipated convict woman. Laura like Voss has early in life discovered the basic value of genuineness, yet unlike Voss she has continued to believe that such genuineness could be found only in other people. She has done more than doubt her own ability to live up to her ideal, and has been burdened with a deep discontent with herself, and with self-pity. Other people have all of them seemed better or at least luckier than she. She has been able to love her cousin Belle, and has been prepared always to see good aspects even in those who have regarded her, the woman who read books and thought her own thoughts, as a freak. Ruthlessly honest and critical with herself, she has curbed her ruthlessness with regard to others in order to keep her illusions about them.

When Voss challenges her to be equally ruthless and honest with him, she discovers that he is no better than herself, but deeply to be pitied in his Luciferic isolation. This reconciles her with herself, at least insofar as it frees her from her self-pity. She is no longer alone in her imperfection but realises that it is inherent in the human situation, or at least in the situation of all who strive for genuineness. Voss is on the other hand struck by Laura's honesty about him, an honesty which he has wanted but has been unable to achieve himself. Her offer to pray for him, which he first finds so unacceptable, nevertheless calls forth some resonance from his deeply buried longing for an understanding authority above him. Laura's love is totally different from the love which he has despised, it is neither soft nor does it promise the unattainable. On the contrary it demands of him that he become more honestly and completely himself.

Their love does not transport Laura and Voss into a world of illusions but leads them to a deeper and more comprehensive awareness and acceptance of themselves. This explains why the physical separation of the lovers does not lead to a mental separation and a mere longing for reunion. They remain united in spite of the lack of physical communication, because each one is part of the other and contains him or her. Their extraordinary awareness of one another in spite of separation is rationally inexplicable but remains credible and is far from striking us as, in any cheap sense of the word, miraculous.

The relationship with Laura makes Voss more human, that is it frees him from his striving to be superhuman, god-like. He becomes less one-sidedly 'manly', dominant, isolated, and he recognises himself more as a finite creature like other human beings or animals. That does not mean that he becomes effeminate, because what Voss calls manly is simply an ideal fantasy, and feminine is to him the cipher for all he rejects in himself. What manly and feminine really amount to is unknown to us; we only have fantastic notions about the question, with their origin in the imaginings of the young child when he has to learn to break from total unity with mother and to realise a self which is different from mother. When we want to overcome these fantastic divisions we use uniting concepts such as 'human' or Jung's concept of the 'Self'. Voss's humanisation is no easy process, the hardship of the journey calls up all his domineering tendencies and makes him more afraid of, and ruthlessly reject, what he regards as softness. In this mood he kills his dog because he will not allow himself the softness of loving him. Yet his own will starts to become ambiguous in its aim. The catastrophe of the overloaded float which causes the loss of a great part of the provisions, and of all the scientific equipment and the findings of the expedition, was foreseeable. Judd actually foresaw it. Yet Voss willed it, thus making the failure of the expedition inevitable. Not only did he thus prove to himself the fallibility of his will, but his will seemed to aim at his destruction, as if something in him knew that only in death could he reach his true humanisation.

That is the reason why he could not return with Judd and try to save his life. Only *in extremis* does he accept himself as creature and become incarnated, submitting to the fate of the body. And while it appears to be the loss of all power it is the homecoming into unity with the cosmos through accepting his finiteness and creaturely limitation. In this sense he reaches Christlikeness as the being whose acceptance of his passion and death fulfilled and consummated the incarnation.

Only in this sense, however, is Voss Christlike, and it seems to me to be the most serious shortcoming of White's book that he tries to make out that Voss dies a sacrificial death. He is sacrificially killed by the natives and we are made to understand that his body is eaten by them in a sacrificial meal. Voss completes his conversion, his healing and becoming whole in his death, but he is no sacrifice for anybody or anything else. Christ is believed to have died for the redemption of our sins; Voss dies for himself only. In vain does White try to convince us that Voss's death is meaningful and effective also for others, repeating at least four times the aboriginal belief that in death the spirit of a living being leaves the body and lives on everywhere in the rocks and waterholes, in the country and in the true love of all men. This vague and primitive belief carries no conviction for me. The belief that all life spirits live on says nothing about the meaningfulness of Voss's death. According to this belief his spirit would also have lived if he had died in bed unconverted in the middle of his Luciferic pride. In addition, nobody except Laura knew of Voss's conversion, and her knowledge was incommunicable. That he died alone as a human being was proof of his peace with the order of the universe, and there White should have left it without claiming more.

Voss's meeting with Laura and his *anima* leads him away from his Luciferic spirituality to incarnation as creature. Laura, on the other hand, in her attempt to accompany and assist Voss on his way to Golgotha, becomes spiritualised to the extent that she nearly loses all hold of the body and comes to death's door. She sacrifices physical fulfilment and motherhood for Voss, but finds help and continued contact with the world of the body, and vitality, through her relationship with her cousin Belle and with Rose Portion. She never ceases to love Belle, who is intellectually superficial but of unbroken animalic vitality, and in Belle Laura admires qualities she has had herself to sacrifice.

Rose is a female figure parallel to Judd. Like him she is an emancipated convict and she lives for the perpetuation of life, in her case by giving birth to a child. Laura before meeting Voss was not on good terms with the cruder aspects of the body, and had difficulty in hiding the repulsion she felt about her ungainly maid. But when the maid became pregnant she grew closer to her, and went through the pregnancy and labour in a state of participation and identification. Thus the child was as if conceived by her in her love of Voss, and borne by herself. In this identification with the pregnant woman she too learned to honour the creature side of our existence, and the child became one of the bonds which kept her alive and part of this world when she had accompanied Voss to his death. In her later life there is from the superficial view of the world nothing uncommon and unconventional in her behaviour apart from not wanting to marry, adopting the child, and taking up a profession without being financially forced to do this. The transformation she went through no more made her a noisy outsider than does any true faith show itself in spectacular behaviour.

Before finishing with some remarks on the general philosophy of the book I have briefly to mention the aborigines and their part in the economy of the story. They live in a world so different from ours that contact with them makes all our life questionable. They exist outside time; the history of the soul and of salvation has no meaning for them. Words, gestures, intentions, letters that one writes, all are meaningless to them, and only on the simplest level of existence is communication possible.

Voss embraces this level in his death, and when life had been reduced to mere survival only Judd could live as one of the native tribes. Jackie, the one native who had tried to share the life of the white men, became in consequence alienated from himself and a freakish madman. Thus the aborigines represent the '*Grenz* (border) situation' which forces us radically to question all our valuations and aims.

White's book is written with such sincerity that a general philosophy becomes visible in it, and we are asked to respond to it and take sides, and cannot read the book as mere entertainment. One would describe this philosophy as a religious humanism without a theology. Laura early on in the same story has come to 'the decision that she could not remain a convinced believer in that God in whose benevolence and power she had received most earnest instruction' and that she had become what might be called a rationalist. This statement is never taken back even when she later learns to pray again. Rational thinking cannot produce a rationally defensible concept of God and no rational statement about God can be true, not even a negative one. This is the end of theology. And because no statements about God are possible, none about the resurrection, the last judgment or about life after death can be made (apart from the vague and primitive belief in the perpetuity of the life spirit which in itself is incompatible with the Christian belief in the day of judgment).

So God comes in not as somebody or something by Himself, but as function in the life of man. We cannot think or speak of God, we can only be related to Him. In our anguish we turn to God as the addressee of prayer. He is the recognition of our limits, the cipher for the experienced transcendence which is only the corollary of the accepted limits of self, the corollary of our humility and humanity. Thus in honouring God we honour the true status of man, God appears as its transcendence. Therefore man's deepest religious concern is to become truly human. This is a dialectical process in which no short cut is possible. If full acceptance of self and all life, simplicity and goodness were the final aim then Judd would have reached it, but it is not the end result alone which counts but also the way by which it is reached. Judd's soul had been maimed by his experiences as a convict and his aims were reduced to securing survival. What was left of any more ambitious aims was symbolically shown in his acquisition of an ineffective telescope. Most other people do not buy even such a telescope. They are content with fulfilling their immediate material needs within the conventions which serve this purpose. This is true not only of the aborigines but also of the bourgeois society which White describes. Or some try to swindle their way through life like Turner.

Yet there are others who in early childhood already realise values which are beyond merely material needs, and who suffer because these values are betrayed by grown-ups and by themselves. They are driven outside the world of mere convention. They are also the great sinners whose quest for a better world will necessarily lead to failure and destruction. It is with them that White's religious humanism deals. His humanism is religious because he believes that there exists a way of salvation for them in the *imitatio Christi*. The sin of these men and women is that they go beyond the confines of the human condition, beyond the limits of our bodily existence and of our human controlling power. They become despisers of human weakness and of what they regard as weakness, namely love and dependence. They deny the powers which transcend them or which may let their controlling will down. Thus their need is to learn to love themselves again in their entirety with their limitations and weaknesses. This is the *imitatio* of Christ's incarnation. The incarnation as miraculous birth interests White as little as the resurrection. It is not regarded as a singular historical event and a revelation. It is the example of Christ's death which moves him and demands imitation.

Historically Christianity was the opposite of Stoic self-deification, as of the deification of leaders, or of nihilism, or rationalism which despises the evidence of our feelings. The Christian answer to paranoid megalomania lies in its valuation of love. This has been criticised by modern rebellion against romanticism, by critics turning against concepts of love which are spurious and rightly to be criticised: against love as a journey into paradise (Musil), as a return to a golden age or to motherly care and shelter, a promise of all goodness which cannot be kept and is insipid; or the passing illusions of erotic ecstasy. Many find only one way out of this, retreat into nihilism and despair, loneliness and drink, like the hero of Beckett's *Krapp's Last Tape*. White avoids such pitfalls with a sounder and more mature idea of love. He too realises that love has its origin in the experiences of childhood, in the child's experience of or longing for unity through mutual understanding, mutual confidence and mutual honesty. Yet there exists too a grown-up way of honouring these values which results in a loving honesty towards oneself, in increased awareness of one's own total existence and the loving acceptance of one's own limitations and those of the beloved one, or that of every man.

Erotic attraction and increase of liveliness promote not illusions but greater truthfulness and realism toward oneself. The demand is not for the *sacrificio intellectus* but only for realisation of the limitations of reason; and if love makes us childlike it should not be as demanding and insipid babes but in return to the genuineness of the child, to authenticity and what Pfaender called '*Echtheit*'. In this sense White's philosophy appears as a valid answer to anti-romantic nihilism and despair, as well as to spurious romanticism and sentimentality. It is a philosophy for inner directed individuals. Compared with the ideas of Jung with which it has much in common it emphasises more the *vita activa* than the *vita contemplativa* which in consequence of his basically therapeutic interests Jung considers more. Compared with some existentialist philosophies with which it has also much in common, it is distinguished by its belief in absolute values which are valid at least for members and descendants of western civilisation; not only the values which are prefigured in the life of the child—such as genuineness—but also the aims which are exemplified in the Incarnation of Christ through His Passion.

It will be obvious that I am impressed by the novel *Voss* and largely in sympathy with the ideas of its author, Patrick White. I am aware that this is easier for me, coming from a Jewish background, than it will be for readers who are Christians. However I do not doubt that they too will regard White as an opponent worthy of being listened to.

On Simplicity

With Reference to Patrick White's Novels
Riders in the Chariot and *The Solid Mandala*

In times of transformation and collapse of traditional moral standards, of disillusionment and growing nihilism, man may look for a new basis of orientation by way of return to that which is essentially human. This may produce a call for a return to nature, or in putting one's trust in spontaneity or simplicity or the naive. There is an optimistic belief that the turmoil of moral disorientation is due to corruption by civilisation, but that there *is* something essentially human which can give lasting guidance for the good life. My concern here is with the belief that that manifests itself in simplicity.

It becomes more obvious that simplicity refers to the manifestation of the essentially human when we consider for a moment the German words for it. The English word 'simplicity' refers to people as well as to things. The German equivalent is *Einfachheit*, yet there is another word too, *Einfalt*, which refers only to man: *Einfalt* is often further defined as *Einfalt des Herzens*. Speaking of the heart we make use of a symbol for the centre of our being, and thus for what is essentially human.

Our language contains a number of words which in a similar way hint at or manifest what is essentially human, such as humility, love, faith, *Gelassenheit*, and others, and about all of these a number of identical statements can be made.

First: all of these terms are interlinked. They all illuminate different aspects of what is essentially human, yet at the some time hint at the whole of it. Simple man is humble: he knows, accepts and lives within his limitations. He has faith, in the sense of trusting himself, trusting that mutual regard and understanding with his fellow men is possible; and trusting in the human sphere: either in religious terms or in the vague awareness that the world is not only hostile but that forces and circumstances exist which support him, which correspond to his essential being or at least fulfil his accepted fate as the finite being he is. And in this trust he is of good cheer. He is open for all that comes to meet him, which is to say that he is *gelassen*. About the link between simplicity and love I shall speak later in greater detail.

Second: neither simplicity nor any of the other manifestations can be willed. The mere fact that one wills simplicity, or faith or love, destroys it. Yet will and moral decision are not totally irrelevant in this regard. One may voluntarily suspend will in order to give simplicity (or any of the other manifestations) a better chance to come to the fore undisturbed. And one may voluntarily strive to avoid what interferes with and contradicts simplicity, for example pretentiousness. Yet one has to remain aware that such voluntary avoidances do not guarantee the manifestation of true simplicity. One may get tangled in a net of prohibitions and negative rules without any positive core becoming visible in their midst, as is so often the case too with religious teaching. To paraphrase Heidegger: the subject's relationship to simplicity cannot be voluntary action but can only be described as 'waiting'.

We can follow Heidegger a step further. He once said that the essentially human can only be found by looking away from man. *Einfalt* or 'love' or 'faith' or *Gelassenheit* are not qualities of the ego but manifestations of openness for what transcends the ego, and for all one encounters in the world, in oneself and beyond the world. One cannot describe simplicity as if it were a thing, an object or a personal quality; it manifests itself only in interaction with what transcends the person.

How can we then speak of 'simplicity' and try to make statements about it which are meaningful? Why do writers like Patrick White, whose novels *Riders in the Chariot* and *The Solid Mandala* occasioned the writing of this paper, believe that 'simplicity' is of importance for people of our time?

The religions of the Far East, as well as the Judaeo-Christian tradition, regard simplicity as the truly human. Even Karl Marx named simplicity as his 'favourite virtue'. In the Gospels simplicity is equated with childlikeness: 'Except ye be converted and become as little children ye shall not enter the Kingdom of Heaven' (Matthew 18, 3). There is an archetypal tendency to look for what is essentially and uncorruptedly human at the beginning of time, whether in Paradise, in a Golden Age, or at the beginning of the individual life in childhood. This archetypal tendency seems to be at work too in this identification of simplicity and childlikeness. Yet also, it is widely held to be an empirical fact that in childhood something truly human is present which is worth preserving and coming back to again in later years. This enables people of our time who do not believe in revealed religion, and want to trust only in their empirical experience, to agree with these biblical teachings. Philosophers as well as theologians and psychiatrists have tried to describe phenomenologically childlike simplicity or, what is synonymous, 'naivety'. Here is for example a resume of how Rabbi Leo Baeck describes childlikeness in a paper on 'rebirth'. He says:

> Childlikeness is first characterised by negatives. Childhood is prior to the development of intellect and of conscious will, prior to the division between subject and object, prior to consciousness and conflict. Childhood is the fullness of potentialities yet without tensions. Nearness and distance, inner and outer world are still one, and there are no memories or expectations. To the child all is play and there is no differentiation between real and unreal or between useful and noxious. And all there is

becomes action and expression. Everything is new and newly discovered, and all is curious and admirable. To the child all is spontaneous
intuition without the need to forget first all that has been learned or is
remembered. And all is concrete, generalising abstractions do not exist
yet. Everything is apperceived as animated and as addressing itself to
the child; and the child is responsive and open. He may reject or fear
what he meets, but cannot yet be indifferent. And all his responses are
wholesome and total, unsparing, free from artifices.

A child psychiatrist, the late Professor August Homburger, also mentions freedom from artifice as characteristic of the naive child. He emphasises '*die Ernst-Gesinnung*', the sincerity of the naive child which disappears
when the child starts to play up to the expectations of grown-ups and begins
to pretend. The Romantic philosopher Novalis emphasises the absence of
conflict when he says that naivety is not '*polarisch*', it is free from awareness
of polarities.

I believe that these descriptions have not been invalidated by modern
psychoanalytical findings. It is true that the child already in the early
weaning period experiences conflicts and responds with defence mechanisms, but these conflicts are experienced as coming from clashes with
outside agencies and are not yet experienced as inner conflicts. Contradictory impulses which exist in the child from very early on, such as the urge to
be at one with mother, and the urge to be independent and have power
himself, can coexist without conflict as long as the child experiences no need
for consistency; and as long as he can wholeheartedly express the tendencies
which are predominant at every given moment.

The Gospels describe simplicity sometimes without explicit reference to
childlikeness, but much of that applies to the naive child all the same: for
instance the advice of Matthew 6, 19ff. not to live in fear of the future or to
protect oneself by laying up treasures upon earth; but to trust that one will
be provided for like the fowls of the air; or, one could add, the infant. One is
not to care about impressing others with splendid raiment, but is to be like
the lilies of the field, or, one could again add, like the infant who is naturally
attractive to his mother. This likeness of the naive child to all living
creatures is most intensely disturbed by excessive spiritual control, spiritual
pride and intellectual dominance; and modern man will read the blessing of
the 'poor in spirit' in Matthew 5, 3 as a warning against one-sided intellectuality, all-controlling intellectual dominance and over-sophistication, though
it is doubtful whether the original Greek text has this meaning. The Greek
uses only one word, πτωχός (*ptochos*), which is an uncommon word for
poor. Its original meaning is 'beggarly' or 'humble' both in the material and
the spiritual sense. My Luther Bible quotes as parallel the saying of Isaiah
57, 15 where man in his humble state is contrasted with the eminence and
majesty of God. In this sense humility is the opposite of spiritual pride, of
giving oneself airs and of being artificial and sophisticated. It is in addition

the knowledge of man's humble and poor estate in comparison with God's exalted state. The *'docta ignorantia'*, the holy ignorance of Nicholas of Cusa, means just this (according to Ernst Simon).

In the Catholic tradition the simplicity of the child is mirrored by the *Einfalt* of the Virgin Mary. Amongst the innumerable paintings of her, none displays her simplicity more clearly than the 14th and 15th century Italian pictures of the Annunciation. Here simplicity manifests itself in the unquestioning acceptance of her most extraordinary fate. Acceptance of whatever fate may bring is one of the signs of simplicity. The German language has a word for Mary's simplicity. It is *'Frömmigkeit'*, or *'fromm'*. In English we have no word which expresses exactly the same meaning. Both 'devout' and 'pious' lay too much stress on the outer signs of faith such as church-going and fulfilling other religious obligations. Only a composite term like 'simple faith' conveys something of the meaning of *fromm*, which refers to the whole of human life and not only to devotional acts. It is however not only the Catholic tradition about the Virgin Mary which has described *'Einfalt'* as an ideal aspect of young womanhood and motherhood. These ideas are so widespread that one could call them archetypal. Some of Shakespeare's female characters, or Goethe's Gretchen, are equally simple and naive. This provides detractors of simplicity with one of their main arguments, namely that simplicity is unmanly. I shall discuss this later.

The child-mother relationship also provides the first pattern of love and mutual trust, and the first pattern for that humble openness and receptivity in relation to one's fellow beings which characterises simplicity. Though the healthy child is dependent on the mother, he is not all-demanding but expects only what he needs and cannot provide himself. He and the mother delight in each other's presence and existence. The mother is concerned for the child's welfare and gives what is needed without expectation of any return. Yet the child soon likes to add to the mother's well-being by enjoying pleasing her. Selfish possessiveness beyond true needs is absent, or subordinate to justified concern for oneself and the other. This may be a one-sided picture of the mother-child relationship insofar as it ignores possessive and destructive aggressive aspects of it, which often are present early on—aggressive tendencies are even necessary for the development of the child into a self-reliant grown-up person — yet one cannot doubt that in the healthy child and healthy mother inclinations towards a loving and trusting relationship are inborn. They become the pattern for all simple love and trust in later life including Christian *agape*.

To regard the relationship of the naive child to others as only loving, would however be sentimental. The naive child can be most sensitive to any form of spuriousness, to any lack of genuineness. He refuses to join in with conventional lies and pretences. For a more or less prolonged period the child remains incorruptible by such antics of grown-ups, and rejects them. This sureness of self in resistance to distortion in the naive child is the prime pattern for genuineness and authenticity which is another aspect of mature simplicity.

In the 18th century naivety became identified with at-one-ness with nature, as for instance in Schiller's famous essay on *Naive and Sentimental Poetry*. According to Schiller, eternal and infinite nature belongs to all poetry either as origin or as aim. Normally we are in unimpeded touch with nature only in childhood, but the naive genius perpetuates this contact beyond childhood. Yet the sentimental poet too tries to re-establish this contact ideally, for all poetry results from the *'Einfalt'*: truth and the necessary order of Nature and man's moral drive forces the poet constantly to seek unity with it. 'Nature' in this sense is a moral entity in contrast to 'raw nature', and 'true human nature' as the concept of ordered totality is differentiated from 'real nature', which is limited and ruled by particular needs and urges. Schiller's concept of Nature is akin to the Neo-Platonic and Stoic *Logos*. It is the *vita vitae*. In the child the *vita vitae* expresses itself immediately. Naive poetry too is its immediate expression, whereas in sentimental poetry it is the object toward which the poet strives. The naive child moves us by his pure and free vitality, his integrity and his affinity with all being (*Unendlichkeit*). As such he is the goal and the ideal of moral man and of the artist.

Schiller also differentiates naivety as childlikeness as contrasted with childishness. By childishness we may mean two different things.

Childish is the ignorance of the child. For instance in *Simplicius Simplicissimus*, the novel which von Grimmelshausen wrote at the end of the Thirty Years' War, the hero gets his name because from his early life with a hermit he emerges into the world totally ignorant not only of all social conventions, and of the ways of the world, but also with the sexual ignorance of *Daphnis and Chloë* in Longus' idyllic story.

Childish is the simplicity of *Simple Simon*. Conventional people are inclined to regard all simplicity in this way as childish and silly. Thus Prince Myshkin in Dostoevsky's novel is regarded as an *Idiot*. Yet the ignorance of the child is unlike Myshkin's simplicity. Kant rightly discerns a state of *'weise Einfalt'*, of wise simplicity, from the state of *'rohe Einfalt'*, the raw simplicity of the ignorant child.

Childish, too, however, is the attempt to remain totally dependent and all-demanding. In this state one exploits others under a mask of helplessness and is anything but simple. It leads to the most elaborate insincerity and deception of others and of oneself, and this type of childishness has features in common with romantic tendencies. When Schiller described the sentimental poet as one who strives after the re-establishment of contact with nature, he anticipated tendencies which became most obvious in the German Romantic movement. These poets strove after simplicity, after childlikeness, and after contact with the mother and all the mother symbols. Yet we saw in the beginning of this paper that striving after simplicity does not produce simplicity. What it most often produces is an artificial harmonisation of the world, a fairy tale-like absence of conflicts or the miraculous solution of them; or a goodness which ignores the real tensions of life.

These are also features of romantic love. The passionate and unrealistic over-valuation of the beloved has to be protected against confrontation with reality; and romantic love ends in separation, in the *Liebestod* together, or leads to platonic relationships when the lovers live permanently apart, like von Risach and Mathilde in Adalbert Stifter's *Nachsommer* (*Indian Summer*), or Heinrich and Judith in Gottfried Keller's *Der Grüne Heinrich*. Another tendency in romantic love is to minimise the polarity of the two sexes. The two lovers are one. Yet even when the tension between the lovers is reduced by being brother and sister (as in Musil's *The Man Without Qualities*), or in homosexual love, the oneness and identification of the lovers with one another cannot last, and the differences between the two people concerned must assert themselves. It was Dostoevsky who in *The Idiot* showed that the essential honesty of the truly simple Myshkin could not fulfil the romantic love expectations of the young Eglaia Epanchin.

The earliest experience of simplicity is the naivety of the child, but this cannot be continued authentically either by perpetuating childish ignorance and dependence, or by the romantic harmonisation of the world. *Die rohe Einfalt* of the child has to become transformed into the wise simplicity of the grown-up. Some religious philosophers have discussed this in greater detail under the heading of 'second naivety' or 'rebirth', and Heidegger wrote about a closely related theme in a paper on *Gelassenheit*. The first who used the term 'second naivety' was a German Catholic, Peter Wust, of whom I know only indirectly through Ernst Simon's 1964 paper on 'The Second Naivety'.

Wust (1884-1940) came from a religious background, but already during High School became estranged from childlike belief. He came under neo-Kantian influence and later became a follower of Max Scheler, with whom he found his way back to the Catholic Church. In 1925 he published a book, *Naivität und Pietät*, which contained a chapter on 'Human Wisdom as Secondary Naivety'. Ernst Simon, Professor of Education at the Hebrew University of Jerusalem, adopted the term 'secondary naivety' from Wust, whilst Leo Baeck discussed similar problems under the heading of 'rebirth'. All three came to the question through a religious conversion, which resulted in a new grown-up *Frömmigkeit* and the ability to pray.

I do not feel happy about the terms 'second naivety' or 'rebirth'. The term 'second naivety' seems appropriate only under certain sociological conditions. It fits the Catholic situation, the educational ideal aims of which are to perpetuate the primal naivety long past early childhood and if possible for all one's life. If a Catholic has broken away from it he may well experience his return to the Church as his second naivety. The traditional orthodox Jewish background is in some senses the opposite of the Catholic. From the age of three the child spends his day away from home in the *cheder*, that is with a teacher of Hebrew and the Bible, and is instructed in the Biblical laws and their traditional interpretations. His first naivety is broken early, and spontaneity is replaced by obedience to the Law and its all-comprehensive interpretations. Often older or old men regain a new spontaneous childlikeness which differentiates their new outlook clearly from their previous rigidity. It is a well-defined 'second naivety'. Outside the Catholic and Jewish setting, mature simplicity does not belong to such a well-defined stage in life. It may manifest itself at any age, yet like wisdom it is not a permanent possession of man but the essential humanity which more or less clearly manifests itself anew from occasion to occasion.

Mrs Hare in Patrick White's *Riders in the Chariot* remained simple, for she retained a child's limited mental capacity all her life. The aborigine Dubbo in the utter isolation of the outcast evolved a simple honesty with himself in his artistic creations. In Mrs Godbold her simple humanity steadily deepened a life in which responsibility and tragedy were present from the start; and there was little temptation to indulge in grand expectations other than those which her joyful Christian faith provided. Only the Jew Himmelfarb has found simplicity though an act of conversion, a homecoming to himself and to the faith of his people, promoted by his love for his wife, Reha.

In *The Solid Mandala* White tries to describe in Arthur a being who is essentially simple and human from the beginning of his life. I do not think he succeeds in making Arthur's childhood psychologically acceptable and visible: he relates a string of incidents and aspects of Arthur's early life which highlight essential features of simplicity, particularly when seen against the background of Arthur's complete opposite, his twin brother Waldo. White is much more successful in showing the transformation of the *rohe Einfalt* of Arthur's childhood into the *weise Einfalt* of his later life. I want to dwell a bit longer both on the pairs of opposites which help White to apperceive and describe simplicity, and on the features which distinguish mature simplicity from the child's simplicity.

Arthur is born a healthy and sturdy child. Waldo is sickly and delicate. Arthur has the red hair of the biblical Esau, the father of the Edomites, the Earth-men. He likes all earthy jobs, looking after a cow or a horse, and is the friend of all animals; if he cannot be the grower of food he is at least the maker of bread and butter; later he becomes an assistant in a grocer's shop, and after his and his brother's retirement he cooks their simple meals.

Waldo is the intellectual, interested in words and books and in what he is taught. Arthur is no scholar; he does not know what he is taught, only what he has learned from immediate experience. Thus he is spared distortion by the great ideas and expectations which come to most of us far too early in life from literature, art and religious teaching. And he has assimilated only those experiences which he has been able to understand, and by-passed those which have been beyond his understanding. He has thus appeared to others as dull-witted. He has taken natural things naturally and has not turned away from them because they have, like the death of his parents, been unpleasant. When in old age his brother on one occasion loses control of his bowels, it is Arthur who cleans up the mess. Being in touch with present reality is *being*, whereas Waldo is constantly running away from *being* into imaginary wished-for identities, into something he wants to become but is not. Thus he cares obsessively about what other people think, about making the right impression, about upholding his own illusions of being the great author he wants to become; or belonging to the superior English gentry from which his mother came, and which she left when she married Mr Brown and emigrated to Australia.

This care for pretence makes Waldo progressively isolated, misanthropic, over-cautious, dry and empty. Arthur by contrast is glad if he is liked but does not go out of his way to bring that about. Least of all does he for that purpose pretend to be anything other than himself. In this sense he does not care what other people think of him. He is immune to any snobbishness, he likes to meet people and accepts them as he finds them, infinitely tolerant of their eccentricities and peculiarities. He meets the uneducated, poor Mrs Poulter with the same ease as he does the scatterbrained, wealthy Mrs Musto; the well-to-do Jews Feinstein and Saporta as the phoney Christians Mrs Allright and Mrs Mutton. And he understands his mother's drinking with sympathetic tolerance.

All this has been almost theoretically thought out and stated. On the other hand, some aspects are not mentioned at all which are necessary to comprehend Arthur as a real person. For example, this strong boy who lived in such intimate contact with concrete reality, and his immediate emotions, must have gone through considerable turmoil at puberty due to his sexual desires. Nothing of this is mentioned. This gives the book not only an intellectual but also a prim flavour, in spite of its author's tendency to speak freely and often about excretion. The artistic value of the book lies in the description of Arthur's progress from the raw simplicity of childhood to the wise simplicity of maturity.

This development was promoted by three events. The first was Arthur's love for Dulcie Feinstein. There he experienced a love which was neither demanding nor giving (as the child-mother relationship is) but was evocative, so that each lover became more completely what he and she really was. Each lover found his or her true self more fully. This led to lasting friendship and respect between the Feinsteins and Saporta and Arthur. Arthur could even repeat the evocative function later, in the consolation he could offer to the dying old man Feinstein. In his relationship with Dulcie Arthur experienced that wholeness of self about which he had read when he found the description of the mandala as a symbol of wholeness in Mrs Musto's library.

The second move forward towards mature simplicity resulted from Arthur's relationship with Mrs Poulter, and particularly their outing to the country, when Arthur danced a mandala for Mrs Poulter. Arthur's love for her was much more sensual than his love for Dulcie. With this sensuality something entered the relationship which carried it beyond the experience of wholeness of self. Something ecstatic and creative entered Arthur's life, an awareness of the Spirit which later on led Arthur into libraries to become deeply involved with Dostoevsky's writings, with mystic texts, and also with the free joyous play of creativity in books like *Alice Through the Looking Glass*. It was at this time that Arthur also started to write serious poetry himself.

The third and final step towards maturity was the discovery that simplicity does not ensure childlike innocence in perpetuity; and that he, Arthur, had become involved in guilt toward Waldo, whom he loved and was intent on protecting.

Like many other readers, when I first read this book I was struck by the apparent similarity of its ending to that of Dostoevsky's *The Idiot*. Yet *The Idiot* is nowhere mentioned in White's book, though it expressly refers to Dostoevsky's *The Brothers Karamazov*, and particularly the story of the Grand Inquisitor in it. On re-reading *The Solid Mandala* I saw the rightness of this. Figures like Myshkin or Himmelfarb and Arthur have a disturbing effect on others. Some just want to remove and destroy the disturbers. Others are deeply affected by them and may perish through inability to follow their example consistently. Just because they are perceptive of Grace they die through their inability to honour it. Thus in *Riders in the Chariot* the factory owner Rosentree shares the fate of Judas in the Gospels. Nastasia Philippovna in *The Idiot* perishes in a similar way, and Myshkin breaks down over the realisation that he has been partly responsible for her death.

Waldo never understood the essence of Arthur's being, or experienced it as something worth emulating. Once he nearly perished in an 'accident' when he became aware of Arthur's friendship with the Saportas. In the end he feels murderous against Arthur when he discovers one of Arthur's poems; but this is sheer envy of Arthur's achievements without insight into the essence of his being. Waldo is like the soldiers who torture and kill Jesus without knowing who he is. He is unlike Judas, who swithers between discipleship and betrayal.

Arthur knew from early on in their life that Waldo needed his protection, although people would have expected it was the other way round. He was clear that Waldo was a lost soul, at least after the scene in the library when Waldo denied that he was Arthur's brother. In his love for Waldo Arthur tried to keep him as happy as was possible in this state, by not facing him with truth. Yet even in this he failed. His guilt is that of the Grand Inquisitor, who despaired of the possibility of making people free, and therefore tried to give them the illusion of happiness through denying them freedom and keeping them away from truth. This behaviour like that of the Grand Inquisitor is what has driven Arthur into paroxysms of guilt at the end of the book. Finally he returns to Mrs Poulter, to be consoled as a child is consoled by his mother when something has to be accepted as unalterable.

He is not annihilated as was Prince Myshkin by the tragic events, but the task is over which has absorbed his energies during the last years, that of keeping Waldo alive. Now he can retreat to the asylum which is his rightful place, as the old tired man he has become, and as the childlike being he always has been.

At the start of this paper I called it a belief that in simplicity that which is essentially human manifests itself. Those who do not share this belief (and who do not reject it on the wrongful assumption that simplicity is identical with romantic illusions and harmonisations) voice mainly the two criticisms that simplicity is unrealistic, and that it is unmanly.

I feel that Patrick White, in the books I have mentioned, gives a valid refutation of the reproach that it is unrealistic. As for the reproach that it is unmanly, it is necessary to clarify the concept of manliness that that involves. It seems to me to a large extent to be based on early childish apperceptions of what differentiates and separates the young child from the mother. All men and women come from the total oneness with mother, and the necessary separation from her follows quite fantastic lines.

The child (and this applies both to boys and girls) may reject the frustrating mother and not want to be like her. She is seen as a big physical power, and it seems dangerous to compete with her or to annoy her. Thus the child may leave the material realm to her alone and try to be 'immaterial', intellectual, spiritual, or in other ways superior to the material realm. This then may be called manly, as the only human beings who seem to be unlike mother seem to be men. The child is also aware that feelings and emotions link him with the mother and express and acknowledge his dependence on her. In order to renounce this dependence the child may suppress his feelings and again regard this as manly. Feelings are then regarded as feminine. In the name of manliness the child may try to abstract himself from emotional responses to the concrete situation, and may leave it to the woman to respond concretely. Even the identification of active with masculine and of passive with feminine, which Freud uncritically accepted as valid, probably originates in fantasies about the mother-child relationship. The child originally is identified and totally united with mother. Later in retrospect this state may be fantastically regarded as passive and the passive identification with mother regarded as feminine. The active child who self-reliantly separates from mother is then seen as essentially male. Yet this equation of active with masculine and passive with feminine is in every respect fantastic. It is even unrealistic with regard to sexual activity. All one can say with any justification is that passive attitudes are more pronounced in women than in men, though both are active as well as passive.

All these early child fantasies of what is mother-like, and what is by contrast manly, produce an archetypal image of masculinity characterised by being active, rational and not emotional, and superior to the material world and femininity in particular. They produce a corresponding feminine image

which is passive, emotive, non-rational or irrational, and bodily or material.
These are archetypal fantasies which have to do with human reality only
insofar as people may sometimes strive to correspond to them. Yet neither
man nor woman insofar as their essential humanity manifests itself in
simplicity, is superior to the other sex; nor alien to any aspect of human life,
whether activity or passivity, the material or the spiritual, the rational or
the emotive. It is on the contrary an essential aspect of simplicity that man is
not stretched away from concrete and material reality, and that he uses all
his faculties, reason as well as feelings, intuition and sensation, for his
orientation in the world. This does not make him unmanly; only thus is he
truly human.

Patrick White is aware of all this. In his blindness to Arthur's true being,
Waldo sometimes calls him 'a big fat helpless female'. Arthur knows how
phoney is Waldo's male superiority over him and women, and that essentially human men and women have much in common. Already as a child he
liked the story of the Greek seer Tiresias, who for a short while was changed
by the gods into a woman. Later on a mystic text impressed him which runs
like this:

> As the shadow continually follows the body of one who walks in the sun,
> so our hermaphroditic Adam, though he appears in the form of a male
> nevertheless always carries about with him Eve, or his wife, hidden in
> his body.

The belief that in simplicity something essentially human becomes
manifest found its clear expression in the Bible; and some modern philosophers who speak about it still find religious language and religious practice
the most appropriate expression of it. Others like Patrick White regard
religious language and practice as an obstacle today to sincere simplicity. In
The Solid Mandala Mrs Poulter had been a believer in Christ. Over the
catastrophic events at the end of the book she loses her Christian faith but
retains her faith in simplicity. She expresses this paradoxically when she
says of Arthur, 'This man would be my saint if we could still believe in
saints'.

In times when alienation is widely felt, when man suffers from self-
isolation and distrust in all, simplicity may be seen as the cipher for the
opposite of all these tendencies. One may dwell on simplicity in order to
fortify oneself against paranoid tendencies in one's self. It is probable that
Patrick White became preoccupied with simplicity for this reason. He states
this indirectly in the earlier novel *Voss*, dealing with the progress of his
hero from paranoid self-isolation and selfcentredness to simplicity. It certainly was also one reason for my writing this paper.

I finish with an anecdote from Ernst Simon's paper on 'Secondary
Naivety'. This deals with a poet of the Franz Rosenzweig circle in Frank-
furt, Ludwig Strauss. He was a true believer though he did not in practice
embrace the Jewish ritual. He wrote once:

As a young man I always crossed out the word 'God' whenever in unguarded moments it had slipped into one of my poems, and I replaced it by the word 'Spirit' or something similarly non-committal. Until one day the rejected word had gathered enough substance onto itself and onto me who used it, to insist irrefutably on remaining there.

And Ernst Simon makes the comment that the poet who could use the word 'God' had recovered his ability to pray.

Acknowledgement

I am gratefully obliged to Dr Lola Paulsen, who read the first draft of this paper and helped me with many useful suggestions and corrections.—*K.M.A.*

References

L. Baeck/'Individuum Ineffabile' in *Eranos Jahrbuch* 1947
M. Heidegger/'Gelassenheit' 1959
A. Homburger/*Psychopathologie des Kindesalters*, 1926
E. Simon/*Brücken, Gesammelte Aufsätze*, 1965
B. Snell/*Die Entdeckung des Geistes*

APPENDICES

From 'Jung in His Letters'

Before he met Freud Jung had been influenced by Nietzsche, and his influence on Jung's political thinking persisted throughout Jung's lifetime. For example in a letter of 26.5.1923 he wrote:

> We need some new foundations. We must dig down to the primitive in us, for only out of the conflict between civilised man and the Germanic barbarian will there come what we need: a new experience of God.

And in a letter of 31.12.1949 he elaborates on this:

> Something in us has remained barbarian . . . when we European barbarians had that sudden and shattering collision with the ripest fruit of antiquity—Christianity—not to the advantage of our inner development.

Like Nietzsche he despised the masses, whom he sometimes referred to by the Nietzschean term 'herd', and he spoke out against socialism, communism, and the predominant concern with social welfare. This Nietzschean outlook explains the optimistic expectations with which Jung welcomed the Nazi revolution in 1933. He never was a Nazi but an onlooker from across the Swiss border, and as little as Nietzsche was he anti-semitic. On the contrary he did all he could to help Jewish refugees, and he had all his life intimate Jewish friends.

The published selection of his letters contains none of the positive remarks on Hitler and the Nazis which Jung made in 1933, for instance during a seminar in Berlin in the summer of 1933 which the present writer attended, but there are letters from March 1934 and later in which he defended himself against the public attack by a Swiss psychiatrist who had reproached him for his indiscretions during 1933. Jung was no politician, as he repeatedly stated himself, and the political opinions he voiced were amateurish. He did not believe that society could be benefitted by political means, only the improvement of the spiritual welfare of the individual could help . . .

In earlier years Jung often answers requests for therapeutic advice or interprets dreams which the addressees have sent to him. Later his interests change somewhat, as he describes in a letter of 20.8.1945:

> . . . the main interest of my work is not concerned with the treatment of neuroses but rather with the approach to the numinous. But the fact is that the approach to the numinous is the real therapy, and inasmuch as you attain to the numinous experiences you are released from the curse of pathology.

By 'the numinous' Jung means the awareness of powers acting upon us which transcend ordinary conscious knowledge, powers the true nature of which we can only vaguely apprehend. Jung's own numinous experience occurred mainly in connection with numinous imagery, and he made enormous efforts to validate his subjective experiences by the study of every form of religious imagery as it appears in orthodox as well as heretical literature all over the world. He therefore felt he could speak about the numinous not only on the basis of his subjective experience but objectively as an empirical scientist.

Jung's preoccupation with numinous imagery hides from him somewhat the fact that in the present period the numinous is often experienced not in imagery but in the transforming power of love, or in awareness of 'ultimate concerns', transcending doubt by an inexplicable ultimate certainty.

Jung's preoccupation with religious questions produced an extensive correspondence with theologians. Many objected to his describing 'God' as a psychological complex, or identifying Him with 'the Self' or 'the unconscious.' Jung replied that as a scientist he is not speaking about God but only about the images of God as they are psychologically experienced.

This seems a peculiarly insincere argument. An image of God is of interest to someone only if it is experienced as a symbol of mysterious and transcendent powers. Otherwise it is like an African sculpture an art dealer buys without caring about its meaning. Jung is either speaking as a scientist, about what is symbolised in the God image, in which case it must be an object of empirical observation, for example 'God is a psychological complex'; or he is expressing psychological beliefs in pseudo-psychological terms such as 'the unconscious' or 'the self'—that is, he is not speaking as an empirical scientist. Even in this case he will clash with the theologians: to them God is a person, and 'the unconscious' is not; and God is infinite, and 'the self' must include the awareness of our corporeal condition, of birth and death and the frailty of the body.

Not only are Jung's statements on God and the numinous not scientific, in addition his scientific teachings on psychology are combined with metaphysical beliefs which can neither be proved nor disproved. If he says that the unconscious is relatively independent of time and space, so that events in a distant part of the world can be parapsychologically experienced here, he is expressing a metaphysical belief which in addition is beyond the comprehension of most people, including the present writer.

What is the explanation of these contradictions, and what are the pre-conditions which make them understandable?

The basic attitude of Jung the psychologist is his deep respect for all that he actually experiences, which he refuses to allow to be explained away by any theory, or to ignore because it appears inexplicable. On the contrary he wants to keep his mind open to meet the inexplicable, surprises and mysteries.

Jung has relatively little respect for thinking as such. He has seen the abuse of thinking by positivistic rationalists, for their purposes of debunking experience. Thinking ought to be the servant of experience, by itself it adds nothing to experience. Methodical rules are taken lightly as mere 'sanitary rules'.

Jung was not trained in philosophy and he spoke disdainfully of the post-kantian philosophers whom he dismissed as neurotics. He studied Kant's critical analysis of scientific thinking, but he knew nothing of the methodology of the human studies which was explored only after Kant in the nineteenth and at the beginning of the twentieth centuries.

He did not realise that his subject-matter belonged to the human studies and not to the natural sciences. He was trained as a natural scientist and knew that nothing was acceptable to his colleagues but what was presented in terms of natural science. In addition his powerful mind strove for unity of experience. When his observations and the methods of scientific thinking clashed, he did not mind bending the latter a bit, or supplementing these methods with excursions into metaphysics. The alchemists whom he studied so thoroughly, and all the pre-sixteenth century scientists and the scientists of the East did the same as a matter of course. Jung's powerful personality created unity out of the most disparate material, out of religion and science, Christian faith and every form of heresy, science and mantic and astrological practices. He could even combine with his medical knowledge the belief that a saint actually lived for twenty years without food.

This is impressive but not to be imitated. Where Jung remains a lasting example is in his respect for experience and his discovery of how typically human all our experience is: that is, how much it is archetypally determined.

(*Glasgow Herald* 18th August 1973)

'The Abenheimer-Schorstein Group'

Schorstein was a neuro-surgeon, and had been not merely a precociously intelligent child but was the son of an almost certainly insane father. Rabbi Schorstein's frequent spasms of tyranny had in different style pressed his son into an education as hothouse as J. S. Mill's. The son had graduated MD in Vienna at the age of 21, not least by telling lies about his age. A former communist, he spoke of having met Trotsky, and touring Europe in his teens and in the 1930s. Phenomenally well-read in philosophy and psychology, trained in psychiatry, a man of strong intellectual passions, his various writings deal with Jewish religion and mysticism, and existentialism (including brief report of an interview with his much-admired Heidegger), and one review which concludes by asking whether Kierkegaard's expressed desire to talk to Christ for all eternity would be reciprocated.

At some stage in the early 1950s Schorstein and Abenheimer thought of forming a general philosophical discussion group in Glasgow, and from vague beginnings impossible to date a group formed. It continued until shortly after Abenheimer's death with more or less regular meetings, every few weeks, at which a paper by one of the members would be discussed . . . usually after it had been read, but if a much longer debate was wanted copies could be sent round for reading beforehand. Abenheimer's 'Some Answers to Nihilism' derives from an early attempt at such a Group meeting, with, besides the *dioscuri*, Penry Jones, later involved with religious broadcasting and associated with George MacLeod's Iona Community, and the most widely-known Group member, an Iona Community associate and star pupil and protegé of Schorstein, the young Dr. R. D. Laing.

Laing remained a member until he went to London in 1957 . . . he returned to give some papers on visits, in later years . . . but the Group had other distinguished members, constituting a very remarkable intellectual milieu, of interesting composition. It was a milieu for all who took part, as much as for Abenheimer, whose psychological insight seems to have sustained it, and the more abrasive Schorstein.

From around 1955 it included classicists, Henry Chalk (killed in a car crash) and Avram Wasserstein, who had left Nazi Germany as a schoolboy and was to retire in the late 1980s as Professor of Greek at the Hebrew University of Jerusalem. Another exile was the Romanian Zevedei Barbu, later professor at Sussex, then in South America. His several books include one on the psychopathology of totalitarianism quite congruent with one interest in Abenheimer's writings. The paper 'Abenheimer and Laing' (*Edinburgh Review,* 78/9) wrongly states that Norman Cohn was a member of the Group. Though a wartime friend of Schorstein, and later Abenheimer's friend (Abenheimer is thanked in *acknowledgements* to the first edition of Cohn's seminal *The Pursuit of the Millenium*) Cohn had left his Glasgow University post in 1951, before the Group began ... though on visits north he delivered papers to it. As well as Barbu and after his departure Dr. Jacob Miller (author of Soviet Russia, first edn. 1955, editor of *Soviet Studies*) and René Beermann came from the Institute of Soviet and East European Studies at Glasgow University. (Beermann, b. 1904, grew up in the Russian imperial court, where his father was a Lutheran chaplain, was a lawyer in the Soviet Union until coming to Scotland during the 1939-45 war; he edits the journal *Co-Existence*, cf. 'Nietzsche, Dostoevsky and Russian Symbolism,' *Co-Existence* Vol. 20, 1983, and 'The Social Psychology of Stalinism: A Literary Approach,' Vol. 27, 1990, representative of some Group discussions).

Ian Henderson (1910-69), pupil of Karl Barth but an existential theologian (*Rudolf Bultmann, Myth in the New Testament*, etc.) is credited with the first coinage of the English term 'demythologising.' His philosophical polemic *Can Two Walk Together* (1947) contains arguments on the meaning of 'Natural Law,' on the necessity of a positive, belief content to ethical discourse; and pungent comment on the German soul not out of keeping with *The Tin Drum*, and garnered from his pre-war student days in Nazi Germany. Henderson's *Power Without Glory* (19??) makes very direct use of H. G. Gadamer's ideas on the 'hermeneutic circle,' at once bringing home the point as to access to continental philosophical literature. Lesser linguists may feel grateful to another Group member, Henderson's student John Macquarrie (b. 1919) for his translation with Edward Robinson of Heidegger's *Being and Time* (1962) published the year he left to become Professor at Union Theological Seminary, New York (he later professed at Oxford) with *An Existentialist Theology* (1955) and *The Scope of Demythologising* (1960) under his belt. Not to mention obligements to the Group from talking on less congenial writers in his ambit.

Until his death R. Gregor Smith (1910-65) was also a highly challenging member, like Henderson a student in pre-1939 Germany, later postwar administrator at the University of Bonn responsible for Barth's appointment there, with a career in publishing and authorship of works on existential theology, translations of Kierkegaard and the first English introduction to J. G. Hamann (which he 'tried out' on the Group, and which Abenheimer reviewed in the *Glasgow Herald*). More to the immediate point is the kind of meticulous, directed persistence which Gregor Smith displayed in discussion, with a definite focus of conviction. In a prevailing climate of English Analytic philosophy, the Group was of great value, as a later member, the theologian Professor A. D. Galloway recalled, having read part of his *Faith in a Changing Culture* (19??) to the Group (Abenheimer reviewed that book too), and welcoming the chance to speak on Hegel.

The principal philosopher present was J. J. Russell (1923-75), who left to become professor in Kansas, then at Kingston, Ontario. His 1966 *Analysis and Dialectic* reflects the existential concerns of the Group with critique of Kierkegaard and sundry references, and operates from a European perspective very much influenced by Edmund Husserl. He also corresponded with Jean Hippolyte and M. Merleau-Ponty in France. His radical programme for a reformed philosophy course in the Scottish Universities alas fell victim to the prevailing Oxbridge philosophy, and poor Russell had by all accounts an unfortunate time prior to a tragic early death. Another philosophy-teacher member was the arch-iconoclast D. R. Bell, 'Nietzschean,' somewhat *advocatus diaboli*, author of a brief monograph on another of his heroes, *Bertrand Russell*, in a series of primers edited by Galloway. In this cast-list of dialogues Bell functioned against theoretic complacencies.

An early Group member was A. C. Craig, a prominent churchman involved with the World Council of Churches, with as well as intellectual strong pastoral concerns ... like the widely popular Murdo Ewen MacDonald, Professor of Practical Theology, author of lighter books and of a forthcoming autobiography. (A biography of Craig is in print, and one of Gregor Smith in progress). If in Galloway' s phrase theology was treated by the group as a 'system of meanings,' the practical and pastoral influenced the point of view of interpretation. And had to, also, for those members professionally specialists in the area roughly of psychotherapies.

R. D. Laing was a founder member, an early one was Paul Campbell, with a background on professional football, the study of law and preparation to enter holy orders, who had before the Group's foundation corresponded with Jung on the prospects of a school of Roman Catholic Jungianism. He retired from the Group, and Glasgow, to an Ashram in India. A somewhat later member, Frederick Stone was Professor of Child Psychiatry at Glasgow University. Dr. Cameron MacDonald, a physician trained in psychotherapy by Abenheimer, and with a keen interest in psychosomatic problems, was present at early ultra-informal Group meetings but not in the longer term of the Group as such. He was, however, of a second Group Abenheimer established, of practitioners of the psychoanalytic psychotherapies, in effect among other things a support group (says Professor Stone) given the strains of such work. While its business has remained the presentation and discussion of cases, Abenheimer certainly circulated one or two papers to that therapists' group for private reading preliminary to discussion. Written records are scarce and memories frail, so that it is possible that the paper on Shakespeare's Sonnets was delivered rather there than to the wider-concerned Group. The initial question posed by it concerns above all psychology, and while Professor Stone (member of both groups) had an acute recollection of hearing it, neither of the literary members consulted did.

One 'literary man' (and this cannot be a full list of members) was Christopher Small, Oxford graduate, critic and essayist of considerable range and ability. There are interesting reflections of psychological and/or political concern in his books, *Ariel like a Harpy*, on Shelley, Mary Shelley and Frankenstein, and *The Road to Miniluv*, on George Orwell, not to mention his essays and more occasional reasoned activist writings on peace issues, and the subject of the Atom Bomb, a major theme of the Group's heyday. Represented by a note, 'Three Phases in the Discussion of the Atom Bomb' among Abenheimer's papers, the topic drew an as ever impassioned paper from Schorstein, 'The Metaphysics of the Atom Bomb' (*Philosophical Journal* 1962), tracing a gradual etherealisation of human consciousness, away from *hyle*, matter, and being ('the fact that there is something rather than nothing:' Heidegger) through the disembodiment, as he saw it, of Christian 'spiritualisation,' to the power-driven physicists leaving of the world behind; or rather so far from contact as to have both the technical and the actual capacity to destroy everything. Schorstein was extremely hostile to the performing of prefrontal leucotomy ('lobotomy') in treating mental illness. There is a report of a discussion in which Abeheimer too took part. For Schorstein the procedure represented a morally untenable, virtually Nazi view of man ... and indeed someone solving their personal problems by having surgery done on somebody else; as he said to parents seeking his approval of the operation being performed on their daughter.

Along with Laing's complaints about orthodox psychiatry, such issues of the day (early 1950s) seem to have got the Group off the ground in discussion of philosophical anthropology; what is man, and what of human experience? The comprehensiveness of the Group was remarked on by Professor Stone, but in fact each discipline represented touched on the others. Although this is not a comprehensive list, there is occasion to mention Jack Rillie, a literary critic and sometime head of the English Literature department at Glasgow University. An 'addiction to teaching' has restricted his literary output, and he has produced no book. He has written a memoir of the Group, which stresses a point hinted at above, that whereas there was nothing to prevent him from reading and admiring the views expressed in Martin Buber's *I and Thou* (translated by Gregor Smith) confidence that he had a perspective on it was very much dependent on the associations maintained by the Group. Not only were dangers of specialisation combatted, consciousness of connections was fostered, of implications, with the depth possible given a freedom of consultation. Interesting especially was Jacob Miller's recollection that in coming to terms with the psychology of certain individuals he had encountered within the Soviet system, his best and immediate assistance came in discussion with A. D. Galloway on the basis of the latter's pastoral experience.

Abenheimer and Schorstein established the Group. Thereafter it grew, allowing a range of concerns to extend itself, each specialist finding another on the boundaries of his professional field, so that there was rather more than hearsay or general reading attended by internal professional uncertainty. Membership was kept at about a dozen, others were invited to contribute . . . including C. F. von Weizsäcker, in Glasgow delivering his Gifford letures . . . and if any established member had left someone asked along to read a paper would be considered by a later meeting as possibly to be invited to join. A keynote was conviviality, that while there was unrestricted criticism, this was encouraged by a friendliness of common intention. If various books were nurtured, from Laing's *The Divided Self* onward, it cannot be doubted that Abenheimer was inspired as much as all the surviving members report having been inspired. If the earlier essays in this book antedate the Group's foundation, the fact that there is a continuing series is also in some wise product too of its nurture. The fact that it did not long survive him, Schorstein by 1973 having declined tragically in health, says a great deal about Abenheimer's part in, as several members put it, letting it happen.

BIBLIOGRAPHY

Introduction
> Critical Remarks on 'Psychological Aspects of the Fantasy of Snow White and the Seven Dwarfs' (by A. S. MacQuisten and R. W. Pickford—Psychoanalytical Review July 1942) is previously unpublished.
> 'Existentialism,' written at the editor J. D. Sutherland's request, was published with a review of J.-P. Sartre's Psychology of Imagination in British Journal of Medical Psychology, Vol. XXIV, part 2, 1951.

On Narcissism, Including an Analysis of Shakespeare's King Lear
> Paper to British Psychological Society, Edinburgh, 6 January 1943.
> British Journal of Medical Psychology Vol. XX Part 3, 1945.

Shakespeare's Tempest, A Psychological Analysis.
> Psychoanalytical Review Vol. 33, pp. 399-415, 1946.

On Narcissism (1968).
> Unpublished typescript, paper to Group.

The Heart of Man (Erich Fromm).
> Glasgow Herald 1965.

Shakespeare's Sonnets 120 and 121.
> Unpublished typescript with emendations noted, 1972-3.

The Problem of Individuation in Friedrich Nietzsche's Writings.
> Guild of Pastoral Psychology, Guild Lecture 59, May 1948.

Rilke and Nietzsche.
> Philosophical Journal (Glasgow) Vol. 4 No. 2, 1967.

Some Answers to Nihilism.
> Unpublished paper to Group, 1954?

The Individualistic Ego.
> Unpublished paper, 19??.

Reflections on the Günter Grass's Novel Die Blechtrommel, (The Tin Drum).
> Philosophical Journal (Glasgow), January 1970.

Patrick White's Voss.
> Unpublished typescript, late 1960s?

On Simplicity (with reference to Patrick White's Riders in the Chariot and The Solid Mandala.
> Revision of unpublished paper to Group, 1972/3.

> *The above-named publishers are thanked for generously permitting previously published papers to appear in this volume.*

SELECT LIST AND PROVISIONAL ARRANGEMENT OF UNCOLLECTED WRITINGS

EARLIER PAPERS

The Integration Of The Personality.
> paper read at the Meeting of the British Psychological Society, Scottish Branch, Edinburgh, 5th November 1938.

Psychological Views on Traumatic Neuroses.
> Paper read to the Scottish Psychiatry Club, October 1939.

Psychoanalysis.
> Lecture Delivered at Lansdowne Clinic, Glasgow.

Weakness and Strength of the Personality.
> Paper read to the Scottish Psychiatric Club, 15th March 1940.

Analytic Psychology.
> Undated typescript.

Changes in the Concept of What Man Is.
> Paper read at the Scottish Refugee Centre, Glasgow, November 1941.

Introduction to R. M. Rilke.
> Paper read at the (Refugee) Centre, Glasgow, 18th September 1941.

On Fear.
> Paper delivered to Scottish Clinic of Massage and Physiotherapy, 21st November 1942.

The Psychology of Social Groups (Jews and Gentiles).
Unpublished address, July 1943.
Jewish Self-Hate.
Unpublished lecture, 1st November 1943.
The Treatise of the Two Married Women and the Widow *(sic)* (with J. L. Halliday, M.D.), on William Dunbar's poem.
Psychoanalytical Review, Vol. 31, pp. 233-252, July 1944.
Studies in the Concepts of the Instincts and the Ego.
Unpublished lecture, June 1946.
The Diary of Vaslav Nijinsky, A Pathological Study of a Case of Schizophrenia.
Psychoanalytical Review Vol. 33, pp. 257-284, July 1946.
The Concept of Instinct in Psychotherapy.
Unpublished lecture, 1947, superseding 'Studies on the Concept of the Instincts and the Ego' of June 1946.
The Animal in Man.
Paper read to the Glasgow Psychological Society, 7th September 1949.

FREUD AND FREUDIANS

Review Article on Freud's *An Outline of Psychoanalysis*.
International Journal of Psychoanalysis, 1941.
Letter to Edward Glover on early chapters of Glover's *Freud and Jung*.
29 December 1948, published, *Edinburgh Review* 78/79, February 1988.
Freud and the Psychology of the Jews.
Paper read in the public lecture course of the B'nai B'rith, 3rd June 1952.
The Psychologist's Difficulty in Being Empirical.
Unpublished typescript.
The Individualistic Ego.
Unpublished paper, 1969, different from version published above.
Reviews of: *The Freudian Ethic,* Richard la Prière; *Freud, Living and Dying,* ed. Max Schur; *Freud, the Man, His World, The Influence,* ed. Jonathan Miller; *Thomas Woodrow Wilson,* by Freud and W. C. Bullitt; *The Letters of Sigmund Freud and Oskar Pfister*; *The Letters of Sigmund Freud 1873-1939* ed. Ernst L. Freud.

JUNG AND JUNGIANS

A Brief Description and Criticism of *Mythology of the Soul* by H. G. Baynes.
Privately circulated paper (8,000 words), June 1940.
The Jungian View of Personality.
Paper read at the Seminar of the Department of Psychological Medicine, University of Glasgow, February 1954: 4000.
Secularism and Religion in Freud's and Jung's Psychology.
Unpublished paper, delivered 9th December 1959.
'Synchronicity' as a New Principle Explaining Natural Phenomena.
Unpublished (and unsympathetic) ts., December 1965.
Dream Symbolism according to C. G. Jung.
Undated paper.
The Psychotherapeutic Use of Painting, with Special Reference to its Use in Jungian therapy.
Unpublished lecture, presented with slides and drawings.
Reviews of: *Memories, Dreams, Reflections,* C. G. Jung; *Contact with Jung,* ed. M. Fordham; *Man and his Symbols,* ed. C. G. Jung; *The Living Symbol,* by Gerhard Adler.

OTHER PAPERS

A Reassessment of the Theoretical and Therapeutic Meaning of Anal Symbolism.
Guild of Pastoral Psychology, Guild Lecture 72, February 1952.
What Do We Mean by 'Unconscious?'
Unpublished ts., undated.
Lou Andreas-Salomé's Main Contribution to Psychoanalysis.
Spring (An Annual of Archetypal Psychology and Jungian Thought) 1971, cf. James Hillman's editorial reference to the paper p. 232.

EXISTENCE PSYCHOLOGY AND PHILOSOPHY

Verstehende Psychologie.
>(Unpublished paper of 1949 submitted with:
Review of Karl Jaspers, *Allgemeine Psychopathologie.*
>*British Journal of Medical Psychology* 1950.
The Concept of the Spirit in Analytical Psychology.
>Unpublished paper of 1947: a much fuller presentation subsequently trimmed and
>adapted as 'Notes on the Spirit as Conceived by Dynamic Psychology,' *Journal of
>Analytical Psychology*, Vol. 1 No. 2, 1956.
Existentialism and Psychotherapy.
>Lecture to the postgraduate seminar of the Department of Psychological Medicine,
>Glasgow University, 24th February 1958; published *Edinburgh Review* 78/79, February
>1988).
Binswanger's Schizophrenia Studies.
>Unpublished typescript, undated.
Reflections on Karl Jaspers' Concept of 'Existence.'
>Ts., published *Edinburgh Review* 74, August 1986: the journal's cover design incorpora-
>tes the tag,'The urge to know what I am is identical to the will to become myself' credited
>to **Karl M. Abenheimer.**
Critical Comments on R. D. Laing's book *The Self and Others.*
>Unpublished review article sent as memo to Laing, 1962.
'Autobiographical Notes of a Schizophrenic' and a reply to R. D. Laing's Review (Inter-
>national Journal of Psychoanalysis, 1963) of Karl Jaspers' *General Psychopathology.*
>Unpublished typescript, 1964.
Reviews on R. D. Laing and his movement: Laing, *The Divided Self, The Politics of
Experience and the Bird of Paradise*; Laing and Cooper, *Reason and Violence*; M. Barnes and
J. Berke, *Mary Barnes*; Morton Schatzman. *Soul Murder.*
Two Ways of Thinking (*Naturwissenschaften* and *Geisteswissenschaften*).
>*Philosophical Journal* Vol. 2 No. 1, 1965.
A Defence of Dualism.
>Undated unfinished ms. draft.
The Logics of Mythical Thinking.
>Undated unfinished ms. draft re. Ernst Cassirer.
Comments on James Hillman's Book *Emotion.*
>Unpublished ts., October 1961.

EGO STUDIES

A Critical Account of *Die Urteilsfunction, Eine Psychologische und Erkenntniskritische
Untersuchung*, by Wilhelm Jerusalem.
>Unpublished typescript, undated.
Critical Observations on Fairbain's Theory of Object Relations.
>B.J.M.P. Vol. XXVIII, part 1, 1955. (*vide* Fairbairn's reply, Vol. XXVIII, part 2).
Three American Psychoanalysts on the Ego Concept (Paul Federn, Heinz Hartmann, Erik H.
Erickson).
>Unpublished ts., October 1959.
On the History of Self-Awareness as Illustrated by Georg Misch's *History of Autobiography
in Antiquity.*
>Undated typescript, 1960s.
On Identity.
>Unpublished paper delivered to psychotherapists' group, 1968.
The Ego as Subject.
>Paper to Third International Congress for Analytical Psychology, Montreux, 1966.
>Published in *The Reality of the Psyche*, ed J. Wheelwright, N.Y. 1968.
+Ego Book
>Various (200+) pages, ms. and ts. dating from 1947/8 with later drafts, presumably
>1972/3 and the opening chapters (30pp. in neat typescript) of a book c.1973.

WRITINGS ON AND REFERENCES TO ABENHEIMER
(the editor would appreciate any information)
Michael Fordham:
  Contact with Jung, 1960. *The Objective Psyche*, 1958.
Robert R. Calder:
  'Abenheimer and Laing', Edinburgh Review 78/9, February 1988.
Jack Rillie:
  'The Abenheimer-Schorstein Group', *ibid.*
James Hillman:
  Re-Visioning Psychology (1977)
Kenneth Collins
  Go and Learn (1988)

OTHER REFERENCES
G. R. Heyer
  The Organism of the Mind (1933)
  cf. C. G. Jung, *Collected Works* Vol. 19 and *Letters*
Frieda Fromm-Reichmann
  Psychoanalysis and Psychotherapy (1959)
  (introduction by Edith M. Weigert)

Index

A Midsummer Night's Dream, 41
Aborigines, 149
Adam, 162
Alice Through the Looking Glass, 160
Allgemeine Psychopathologie
  (Jaspers), 11, 18
An Outline of Psychoanalysis
  (Freud) 116
Andreas-Salomé, Lou, 38, 53, 54, 87,
  97, 171
Anima, 42, 46, 49, 69, 114, 148
Anna Karenina, 106, 107
Antony and Cleopatra, 143
Apollo, 72, 73
Ariadne, 80, 107
Athene, 50
Australian aborigines, 144
Baden-Baden, 134
Baeck, Rabbi Leo, 153, 157, 163
Baynes, H. G., 16, 171
Bayreuth, 74
Beckett, Samuel, 150
Biedermeyer, 136, 139
Bildung, 130, 135
Binswanger, 172
Blonde Bestie, 83, 93
Borgia, Cesare, 84
Bowlby, John, 17
*British Journal of Medical
  Psychology*, 13
Brunnhilde, 22
Buber, Martin, 11
Butler, E. M., 88
Caesar, 79, 84
Calderon, 92
Caliban, 129
Carus, Carl Gustav, 25, 114
Cassirer, Ernst, 172
Christianity, 48, 75, 76, 84, 92, 98,
  114, 123, 131, 143, 150, 159
Christian tradition, 90
Citizen Kane, 31
Cohn, Hans, 88
Communism, 111, 130, 134
Complexes, 20
Coriolanus, 44
Courbet, G.,66
Cymbeline, 50, 51
Dante, 82, 92
Danzig, 133, 134
Danzig, 135
Daphnis and Chloë, 156

Das Stundenbuch (Rilke), 93
Dawn of Day, 77
Der Grüne Heinrich, 65, 66, 157
Descartes, 26
Devil, 102, 108, 114
Die blonde Bestie, 83, 93
Dionysos, 72, 73, 74, 84, 85
Doktor Faustus, 100
Don Juan, 84
Dostoevsky, 156, 160
Duino Elegies, 87, 92
Dunbar, William, 171
Earl of Southampton, 66
Earth-Mother, 77, 83
Ecce Homo, 71, 81, 180
Echo, 35
Eckhart, Meister, 96
Ego, 20, 24, 113-128
Erickson, Erik H., 172
Eros, 123
Esau, 158
Eternity, 79
Eternal Recurrence, 78
Eve, 162
Existence,20
Existentialism, 171
Fairbairn, W. R. D., 172
Fascists, 130
Faust, 100
Federn, Paul, 172
Fordham, Michael, 173
Frazer, J. G., 35, 38
Freudian, 19
Freud, Anna, 116, 117, 123
Freud, Sigmund, 11, 15, 17, 18, 22,
  26, 29, 30, 35, 38, 53, 54, 59,
  103, 113-128, 171
Fromm, Erich, 59-60, 170
Fromm-Reichmann, Frieda, 11, 15,
  16, 173
George, Stefan, 67
Germany, 134, 135, 141
Gide, André, 36, 38
Glasgow Herald, 19
Glover, Edward, 171
God, 108, 149, 75, 84, 91, 98
Goethe, 27, 36, 48, 79, 100, 155
Golden Age, 153
Gospels, 154, 160
Grand Inquisitor, 160
Grass, Gunter, 129-139, 170
Greene, Robert, 50

Halliday, J. L., 171
Hartmann, Heinz, 116, 172
Heidegger, Martin, 25, 57, 131, 153, 163
Hermes, 93
Heyer, Gustav Richard, 11, 15, 173
Hildegard, St., of Bingen, 95
Hillman, James, 172, 173
Hitler, 11, 85, 96, 131
Homburger, August, 154, 163
Homer, 114
Homosexuality, 127
Horney, Karen, 38
Human All Too Human, 70
Husser, Edmund, 25
Hybris, 38
I Ching, 139
Id, 16, 20, 24, 115
Imitatio Christi, 150
Instinct, 122
Jaspers, Karl, 10, 11, 13, 15, 18, 20, 26, 57, 172
Jerusalem, Wilhelm, 172
Jesus Christ, 136, 137, 142, 148, 150, 151, 162
Jews, 130, 151, 159, 171
Jones, Penry, 110
Journal of Analytical Psychology, 13
Judaeo-Christian, 153
Judas Iscariot, 160
Jung, C. J., 11, 15, 16, 18, 23, 34, 39, 48, 54, 57, 65, 73, 80, 82, 114, 121, 123, 127, 131, 147, 151, 171
Jungians, 16
Kafka, Franz, 94
Kaiserreich, 134
Kant, 130, 156
Karma, 114
Kaufmann, Walter, 19, 90, 87-99
Keller, Gottfried, 65, 66, 157
Kierkegaard, 27, 30, 54, 101
King Lear, 36-38, 51, 60, 170
Klein, Melanie, 22
Laing, R. D., 14, 55, 172
Levy-Bruhl, 34
Libido, 22, 116
MacNiven, Dr. Angus, 12
MacQuisten, A. S., 23, 170
Maenads, 92
Mann, Thomas, 100, 101
Marlowe, Christopher, 66
Marx, Karl, 153
Mason, E. C., 88

McDougall, William, 25, 32
Meister Eckhart, 96
Messiah, 85
Misch, Georg, 172
Mother, 30
Muir, Edwin, 88
Musil, 17, 100-108, 157
Mussolini, 96
Myshkin, 160, 161
Mythology of the Soul (Baynes), 16
Napoleon, 79, 84
Narcissism, 53-60, 170
Narcissus, 30, 35
Nazism, 85, 130, 131, 134, 135
Neoplatonism, 123
Nicholas of Cusa, 155
Nietzsche, Friedrich, 18, 19, 27, 70-99, 100, 101, 103, 107, 130, 131, 138, 170
Nihilism, 137, 170
Nijinsky, Vaslav, 171
Novalis, 154
Oedipus, 127
Orpheus, 92
Othello, 51
Ovid, 35
Paranoia, 127
Pausanias, 35
Peace-Emperor Franz Joseph, 103
Peutadius, 35
Pfaender, 33, 151
Piaget, Jean, 16, 114
Pickford, R. W., 23, 170
Platonists, 62
Plotinus, 123
Poland, 134
Principium individuationis, 73, 75, 82
Psychologie der Weltanschauungen, (Jaspers), 10
Rieff, Philip, 120, 121
Rilke, R. M., 18, 36, 38, 87-99, 138, 170
Rodin, August, 94
Romanticism, 138, 141, 156
Roman Catholicism, 90, 135, 137, 155, 157
Roman Catholic tradition, 92
Romeo and Juliet, 65
Rosenzweig, Franz, 162
Rossi, Alberto, 68
Rousseau, J.-J., 26, 130
Rowse, A. L., 66, 69
Russians, 135
Ryle, Gilbert, 114

Sartre, J.-P.,26, 94, 170
Scheler, Max, 157
Schiller, Friedrich, 156
Schmidt, A., 69
Schopenhauer, Arthur, 72
Schorstein, Joseph, 13
Schwarze Köchin, 133
Scotti, Duchess Gallarati, 96
Self, 114, 119, 127, 147
Shakespeare, 36-70, 129, 137, 155, 170
Shakespeare Lexicon, 69
Silberer, 23, 24
Simon, Ernst, 10, 155, 157, 162, 163
Simple Simon, 156
Simplicius Simplicissimus, 156
Snell, Bruno, 163
Snow White, 18, 22-24, 170
Socrates, 72, 73, 79
Sonnets to Orpheus, 87, 89, 92
St. Paul, 79
Stendhal, 145
Stifter, Adalbert, 157
Stoicism, 150
Strabo, 35
Strauss, Ludwig, 162
Superego, 20
Sutherland, J. D., 170
Tao Te Ching, 90
Tauler, 96
The Birth of Tragedy, 72, 73, 74, 85
The Brothers Karamazov, 160
The Divided Self 14

The Ego and the Id (Freud), 116
The Idiot, 160
The Joyful Wisdom, 71
The Man Without Qualities (Musil),
    17, 100-118, 157
The Picture of Dorian Grey, 56
The Tempest, 39-52, 129, 137, 170
The Will to Power, 70
The Winter's Tale, 50, 51
Theseus, 80
Thus Spake Zarathustra, 70, 71, 78,
    79-81, 85
Timon, 44
Tiresias, 162
Titian, 62
Tolstoy, 93
Totentanz, 95
Virgin Mary, 155
Voss, 140-151, 162, 170
Wagner, Richard, 72, 74, 76, 79, 93
We Philologists, 70
Weber, Max, 15, 96
Weltanschauung, 24, 27, 82
Wernicke, 116
White, Patrick, 140-163, 170
Wilde, Oscar, 31, 32, 55, 56, 101
William II, Kaiser, 96
Wind, Edgar, 62
Wust, Peter, 157
Zarathustra, 84, 79
Zen Buddhism, 131, 139